The ASSIST Program

Affective/Social Skills: Instructional Strategies and Techniques

Helping Kids Find Their Strengths

A Validated Washington State Innovative Education Program

This manual is a product of the joint efforts of

Pat Huggins
Donna Wood Manion
Larry Moen
and
Elizabeth Tyler

Artwork by Ernie Hergenroeder and Larry Moen

Lessons in this curriculum are based on the Dependable
Strengthwork of Bernard Haldane, Ph.D. These were written with
the assistance of the Dependable Strengths Project Team, directed
by Dr. Jerald Forster of the University of Washington, Seattle,
Washington.

ISBN #1-57035-006-X

Printed in the United States of America

Published & Distributed by

Sopris West™
EDUCATIONAL SERVICES

A Cambium Learning™ Company

4093 Specialty Place   •   Longmont, Colorado 80504   •   (303) 651-2829
www.sopriswest.com

Table of Contents

A UNIT FOR **PRIMARY GRADES**

Students will understand that they are a mix of strengths and
areas that could be improved.

Students will understand the benefits of focusing on their good
experiences and strengths, rather than on their mistakes or
weaknesses.

Students will identify and share good experiences.

Student will understand that they can discover their strengths
by remembering their good experiences.

Students will start building a vocabulary of words which
describe strengths.

Students will learn to recognize and use a number of new
vocabulary words that describe personal strengths.

Students will continue to identify these strengths in themselves
and others.

Students will practice looking in areas other than kinesthetic
when identifying their strengths.

Students will further develop their ability to detect strengths in
others and in themselves.

A UNIT FOR **INTERMEDIATE GRADES**

Students will participate in small groups, sharing good experiences, practicing good listening skills, and using their new strength vocabulary words to identify others' strengths.

Students will become aware of their own strengths as perceived by others.

Students will continue to expand their repertoire of strength vocabulary words.

Students will learn to avoid common ways of discounting their strengths.

Students will discern their most dependable strengths with the help of their teacher and peers.

Students will prove that they have particular strengths by citing instances in which they have used them.

Students will select strengths important to them and choose a modality for presenting them to the class.

Students will use a public presentation to celebrate the discovery of their strengths.

Students will use their strengths as a springboard for setting new goals.

Students will learn and use a number of strategies for reaching their goals.

APPENDICES

Overview of the ASSIST Program

Affective/Social Skills: Instructional Strategies and Techniques

The ASSIST Program is designed to increase students' growth in self-esteem, self-management, interpersonal relationships, and emotional understanding. ASSIST manuals provide a complete guide for elementary teachers and counselors to actively involve students in developing critical personal/social skills. The ASSIST Program can be sequenced into a grades 1-6 school climate curriculum, integrated into regular academic programs, or each manual can stand alone as a curriculum for personal growth or social competence.

The ASSIST curriculum is the result of an extensive review of child development theory and research, a review of existing social/emotional education programs, and the feedback of many teachers and students who participated in the Program. ASSIST incorporates concepts and procedures from social learning theory, child psychology, and proven educational practices.

Each field-tested lesson includes:

- A "To the Teacher" section which provides a theoretical background for lesson concepts;
- A "scripted" lesson that provides the dialog, examples, and practice necessary to teach lesson concepts and skills;
- A series of transparency masters which make lesson concepts accessible to picture-smart students;
- A series of reproducible worksheets which provide opportunities for students to process the lessons; and
- A variety of "Supplementary Activities" designed to encourage the transfer of training. Some lessons include a parent involvement component.

ASSIST was developed with Title IV-C Innovative Education Funds and was evaluated in elementary school classrooms in four school districts. **Statistically significant gains in self-concept and social skills occurred in eight out of nine assessments.** As a result, ASSIST was validated in Washington State and designated cost-effective and exportable. It is now in the State's "Bank of Proven Practices," a clearinghouse for quality programs.

The ASSIST manuals currently in print include the following:

- ***Building Self-Esteem in the Classroom***—Both the *Primary Version* and the *Intermediate Version* contain all new lessons and activities. Students refine their self-descriptions and acquire an appreciation for their uniqueness. They are introduced to the concept of multiple intelligences and learn a process by which they can determine their own strong intelligences. They learn the cognitive skill of self-encouragement, which enables them to respond to mistakes, failures, or put-downs in a manner which maintains their self-esteem. They learn to take responsibility for their school success by using self-statements to motivate and coach themselves through academic tasks. A unit written for advanced or middle school students is also included in the *Intermediate Version*. (*Primary Version*, 580 pages; *Intermediate Version*, 635 pages)

- *Creating A Caring Classroom*—This manual includes a collection of strategies designed to promote mutual support and strengthen connections in the classroom. Included are: (1) getting acquainted activities; (2) classroom management procedures; (3) a personal/social behavior scale and behavior improvement strategies for students with special needs; (4) a relaxation training program; and (5) a large collection of activities for establishing a nurturing classroom community. (582 pages)

- *Helping Kids Find Their Strengths*—Designed to enable students to identify and utilize their strengths. Based on pioneering research by Bernard Haldane, Ph.D., and the Dependable Strengths Project Team at the University of Washington. Students build self-esteem not by positive thinking, but by analyzing experiences they're proud of for clues regarding their core strengths. Students share their good experiences, then utilize teacher and peer input to "tease out" the strengths that helped them create those experiences. They learn a large strength vocabulary and use their expanded self-identity as a springboard for new successes. In helping others find their strengths, students develop a respect for diversity. (699 pages)

- *Helping Kids Handle Anger*—This manual includes lessons designed to enable students to acknowledge, accept, and constructively express anger. Students learn: (1) to use inner speech to inhibit aggressive behaviors; (2) to use thinking skills for choosing constructive behaviors when angry; (3) appropriate language to express anger; (4) a variety of techniques to release energy after anger arousal; (5) ways to defuse the anger of others; and (6) a model for resolving classroom conflicts. Role-plays and puppets are utilized to encourage active student involvement. (515 pages)

- *Teaching About Sexual Abuse*—The lessons in this manual are designed to provide students with information about sexual abuse in a low-key, matter-of-fact way. Lessons focus on: (1) children's right to reject inappropriate behavior; (2) assertiveness skills helpful in the prevention of sexual abuse; and (3) establishing family and community support systems. (72 pages)

- *Teaching Cooperation Skills*—This manual includes a series of lessons and experiential activities designed to teach students the skills necessary for cooperative learning to take place. Lessons focus on the skills of self-management, listening, collaborative problem solving, and leadership. Students learn to resolve conflicts through negotiation and compromise. Included are 52 activities designed to provide practice of cooperation skills and 55 cooperative academic activities in the major subject areas. (437 pages)

- ***Teaching Friendship Skills***—Both the *Primary Version* and the *Intermediate Version* contain all new lessons and Supplementary Activities for each grade level. Students identify the behaviors in others which attract them and behaviors which alienate them. They examine their own behavior and determine changes they need to make in order to gain friends. They learn how to curb physical and verbal aggression. They discover that the secret to making friends is to make others feel special, and practice specific ways to do so. They learn the value of sharing and how to give sincere compliments and apologies. In addition, the *Intermediate Version* focuses on listening, understanding others' perspectives and feelings, and being honest but kind. It also contains 56 activities designed for a "Multiple Intelligences Friendship Center." Each version provides a comprehensive bibliography of children's books on friendship. Puppets, games, role-plays, kinesthetic activities, and goal-setting are used to increase motivation and transfer of training. (*Primary Version*, 605 pages; *Intermediate Version*, 537 pages)

Introduction

This manual is designed for classroom teachers and counselors to use in assisting children in recognizing, appreciating, and utilizing their strengths. The foundation for these lessons is the pioneering work of Bernard Haldane, Ph.D., and the research of the Dependable Strengths Project Team at the University of Washington, directed by Dr. Jerald Forster. Numerous studies of the Dependable Strengths Process have demonstrated significant enhancements of self-esteem and motivation to achieve in individuals aged 7-55.

"Dependable" Strengths

A **dependable strength** has been defined as a skill or talent a person has used to advantage over the years and is seen as helpful to his or her continued achievement. We don't use the term "dependable" when we talk about the strengths of young children because their particular skills, talents, and abilities are just beginning to emerge and develop. However, some children do manifest definite patterns of strengths. Because they don't always think abstractly, they are often unable to see these strengths. What they **can** do is tell little stories about their successes. Hidden in these little stories are the strengths the child used to create the successful events.

As a teacher you can't increase students' self-esteem. You can, however, show students what they can't see by pointing out their emerging strengths and by helping them see their actions in ways that cause them to feel good about themselves. You can do this during unit lessons as well as throughout the school day by linking a specific success to a more global personal quality.

How Discovering Strengths Builds Self-Esteem

Instilling a sense of competence is essential in building students' self-esteem. Many students have developed a habit of focusing on their weaknesses or on what they can't do well. The first step in helping them feel competent is to help them focus on what they **can** do well.

This curriculum addresses the building of self-esteem, not just by positive thinking, but by enabling students to analyze experiences they're proud of for clues to their unique abilities and potentials. In this process, students review memories or experiences they are proud of, recalling themselves "at their best." They share these moments of good experience, then use both teacher and peer input to "tease out" the strengths that helped them create those experiences. After proving to themselves they have particular strengths by reviewing numerous times they have used them, students prioritize their strengths and articulate them in creative ways. Intermediate age students use their expanded self-identity as an impetus for creating new positive experiences for themselves. Students set goals and consciously use their particular strengths to assist in reaching them.

Naming One Another's Strengths Builds Connections

This approach to self-esteem minimizes the degree to which students feel good about themselves because they think they are better than others. They discover their own particular strengths and develop a respect for the diversity of strengths among their classmates. The process of working to identify strengths in one another tends to create a sense of mutual support and fosters positive social behaviors in the classroom. Students thrive in classroom environments where differing skills and personal qualities are honored. The lessons in this manual also provide numerous opportunities for students to validate one another.

A Language Arts Component

Children's natural vocabulary generally includes many words for things that are "wrong" about themselves and others. Their knowledge of words that describe their own and others' strengths is more limited. In order to name their own and others' strengths, students need at their command a repertoire of strength words. Much time in this unit is spent building a large sight and comprehension vocabulary of words that describe strengths. This teaching effort can be integrated into your language arts program. By the time students have completed the unit, they will have added to their reading and speaking vocabularies a large number of words that describe positive human traits.

An Overview of Concepts and Skills Taught in This Unit

The lessons presented in the unit are sequenced to help students gain the following awarenesses:

- They learn to see themselves and others as multifaceted.
- They learn that strengths are talents, skills, and abilities.
- They learn that they have a unique combination of strengths.
- They learn that they can identify their strengths by looking closely at their good experiences.
- They learn that good experiences are those things they feel they do well—experiences they are proud of.
- They learn that they create their own good experiences by using their strengths.
- They learn to focus on their strengths instead of on their weaknesses.
- They learn to feel comfortable sharing their strengths with others.
- They learn to listen to the good experiences of others and help them identify their strengths.
- They learn a large repertoire of words to describe strengths.
- They learn to give evidence of their strengths.
- They learn to use their strengths as a springboard for creating new successes.
- They learn tolerance for diversity and appreciation for their peers.

How to Use This Curriculum

Lesson Grade Levels

This manual includes both a primary unit and a unit for intermediate age students. Because of the timelessness and generality of most of these concepts, the same lessons can be taught to students as they advance through the primary or intermediate grades. Each time students are exposed to the concepts in a lesson, they are able to consider them from a new frame of reference and make new and more precise applications. Supplementary Activities following the lessons can also be used at different grade levels.

The primary unit can be taught in any primary grade and the intermediate unit in any intermediate grade. If your school follows the suggested ASSIST Program Scope and Sequence in Appendix B, students would be taught the lessons in the primary unit in grade two and would be introduced to the intermediate unit in grade four.

To the Teacher Section

Each lesson has a clearly stated objective, a list of all the materials needed to teach the lesson, and a "To the Teacher" section. This section outlines the planning necessary for the lesson and provides theoretical background on the concepts presented. It also includes a summary of the skills taught in the lesson, the methods used, and suggestions for effective teaching.

Lesson Presentation Section

The "Lesson Presentation" section gives step-by-step instructions on how to conduct the lesson. To facilitate the use of teaching techniques in affective education, scripts are provided in boldface type. These scripts are not intended to be used verbatim, but are models of effective teacher comment and interaction. You will want to rephrase this script, saying things in your own words to accommodate aspects of your particular students' frames of reference. The success of the lesson will depend on your ability to provide examples and illustrations of lesson concepts that your students will relate to. It will also depend on your sense of how to pace the lesson, expanding or shortening sections to fit your students' needs. Feel free to exercise wide latitude in spending additional time on a lesson that seems of particular interest to your students.

Names of fictitious children are used throughout the lessons. You may want to substitute other names if there is any chance of embarrassment to your students. You may also wish to change names in order to focus positive attention on students of various ethnic origins.

If you are to tailor a lesson to the needs of your students, you will need to be very familiar with it before you teach it. One way to gain this familiarity is by taping a lesson and listening to it as you travel to and from school. Becoming familiar with lesson format in this way will enable you to "ad lib" the lesson, freeing you to more easily handle the many transparencies that accompany the lessons.

Each lesson concludes with a debriefing. The teacher page that follows this introduction, "Promoting Cognitive Summaries and Transfer of Learning to Real Life Situations," can be used to facilitate "transfer of training."

Transparencies

Each lesson includes a series of transparency masters for picture-smart students whose learning style is "Don't just tell me—show me!" You may wish to color the transparencies or ask an "art-smart" student to do so. You'll be writing on many of the transparencies during the lesson and will need to clean them when the lesson is concluded. For coloring purposes, therefore, you'll need to use permanent-ink markers. Berol Prismacolor™ Art Markers come in a wide variety of colors and would be a good choice. If you color the transparencies on the back side, the markers will not dissolve the black lines of the transparencies.

Handouts

Reproducible student handouts/worksheets also accompany each lesson. These worksheets give students an opportunity to process lesson concepts as well as to demonstrate that they were "attending and receiving" during the lesson presentation and discussion.

Parent Involvement

Keep parents informed regarding what you are teaching and invite their participation by using the "Keeping In Touch" form following this introduction.

Supplementary Activities

Following each lesson are a number of "Supplementary Activities" designed to appeal to students of varying abilities. These activities are designed to help students process the ideas presented in the lesson and to provide opportunities for them to practice targeted self-concept skills. Many of these activities provide practice of basic skills in the academic areas.

Scheduling the Lessons

Lessons should last 30-45 minutes, depending on your students' attention spans. Some lessons can be divided and taught in segments without undermining their effectiveness. Teaching the lesson early in the school day allows you to capitalize on opportunities during the remainder of the day to use lesson vocabulary and encourage the students to use skills that were introduced that morning.

Every school and classroom has its own particular set of characteristics, and you will want to utilize these materials in your own unique way. Some teachers integrate lessons into their health, social studies, and language arts/communication curricula. Others set up a formal "personal/social skills" period and teach lessons once per week or use a "unit" format, teaching a lesson or doing an activity on a daily basis for a period of time.

Integrating Lesson Concepts Into Classroom Life

You can achieve maximum results with this curriculum by finding ways for the students to practice and review the concepts regularly and by extending the learning to other areas consistently throughout the school year. You can be alert for teachable moments—times you can verbally link present events to self-esteem concepts you have presented previously. Just as a single vitamin tablet administered on a regular basis is a more effective regimen than a handful once per month, growth in self-esteem is more likely to occur with regular skill applications.

You may want to weave lesson concepts and activities into your art and creative writing programs, as well as into integrated units in the content areas. You will also find that students enjoy repeating some of the games included in the lessons. A particularly effective technique for achieving transfer of training involves asking students to write down or state a specific time when they will implement a behavior that is encouraged in the lesson. Follow-up might involve asking students to write you a note or to indicate on a class chart when they used the behavior. This type of consistent reinforcement will not only combat the tendency of new learning to diminish but will model for students that you are genuinely interested in them as people who have needs and concerns beyond the realm of academics.

Using the Technique of Class Discussion to Teach Self-Esteem Skills

Class discussion is a valuable teaching tool, especially when the discussion is structured so that students who are functioning on a high social level can share their knowledge, experience, and opinions with their peers. Studies have shown that, even at the kindergarten level, students are influenced more by the comments of peers than by the comments of their teacher.

Following are some suggestions to make class discussion more effective:

- If possible, seat students in a circle so they can all see each other.
- Ask open-ended questions such as, "What can you tell us about . . . ?" or "Can you tell us more about . . . ?"
- If a student who is not attending well is not ready to give a response to a question, say you will come back to him or her shortly for a response.
- If a student is dominating the discussion, say something like, "We have to move on, but I would be interested in hearing more later."
- Use the technique of "thumbs up or down" to get all students to respond to general questions.
- Remember that repeating a question after calling on a student trains students not to listen to you.
- Encourage students to give complete answers and refrain from repeating or elaborating on their answers for them.

- Encourage discussion and avoid "sermonettes" about lesson topics.
- Structure discussion to encourage students with high social functioning to suggest examples of the concepts you want to get across.

Additional Things You Can Do to Aid the Development of Self-Esteem in the Classroom

- **Teach well!** A student who is failing to learn won't feel good about himself or herself no matter what else is done. Careful instruction makes learning easier and leads the student to success. There is nothing more important for any student than believing and experiencing that he or she is able to learn!
- **Help students find success in an area that is challenging for them.** Self-confidence is very much the result of having successfully met a series of challenging situations.
- **Demonstrate that you accept and care for students.** During elementary school a correlation exists between children's perceptions of their teacher's feelings towards them and their own self-image. The best way to demonstrate care and acceptance is by listening with real interest and focus.
- **Use other techniques to help students build their self-esteem.** Teach the lessons on uniqueness, multiple intelligence, encouraging self-talk and handling put-downs in the primary or intermediate versions of the ASSIST manual *Building Self-Esteem in the Classroom.*
- **Help each student feel a sense of belonging in the classroom group.** The ASSIST curriculum manuals *Teaching Cooperation Skills*, *Teaching Friendship Skills*, and *Creating A Caring Classroom* contain numerous strategies for establishing a caring, cohesive classroom community.
- **Use notes, awards, and certificates to make students feel special.** Take a few minutes after school to write a short affirming note to a student and tape it to his or her desk—then watch his or her expression the next morning! (See the ASSIST manual *Creating A Caring Classroom*, Section D "Praise and Reward.")
- **Give students responsibility.** A student with low self-esteem is often surprised and pleased when someone thinks he or she can handle responsibility, because this demonstrates a level of trust in the student's ability to behave in a mature manner.
- **Create an environment in the classroom where students learn to accept and express their feelings without fear of criticism or rejection.** A student who is allowed to "own" his or her feelings can comfortably say, "It's all right to be me. Having certain feelings does not mean I'm a bad person."
- **Help parents understand the tremendous influence they have on children's self-concept.** Take the opportunity at parent conference time to help parents be aware of the direct relationship of self-esteem to academic achievement. This is also a time to stress to parents their own importance in the development of their child's self-esteem. Explain that their child desperately needs their positive feedback regarding even small successes. This is expressed cogently by

the boy who said, "Mother, let's play darts. I'll throw the darts and you say, 'Wonderful.'"

Suggestions for Enhancing the Teaching of This Curriculum

- Assign students a "Learning Partner" with whom they can discuss lesson concepts when you direct them to do so.

- Emphasize the fun activities that accompany each lesson.

- Supply students with a "think pad" to write on during lessons.

- Make sure students keep all handouts and materials from the lessons in a special folder.

- Let students' interests, responses, needs, and contributions shape the lessons rather than trying to complete a lesson in a given time.

- Incorporate vocabulary lists and writing activities in the lessons into your language arts program.

- Make notes about lesson content on index cards for reference as you teach from lesson transparencies.

- Make audio tapes of lessons that you can listen to on your way to or from school to gain familiarization with lesson content.

- Use the form "Take a Minute to Think About Your Good Points" that follows this introduction in conjunction with either the Primary or Intermediate Unit as an informal Pre-Post Test. Simply asking students to list their strengths before and after you teach the unit will give you a sense of the efficacy of this curriculum.

- Send home the parent letter included in Lesson Five when teaching that lesson. Additionally, use the parent communication form "Keeping In Touch" that follows this introduction to inform parents of lesson activities as you proceed through the unit (either the Primary or Intermediate Unit). Family members can then assist you by reinforcing lesson concepts and helping students focus on their strengths.

Promoting Cognitive Summaries and Transfer of Learning to Real Life Situations

THINKING BACK

1. What do you think was the purpose of this lesson?

2. What did you learn from this lesson?

3. Is there anything you are still confused about?

4. Did you change your mind about anything?

5. Are there any questions you still have?

6. Did anything surprise you?

7. Is there anything you'd like to talk more about next time?

8. What are you going to do differently as a result of today's lesson?

FINISH ONE OR MORE OF THE FOLLOWING SENTENCES:

- A way I'm going to use what I learned today is . . . .
- I realized that . . . .
- The main idea we've been talking about is . . . .
- I liked . . . .
- I didn't like . . . .
- I changed my mind about . . . .
- I hope that . . . .
- A behavior I'm going to work on is . . . .

Keeping In Touch

Date _____

Dear Family Member,

In our classroom your child is learning:

Your child's homework this week is:

If you wish, you can help by:

If you have any questions or concerns, please call me at:

Thank you for your support.
Sincerely,

Pre-Post Test

 # Take a Minute to Think About Your Good Points

List the good things about yourself: your talents, skills, strengths, good qualities, things you're proud of, or things about yourself that you like.

Your Name:

_____

_____

_____

_____

_____

_____

_____

_____

_____

A UNIT FOR
PRIMARY GRADES

Learning to Focus on Good Experiences

Objective

Students will understand that they are a mix of strengths and areas that could be improved.

Students will understand the benefits of focusing on their good experiences and strengths, rather than on their mistakes or weaknesses.

Materials

Transparency #1 - "Everyone Is a Mix of Strengths and Things That Could Be Improved"

Transparency #2 - "Sometimes We Only Notice a Person's Strengths"

Transparency #3 - "Sometimes We Only Notice a Person's Weaknesses"

Transparency #4 - "Some People Hide Their Good Qualities"

Transparency #5 - "What If There Were a Video . . . ?"

Transparency #6 - "Bad Experience Channel"

Transparency #7 - "Bad Experiences"

Transparency #8 - "Good Experience Channel"

Transparency #9 - "Good Experiences"

Transparency #10/Handout #1 - "A Good Experience I Have Had"

One large piece of construction paper for each student to make a "Strengths Folder"

To the Teacher

In this lesson students learn that they are multifaceted, a mix of strengths and areas that may need improvement. They are cautioned against seeing their negative traits as a whole picture of themselves. Their deficits are not denied, but the benefits of focusing on their strengths are emphasized. The fact that some students hide their positive characteristics with "tough" behaviors until they feel safe enough to reveal their more sensitive aspects is also discussed , and students are encouraged to look beneath the surface for these positive characteristics.

Students learn that they can choose to focus on unpleasant past experiences or positive ones and discuss the fact that trying something new or difficult is easier to do when they remember past successes. Watching videos on TV is used as a metaphor for memories, and students are encouraged to practice "changing the channel" from memories of discouraging past experiences to those of a more positive nature.

Students practice focusing on encouraging memories by drawing a picture of a past good experience and sharing it with their classmates. In order to "set the stage" for the students to learn in the future to identify the strengths that they and their classmates use to create their good experiences, you can identify the most obvious strength demonstrated in each of their drawings.

You will lead students in a review by asking them to respond to several sentence starters and giving them large sheets of construction paper so they can each make a "Strengths Folder." Students will keep all handouts from this unit in their folders so they can refer to them during future lessons.

Lesson Presentation

Say or paraphrase: **Over the next few weeks I'm going to ask you to be thinking about things you've done that you felt good about or were proud of in some way. As you remember things you've done that you're proud of, you're going to discover that you have some special strengths that helped you do these things.**

EVERYONE IS A MIX OF STRENGTHS AND WEAKNESSES

One of the things we're going to talk about today is the fact that each person is a mix of strengths and areas that could be improved, and that it makes more sense to focus on your strengths than always to be thinking about your weaknesses.

Transp. #1

Show Transparency #1, "Everyone Is a Mix of Strengths and Things That Could Be Improved." Explain: **We all have strengths and things we're good at, and we also have things that we aren't so good at. For example, maybe you're really good at making friends and you like being with people, but when it comes to finishing your schoolwork you have a hard time. Maybe you're great at schoolwork but don't feel so good about your ability to make friends.**

Transp. #2

Show Transparency #2, "Sometimes We Only Notice a Person's Strengths." **It might seem to you that some people have all** pluses—that they're almost perfect. That's because you're just looking at their strengths. You don't know about, or you choose not to look at, the things they need to improve.

Transp. #3

Show Transparency #3, "Sometimes We Only Notice a Person's Weaknesses." It may seem as if other people are all minuses. That's because you're not noticing their strengths, or what's good about them—you're only looking at the things about them that you don't like. It also might be that some of these people are not showing their pluses.

Transp. #4

Some people hide their good qualities—especially when they don't feel safe. *Show Transparency #4, "Some People Hide Their Good Qualities," covering the bottom half.* Some kids think they need to look tough, so they only show their mean side. When you really get to know a person like this and they feel safe enough to be themselves, it's amazing how you find that they have lots of strengths or good qualities, like this boy does. *Show the bottom half of the transparency.* He's good at taking care of animals. If you study people, you'll find that everyone is a mix of strengths and weaknesses.

WHY IT'S IMPORTANT TO FOCUS ON STRENGTHS INSTEAD OF WEAKNESSES

In our class I'd like it if we all tried to think more about the things we do well instead of the things we don't do well. When you think a lot about the mistakes you make, it makes you feel bad. When you think about the things you do well, it makes you feel good and feel encouraged. When you feel encouraged, it helps you do better at things like school-work or sports.

WATCHING "VIDEOS" OF OUR GOOD EXPERIENCES INSTEAD OF OUR MISTAKES

Transp. #5

Let's pretend for a minute that someone has been following you around with a video camera and has made two videos of your life. One of these videos shows all the mistakes you've ever made. The person with the video camera recorded all your most embarrassing moments, all the times you weren't good at something. *Put Transparency #5, "What If There Were a Video . . . ?" on the overhead and discuss how we've all had times when we have "crashed" trying to do something.* This video also has a record of every time someone criticized you. How would you feel sitting down watching this video of yourself? *Allow for student response.* It would be pretty depressing, wouldn't it?

Now let's think about the other video of your life. Let's suppose this video shows all the things you have done well—all the things you've tried that turned out O.K. The person who shot this video got on film all the times you learned how to do something new—all the times you did something well or felt proud of something. Which of these videos would you rather watch? *Allow for student response.* How would you feel about trying something new if you always watched the video of yourself making mistakes? *Allow for student response.* How would you feel about trying something new if you watched your "good experience video" about the times you did well? *Allow for student response.*

"BAD EXPERIENCE CHANNEL"

Imagine you have a special kind of television set in your head. Imagine this television has two different channels that play videos about your life.

Transp. #6

Show Transparency #6, "Bad Experience Channel." Let's pretend one channel shows videos of all your bad experiences: all the mistakes you've made; all your goof-ups or times you've done something the wrong way; all the times you've felt like a flop.

Transp. #7

Show Transparency #7, "Bad Experiences." Go over the examples on the transparency with the students. Then ask for a student volunteer to suggest an example for the last frame. Draw a stick figure of the suggested example in the blank box.

"GOOD EXPERIENCE CHANNEL"

Transp. #8

Show Transparency #8, "Good Experience Channel." **Let's pretend that another channel has videos of all the things you've done that have worked out well and that you've felt good about. These videos show the times you were proud of something you did. All these videos are about the things you've done well.** *Discuss times the students felt proud, especially for something that was hard to learn or took practice.*

Transp. #9

Show Transparency #9, "Good Experiences." Go over the examples on the transparency with the students. Then ask for a volunteer to suggest an example for the last frame. Draw a picture of the suggested example in the blank box.

CHOOSING WHICH CHANNEL TO WATCH

Your mind is very much like a television with different channels, because you can choose to remember and think about your <u>failures</u> or your <u>successes</u>. If you wanted to feel happy, which channel would be best to watch? *Allow for student response.* **Right—the channel of your good experiences. This would be your "Happy Channel."**

You can also choose to watch the channel that shows you all the times you didn't do something well or the times you've goofed up. If you only watch this channel, how do you think you'll feel? *Allow for student response.* **I agree with you! I would feel pretty sad watching all my mistakes.**

Luckily, you can "change the channel" any time you want to because you can decide to think about the times you've done things well instead of thinking of all your past

mistakes. **How do you think you'd feel watching videos about your good experiences?** *Allow for student response.* **I think I would feel pretty good, too!**

Some people get in the habit of watching their "Sad Channel" or thinking about their past mistakes all the time. This causes them to feel discouraged. They'd be much happier if they would "change the channel." To help us learn to be better able to change the channel ourselves, we'll be spending some special time each week when we look only at our "Happy Channel." We'll be taking time to think about our good experiences and telling each other about them. Remembering the things we've done well in the past can help us feel encouraged about trying new things.

MODELING "CHANGING CHANNELS"

Transp. #10

Show Transparency #10, "A Good Experience I Have Had." **I'd like to tell you about one of my good experiences that I like to watch on my "Happy Channel." This was a time when I felt I did something well; I put in a lot of effort on something and I was proud of the way it turned out.** *Model for the students by sharing a good experience of your own. Make a sketch on the transparency that illustrates your good experience. Summarize your good experience on the lines under the phrase: "What this picture is about."*

Take a moment to explain to students why it makes you feel good to remeber this experience. Then say: **I've had some discouraging experiences in my life, too, when I wasn't able to do well at something. Sometimes it's useful for me to remember these so I'll be sure to try other ways of doing things. But when I want to feel happy and encouraged so I'll do well at something, I try to "change the channel" to my good experiences.**

STUDENTS SHARE GOOD EXPERIENCES

Is there anyone who would like to share one of your good experiences—something you tried hard to do and it turned out the way you wanted it to—something you were proud of? *Allow for student response. If the students have difficulty thinking of good experiences, say:* **Here are some good experiences some other kids have told about:**

- **"I dug a three-foot hole in the sandbox when I was in preschool."**

- **"I finally learned to color inside the lines."**

- **"I learned to spell a long word."**

- **"I learned to whistle."**

- **"I saved a mouse by opening my aunt's cat's mouth and taking the mouse out."**

- **"I was nice to a new student and he became my friend."**

- **"I made a gift for a person in a nursing home."**

- **"I gave my sister a present for no reason at all."**

If the students continue to have difficulty recalling their good experiences, use the following list of experiences to trigger their memories. Read a few of the words until hands start to go up; call on a couple of students to tell about their good experiences. Then read a few more trigger words until the students start to raise their hands again, etc:

- acting
- art
- building forts
- building models
- coloring
- cooking
- dancing
- digging holes
- diving
- doing cartwheels
- doing math
- drawing
- fishing
- helping people
- ice skating
- jumping rope
- karate
- learning new things
- making friends
- making things
- painting

- planting things
- playing baseball
- playing basketball
- playing checkers
- playing computer games
- playing football
- playing games
- playing hopscotch
- playing an instrument
- playing soccer
- reading
- riding a bike
- rollerskating
- running
- singing
- skiing
- swimming
- taking care of pets
- telling jokes
- thinking
- writing

STUDENTS ILLUSTRATE AND SHARE A GOOD EXPERIENCE

Handout #1

Now you're going to have a chance to draw a picture about one of your good experiences, just as I did. *Point to Transparency #10.* **Think about the different kinds of good experiences we've been sharing with each other and see if they help you remember one of your own. I'm going to give you a TV page just like mine, and I want you to draw a picture of your good experience. You can write what your picture is about on the TV Guide at the bottom of the page, if you like.** *Point to the lines at the bottom of the transparency.* **When you're finished, you may want to share your pictures with the rest of the class.** *Distribute copies of Handout #1, "A Good Experience I Have Had," and give the students time to complete it. If the students have difficulty remembering their good experiences, whisper some of the phrases from the above list to the students having difficulty.*

SHARING COMPLETED WORK

When the students have completed their handouts, give those who wish an opportunity to show their pictures and tell about their good experiences. After each volunteer has shared, say something like: **You must have been very <u>(athletic, determined, brave, patient, strong, coordinated, generous, etc.)</u> to have had a good experience like that!** *In this way you will "pave the way" for students to learn to identify their own and others' strengths in future weeks.*

LESSON REVIEW

Review the lesson by asking the students to respond to one of the following sentence stems:

- *I learned . . . .*

- *I liked . . . .*

- *I hope . . . .*

- *I'm confused about . . . .*

STRENGTHS FOLDERS

Give each student a large piece of construction paper that can be made into a "Strengths Folder" to hold all the materials from this unit. Have them put their completed copies of Handout #1 in their folders. Say or paraphrase: **We'll be adding lots of pages to our "Strengths Folders" over the next few weeks.**

Instruct the students to draw three horizontal writing lines toward the bottom of the cover of their folders, showing them a completed model. Say: **By the time we've finished studying about our good experiences, you will all be able to write down three of**

your best strengths on these three lines. We're going to have a lot of fun finding out what those are.

Between now and Lesson 2, give the students an opportunity to decorate their "Strengths Folders" in any way they wish.

SUPPLEMENTARY ACTIVITIES

Use the Supplementary Activities to provide additional practice with lesson concepts:

- *"Fish for Good Experiences"*
  (Supplementary Activity #1)

- *"The Most Wonderful Egg in the World"*
  (Supplementary Activity #2)

- *"A Time When You Were Little and You Learned to Do Something Well"*
  (Supplementary Activity #3)

TRANSPARENCY #1

Everyone Is a Mix of Strengths and Things That Could Be Improved

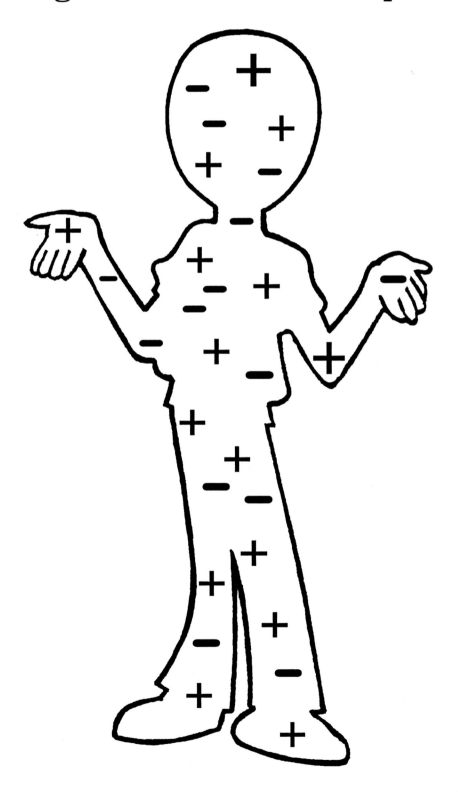

TRANSPARENCY #2

Sometimes We Only Notice a Person's Strengths

TRANSPARENCY #3

Sometimes We Only Notice a Person's Weaknesses

TRANSPARENCY #4

Some People Hide Their Good Qualities

TRANSPARENCY #5

What If There Were a Video . . . ?

TRANSPARENCY #6

Bad Experience Channel

TRANSPARENCY #7

Bad Experiences

TRANSPARENCY #8

Good Experience Channel

TRANSPARENCY #9

Good Experiences

TRANSPARENCY #10/HANDOUT #1

A Good Experience I Have Had

SUPPLEMENTARY ACTIVITY #1

Fish for Good Experiences

Objective   Students will remember more of their good experiences by completing sentence starters in a fun activity.

Materials   Teacher Page - "Fish for Good Experiences Pattern"

Construction or other stiff colored paper

Glue or rubber cement

Medium-sized cardboard box or similar container

For Option 1:
Stick to be used as a "fishing pole"
String and paper clips
Small magnet that can be attached to the string

For Option 2:
String, cut into $2\frac{1}{2}'$ long pieces
Paper punch

Procedure   This activity provides a lot of enjoyment for students while at the same time prompting them to remember more of their good experiences. Students will "catch" a fish which has a sentence starter on it, and then will finish the sentence by recalling a good experience that fits the sentence stem. This can be done verbally or as a seatwork assignment where the students draw a picture or write about the good experiences. If the students can't think of a good experience to use to complete the sentence on the first fish they catch, they may "throw it back in" and try once more.

Prepare for this activity by cutting colored construction paper into fish shapes, enough for at least one per student. Use the fish on the Teacher Page ("Fish for Good Experiences Pattern") as a template. Cut out the sentence starters found on the Teacher Page and glue or rubber cement them onto the fish. If you have more students than the 24 sentence starters, you may need to make duplicates of these.

Students may "go fishing" in either of two ways:

OPTION 1

Make a "fishing pole" by attaching a magnet to the end of a length of string, then tying the other end of the string to a stick. Place a paper clip over the head of each of the fish, and put the fish into the cardboard box. Have the students take turns casting the magnet into the box and pulling out whichever fish becomes attached to the magnet.

OPTION 2

Punch a hole in the mouth area of each fish and attach a length of string. Put the fish into the cardboard box with the strings all hanging over the edge. Each student in turn will select a string and "reel in" his or her fish.

SUPPLEMENTARY ACTIVITY #1 TEACHER PAGE

Fish for Good Experiences Pattern

I realized I was good at
_____ the time I . . . .

It was hard but I finally . . . .

Something I learned to do
by myself was . . . .

I felt good when I helped . . . .

Something new I've learned
to do recently is . . . .

I was afraid but I did it anyway and felt great the time . . . .

When I was younger I think people
were proud of me the time I . . . .

A talent I have that makes me
feel good is . . . .

It felt good to stick with a job
and finish it the time I . . . .

I didn't feel like doing it but I made
myself and then felt great when . . . .

I did my best the time I . . . .

Nobody else noticed, but
I felt good when . . . .

I didn't think I could
do it but . . . .

It took some doing but I finally . . . .

I really felt proud the time I . . . .

I was glad I kept trying
after I finally learned . . . .

I felt good making someone
happy the time I . . . .

I got a lot of congratulations
from others when . . . .

I was glad I practiced
the time I . . . .

I've always had a talent for . . . .

Even I was surprised how well
things went the time I . . . .

I deserved a pat on the back
the time I . . . .

Pattern for Making Fish
Tape or glue a sentence starter here.

The Most Wonderful Egg in the World

Objective   Students will understand that a person's strengths are more important than their physical appearance and will identify something that they do well.

Materials   Children's book: Heine, H. (1983). *The most wonderful egg in the world*. London, England: J. M. Dent & Sons, Ltd.

Supplementary Activity #2 Handouts #1A and #1B - "The Most Wonderful Egg in the World"

Supplementary Activity #2 Handout #2 - "The Most Wonderful Egg in the World Cut-Outs"

Procedure   Tell students you're going to read them a story about three hens who found out that they were special, not because of the way they looked, but because of something they could do. Tell students that as they listen to the story, they should try to think of something special that **they** are able to do. Read the story aloud, showing the illustrations.

Distribute copies of the handouts. Students may color the hens and eggs on the handouts, but for now they should leave the big egg in the nest on Handout #1B uncolored. Ask students to cut out the three eggs on the "Cut-Outs" sheet (Handout #2). Instruct them to glue the three eggs on the Xs next to the three hens, being sure to match them correctly (the square egg for Plumy, the first hen; the giant egg for Stalky, the second hen; the perfect egg for Dotty, the third hen). On the big egg in the large nest at the bottom of Handout #1B, have the students draw and color something they do well.

The Most Wonderful Egg in the World

SUPPLEMENTARY ACTIVITY #2 HANDOUT #1B

The Most Wonderful Egg in the World (continued)

Dotty

X

Something I do well.

The Most Wonderful Egg in the World Cut-Outs

Directions:

Cut out the three wonderful eggs and glue them to the Xs by the three hens on your other handout pages.

SUPPLEMENTARY ACTIVITY #3

A Time When You Were Little and You Learned to Do Something Well

Directions:

Draw a picture or write about something you learned to do when you were little.

At Home

Indoors

Outdoors

Away From Home

Indoors

Outdoors

Discovering Our Strengths

Objective

Students will identify and share good experiences.

Students will understand that they can discover their strengths by remembering their good experiences.

Students will start building a vocabulary of words which describe strengths.

Materials

Transparency #1 - "The Definition of a Good Experience"

Transparency #2 - "Why Are They Proud and Happy?"

Transparency #3A/Handout #1A, Transparency #3B/Handout #1B, and Transparency #3C/Handout #1C - "A Good Experiences Survey"

Transparency #4 - "My Good Experience Channel—Examples"

Handout #2 - "My Good Experience Channel" (run two copies for each student)

Handouts #3A and #3B - "Possible Good Experiences"

Transparency #5 - "Being Determined Is a Strength"

Transparency #6 - "Being Kind Is a Strength"

Handout #4 - "Strength Word List"

Strength Word Card Pages #1-#12 - "Strength Word Cards"

Standard pocket chart (available in educational supply stores)

To the Teacher

In this lesson students learn the definition of a good experience: something that they feel they did well—something they were proud of. They begin to recall good experiences of their own and to discover some of the strengths they may have used to create those good experiences. The lesson emphasizes that a good experience is something students did that took some effort, not just a passing experience where something good happened to them.

The strengths students used are identified initially through teacher input. Then, as students become more familiar with the concept of strengths, they are asked to try to identify the strengths that they and others used to create a good experience. Students are also asked to identify strengths in others. To help facilitate the strengths discovery process for students, it is suggested that you model identifying strengths in one or two of your own good experiences, choosing experiences in which it would be easy to point out the strengths.

Students will record their good experiences on "My Good Experience Channel" handouts. They should be reminded of the concept presented in the previous lesson—that we feel better if we remember (or "watch videos" of) our good experiences, rather than remembering our bad experiences or picturing our past mistakes. Initially, three or four blank channel pages could be given to students for them to record their good experiences. More sheets can be added if students want to record more good experiences as time goes on.

"Strength Word Cards" describing strengths are provided in this lesson for you to use as a teaching aid. These are designed to fit in a standard pocket chart. As strengths are identified in your class discussions, the appropriate strength word card should be placed in the pocket chart. Pictures are included on each card to help nonreaders learn the words. The copies of the "Strength Word Cards" in the lesson can also be made into transparencies. Instead of putting the cards in a pocket chart, you can show the words on the overhead projector.

You may also wish to keep an extra set of these "Strength Word Cards" in a "Strength Box" at the front of the room to use at various times during the day. Then when you notice students demonstrating particular strengths in class, you can pull out the appropriate strength cards and tape them to the students' desks.

In addition to using these "Strength Word Cards" to build vocabulary, students are also given a list of strength words to help them name more strength words for themselves and others. These word lists can be kept in their "Strengths Folders" (from Lesson 1). Any new strength words that are later identified can be added to these lists.

This lesson is designed to extend over several sessions, allowing time for each student to share one or more good experiences with the class and to become familiar with the process of identifying strengths using a strengths word vocabulary. By the conclusion of all the activities suggested in this lesson and the Supplementary Activities that follow, the students should have identified some of their good experiences and have an understanding of how they used their strengths to make these good experiences happen. They should also have a larger working vocabulary of words to use to describe strengths.

Lesson concepts can be modified for students of younger ages or lower ability levels. A list of lesson extension ideas is provided at the end of the lesson to help meet the individual needs of your students.

REVIEW OF PREVIOUS LESSON

Lesson Presentation

Say or paraphrase: **In our last lesson we talked about how no one is perfect—how we all have some things we do well and some things that we don't do so well. We all have pluses and minuses, and it's O.K. to have both.**

Remember when we talked about pretending to watch videos of ourselves in our minds? What kind of videos did we decide we should watch if we want to feel good about ourselves? *Allow for student response and remind the students of the importance of focusing on things that they have done well or focusing on their good experiences. You might end this review by saying:* **When we remember to think about what's on our "Happy Channel," we feel good about ourselves, and that can help us to do more things well.**

DEFINING A GOOD EXPERIENCE

Transp. #1

Say or paraphrase: **I want to tell you exactly what I mean when I talk about a "good experience."** *Put Transparency #1, "The Definition of a Good Experience," on the overhead. Point to the first part of the definition and say:* **For something to have been a "good experience" it must be something you worked hard on and were at least a little bit proud of doing. It should be something that turned out the way you wanted it to. You're the one who decides if you did it well enough to be proud of it—it doesn't matter what someone else thinks. If you think you did a good drawing or wrote your name well, yours is the only opinion that counts!**

A good experience also has to be something you <u>did</u>—not something that happened to you. Let's think about some

examples and decide if they would be called a "good experience" the way we're using the words.

What if you got a puppy that you wanted for Christmas? Would that count as the kind of a good experience we're talking about? *Say or paraphrase:* Getting a puppy wouldn't count as the kind of good experience we mean because it's not something that <u>you did</u>. It was given to you. You have to actually <u>do</u> something to make a good experience happen. If you took really good care of the puppy, trained it, and took responsibility for it, you could say "taking care of your puppy and training it" was a good experience. You have to <u>do</u> something to have the kind of good experience we're talking about.

What if you studied and studied your math facts until you got all of them right one day? Would that be a "good experience?" *Allow for student response.* Yes, it would count as a good experience because you did something to make it happen.

Transp. #2

Show students Transparency #2, "Why Are They Proud and Happy?" Say or paraphrase: Let's see if we really understand what a good experience is. Take a look at this little boy. He can hardly wait to tell his dad something! Notice how proud he looks. He also looks as if he just had a great time doing something. What kind of good experience do you suppose he had that he wants to share with his dad? *Allow for student response.*

Point to the lower picture on the transparency. Now look at this girl. She's dying to tell her best friend about something. It looks as if she has accomplished something that's really made her feel happy. What good experience do you suppose she might want to share with her friend? *Allow for student response. You might want to put the definition of a "good experience" up on a chart that students can see in the classroom or enlarge a copy of Transparency #1, "The Definition of a Good Experience," to refer to throughout the rest of the lessons.*

A "GOOD EXPERIENCES" SURVEY

Handout #1A
Handout #1B
Handout #1C

Sometimes it's hard to remember some of our good experiences. I think it would be fun to do a survey of good experiences in our class. This might help you remember some of the things you've done well or felt proud of. *Distribute copies of Handouts #1A-#1C, "A Good Experiences Survey." Because this is a long checklist, you may wish to distribute only one or two pages for the survey and reserve the remaining page(s) for later use. (See the Lesson Extension Ideas at the end of the lesson.)*

Transp. #3A
Transp. #3B
Transp. #3C

Show the corresponding Transparencies #3A-#3C ("A Good Experiences Survey"), using a covering sheet of paper so that you only reveal one statement at a time. Read each experience aloud for the class and instruct students to put a check mark in the box on their handouts if they have had that good experience. (You may want to stop from time to time to let student volunteers give a few details about their particular experiences.)

After completing the survey, your class might enjoy taking a class tally of good experiences. Do this by reading aloud the items on the survey once again, asking students to raise their hands if they marked the item. Count the number of raised hands and record the number of responses on the transparency. Point out the three most common experiences.

RECALLING A GOOD EXPERIENCE

Remember when we talked about our pretend television sets, the ones where we can watch discouraging or encouraging videos about ourselves in our minds? We drew some pictures of our good experience videos on our TV sets. I want to show you some examples of good experiences other kids drew pictures about.

Transp. #4

Show Transparency #4, "My Good Experience Channel—Examples." Uncover the pictures one at a time, first showing the student "saving a friend" from a bully and then the student "learning to do a somersault dive." Read the descriptions of the two experiences as written on the "TV Guide."

Say or paraphrase: **You've all had many good experiences. The important thing is to <u>remind</u> yourself of them because this will give you encouragement to try new things.**

I want you to try to "tune in" a good experience now. It could be anything you remember you did well—a time when you didn't blow it, but things turned out the way you wanted them to. Maybe it was a good experience you had when you were little, before you started school. Maybe you'll remember something you did recently that you did well. Try to think of something different from the two examples I showed you if you can. Tune in your "Happy Channel" and see if you can remember at least one good experience right now.

Handout #2

Give students Handout #2, "My Good Experience Channel," and ask them to draw a simple picture of their good experience. Tell students not to worry if drawing pictures is sometimes hard for them—the most important thing is just to show what their good experience was about. Have several copies of this handout available for those students who want to do more than one picture.

If students want to write down a few words to help describe their good experience, they can do so in the "TV Guide" section at the bottom of the page.

It is recommended that you circulate through the room while students are drawing their pictures. Assist those students who are finding it difficult to write down words describing their experiences. You may also allow students to leave this section blank. Give extra copies of the handout to students who wish to draw more than one good experience.

Handout #3A
Handout #3B

Note those students who may be having difficulty retrieving a memory of a good experience. Read them examples from Handouts #3A and #3B, "Possible Good Experiences," to trigger their memories. Give them a copy of the handout if appropriate. Remind students again that a good experience can be anything they did that they are at least a little bit proud of.

As you circulate through the room looking at the students' drawings, see if you can find a picture of a good experience that could be used to illustrate the strength of being <u>determined</u>. Ask the student who drew this picture if he or she would be willing to share the good experience when the time comes for student sharing.

BUILDING A CONCEPT OF STRENGTHS

When most of the students have finished their good experience drawings, explain that it's now time to start sharing some of their good experiences. Ask the previously identified student to tell the class about his or her good experience. After that student has shared, ask: **Did you have to try again and again until you got it right?** *If the student indicates "yes," say:* **It sounds like you had to be pretty <u>determined</u> to have that good experience. You kept trying even when it was hard to do. We can say that you have the "strength" of being <u>determined</u>. A "strength" is an ability we use to make a good experience happen. If <u>(determined student)</u> had not been <u>determined</u>, he *(she)* could not have made this good experience happen. His *(her)* strength of being <u>determined</u> helped him *(her)* to <u>(reiterate good experience)</u> .**

Transp. #5

Show Transparency #5, "Being Determined Is a Strength." **When you have the strength of being <u>determined</u>, you can make a lot of different good experiences happen.** *Point to each illustration and talk about the role determination plays in each good experience. Ask students if any of them have had a good experience where they used the strength of being determined. Illustrate or write them in the blank space on the transparency.*

Transp. #6

Being <u>kind</u> is a strength I often see in our classroom. *Give an example of a kindness you've seen shown in your classroom and show Transparency #6, "Being Kind Is a Strength."* **Being kind helps us to make new friendships or keep old ones. There are lots of ways we can use the strength of being kind.** *Discuss with the class each of the good experiences illustrated on the transparency, talking about the way the strength of being kind helped to create each experience. Ask for other examples of kindness; illustrate or write these in the blank space at the bottom of the transparency.*

Strength Word Card Page #2
Strength Word Card Page #4

When someone says the word "strength," people often think that it means being physically strong. That's just <u>one</u> kind of strength. We're going to be talking about lots of different kinds of strengths. Being <u>determined</u> is one; being <u>kind</u> is another. *Show the "determined" and "kind" "Strength Word Cards" to the class and display them in a pocket chart or as transparencies on the overhead.*

Strength Word Card Page #1

Another strength many of you have is the strength of being <u>brave</u>. Being <u>brave</u> is a strength that helps us do things that might seem scary. Being <u>athletic</u> is a strength that helps you do well in sports or in using your hands. It means your legs and arms or hands do what your brain tells them to do. *Find the "brave" and "athletic" "Strength Word Cards" and place them in the pocket chart or on the overhead projector. Blank cards are also provided for you to write in any additional words you feel would be appropriate for your students. (Keeping all the "Strength Word Cards" in alphabetical order will make retrieval easier.)*

DISCOVERING STRENGTHS IN OUR GOOD EXPERIENCES

Say or paraphrase: **Now let's hear about some more of your good experiences. I'll try to help you discover the strengths you used to create your good experience. Who else will share his or her picture with us and tell us about their good experience?**

Call on student volunteers to describe their good experiences and attempt to pinpoint the strength(s) they used. Pick out the corresponding "Strength Word Card." Ask each responding student if he or she thinks this skill or ability was used to create the good experience, explaining the meaning of the word and possible ways to use that strength. If the student indicates that he or she did indeed use that strength, ask him or her to write down the strength word under the "Strengths I used to make this good experience happen" phrase at the bottom of the handout. (You can temporarily place the appropriate "Strength Word Card" on the student's desk for spelling help.) Rather than always asking students if they used a certain strength, at times say: **"You must have used the strength of being ____ in order to create that good experience for yourself."** *Ask your volunteer what other strengths he or she may have used to create the good experience. The student should write these strengths on his or her handout as well.*

Note that the emphasis at this point is on helping students understand the concept that strengths are used to make good experiences happen. There should be no pressure on students to think of underlying strengths right away. Although some students will be able to do this easily, others will need more modeling of the strength identification process and more of a strength word vocabulary before they are able to do this on their own.

Invite another student to share his or her picture and describe his or her good experience. Identify this student's underlying strengths in this same manner, asking the student if he or she used the strength you suggest.

So there are many different kinds of strengths that help us do things well. We're going to keep adding to our list of strength words as we discover them. If any of you discover a strength that we haven't already talked about, be sure to tell me so we can add it to our list.

Continue this strength discovery exercise as long as it holds student interest. You can extend this strengths discovery lesson over several days, so that each student in the class gets a chance to share a good experience.

STUDENTS IDENTIFY ONE ANOTHER'S STRENGTHS

After you have modeled identifying strengths a number of times, begin the process of having the students learn how to identify strengths in good experiences for one another. Have two or three students "show" their good experience drawings on their "My Good Experience Channel" handouts and then "tell" what their good experience was about. Guide the class in identifying the strengths that the volunteers used to create their good experiences.

As you proceed, try to step more and more out of the role of being the "authority" regarding what strengths were used. The goal here is for the students to begin to identify strengths in their classmates' good experiences and to be able to decide what strengths they themselves used to create their own good experiences. Facilitate this sense of self-assessment. In the process, the students will sharpen their discernment of the many strengths that they and their classmates have and are using but have been unaware of.

BUILDING A STRENGTH VOCABULARY

Handout #4

After several students have shared a good experience and they have identified some strengths, give the class Handout #4, "Strength Word List." Say or paraphrase: **I'm going to give each of you a list of strength words that will help you think of even more strengths that you can find in good experiences.** *Read some of the words to the class, using them in a sentence to help build vocabulary. Explain to students that you'll be going over these words and their meanings many times; students should not worry about remembering them all right now. Students should keep their word list handouts in their "Strengths Folders" for easy reference.*

End this part of the lesson after: (1) every student who wants to has had a chance to share at least one of his or her good experiences; and (2) the students have listed the strengths noticed by you, their class- mates, and themselves on their "My Good Experience Channel" handouts. Compliment everyone on identifying some "good experi- ences" and on helping discover some of the strengths in themselves and their classmates.

LESSON REVIEW AND PREVIEW OF NEXT LESSON

Ask a number of students to respond verbally to one of the following questions:

- *What do you think was the purpose of this lesson?*

- *What did you learn from this lesson?*

- *Did anything surprise you?*

Tell students that you will be teaching them some fun new strength words in the next lesson so they can do a better job of helping each other find their strengths.

SUPPLEMENTARY ACTIVITIES

Use the Supplementary Activities to provde additional practice with lesson concepts:

- *"I Wish I Were a Butterfly"*
     (Supplementary Activity #1)

- *"Cracking the Meaning of Strength Words"*
     (Supplementary Activity #2)

- *"My Good Experience Pop-Up Page"*
     (Supplementary Activity #3)

LESSON EXTENSION IDEAS

In addition to the Supplementary Activities, you may wish to use one or more of these lesson extension ideas:

- *End each school day by asking students to share their best "good experience" of the day. Have the class as a whole deduce the strengths which made those good experiences possible.*

- *The words on the "Strength Word Chart" can be used as a source for weekly spelling words. The students can use each word in a sentence or create a story using words on the chart.*

- *When you notice a student using a strength, give him or her that strength word card to tape on his or her desk for the day.*

- *Since most students love to do charades, have them perform a charade of one of their good experiences. The class can try to guess what their good experience was and what strengths they may have used.*

- *Turn strengths into encouraging statements, such as "I'm a kid who is creative" or "I'm good at art." Print these on cards for the students and tape them on their desks.*

- *Use any reserved pages of Handouts #1A-#1C, "A Good Experiences Survey," for seatwork. Distribute one survey page to the students, along with three "My Good Experience Channel" pages (Handout #2). Have students complete the survey page and then star their "best" good experience from each box. Then have students complete a "My Good Experience Channel" page for each of their starred experiences.*

- *Use puppets to role-play the strength discovery process. One puppet can tell of a good experience while the other puppet can first show good listening skills and then "think aloud" what strengths might have been used to create the good experience.*

Write the strengths the puppet decides were used on the chalk-board or on the overhead.

- *Point out strengths in characters you and the students read about in literature, social studies, or when studying historical events. For example, on Martin Luther King Day have the students imagine what some of his good experiences might have been (or focus on his accomplishments) and identify strengths Dr. King had that helped these occur.*

TRANSPARENCY #1

The Definition of a
Good Experience

Something
that you feel
you did well.

You were
proud of it!

TRANSPARENCY #2

Why Are They Proud and Happy?

TRANSPARENCY #3A/HANDOUT #1A

A Good Experiences Survey

❑ I wrote a good story.

❑ I learned my math facts.

❑ I shared something of mine with someone else.

❑ I gave my brother or sister a present for no particular reason.

❑ I made my first best friend.

❑ I stuck up for someone when others made fun of him or her.

❑ I helped an animal who was hurt.

❑ I helped a person who was hurt.

❑ I did a good job on an art project.

❑ I built something all by myself.

❑ I learned to play a musical instrument.

❑ I taught my little brother or sister something.

❑ I made an especially good play in a sport.

❑ I helped someone who was younger than me.

❑ I made a good grade on a hard assignment.

TRANSPARENTY #3B/HANDOUT #1B

A Good Experiences Survey (continued)

❑ I drew something that looked exactly right.

❑ I learned to tie my shoes.

❑ I got an award.

❑ I learned to do a difficult gymnastics mo

❑ I learned to swim.

❑ I learned to dive.

❑ I made someone in my family proud of me.

❑ I taught an animal a trick.

❑ I saved my money and bought something special.

❑ I read a hard book.

❑ I felt scared about something and did it anyway.

❑ I cooked something that everybody liked.

❑ I learned to ride a two-wheeled bike.

❑ I learned to cut out a perfect valentine heart.

❑ I learned to do a difficult jump-rope move.

TRANSPARENCY #3c/HANDOUT #1c

A Good Experiences Survey (continued)

❑ I made someone who was sad feel better.

❑ I acted in a play or skit.

❑ I did something that was hard and was told I did a good job.

❑ I felt good about something I did even though no

❑ I controlled my temper when I was really mad.

❑ I stuck to a hard job until I finished it.

❑ I surprised myself at how well I did at something.

❑ I made someone else happy.

❑ I learned to do something I thought I could never do.

❑ I got better at something because I practiced and practiced.

❑ I made myself do my work even though I wasn't in the mood.

❑ I surprised someone by doing a chore or task for them.

❑ I didn't let a put-downer get me mad.

❑ I made someone a present that they really liked.

❑ I took good care of a pet.

TRANSPARENCY #4

My Good Experience Channel—Examples

HANDOUT #2

My Good Experience Channel

HANDOUT #3A

Possible Good Experiences

acting

art

building forts

building models

chopping wood

coloring

computer games

cooking

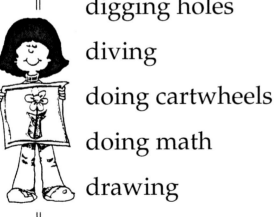

dancing

digging holes

diving

doing cartwheels

doing math

drawing

fishing

helping
 people

hitting a ball

ice skating

jumping rope

karate

learning new things

making friends

making things

painting

planting things

playing baseball

playing basketball

playing checkers

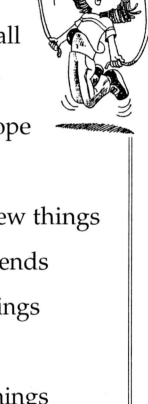

HANDOUT #3ʙ

Possible Good Experiences (continued)

playing football   running

playing a game   singing

playing hopscotch   skiing

playing an instrument   swimming

playing soccer   taking care of pets

playing tennis   telling jokes

reading   thinking

riding a bike   writing

rollerskating

TRANSPARENCY #5

Being **Determined** Is a Strength

Determined

TRANSPARENCY #6

Being **Kind** Is a Strength

Kind

HANDOUT #4

Strength Word List

artistic

athletic

brave

caring

cheerful

cooperative

coordinated

creative

determined

energetic

fair

fast

friendly

generous

good memory

hard worker

helpful

honest

imaginative

kind

musical

organized

patient

positive attitude

problem solver

responsible

sense of humor

sharing

strong

unselfish

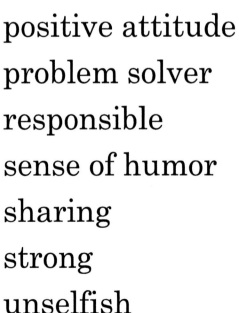

STRENGTH WORD CARD PAGE #1

Strength Word Cards

athletic

artistic

brave

caring

Strength Word Cards (continued)

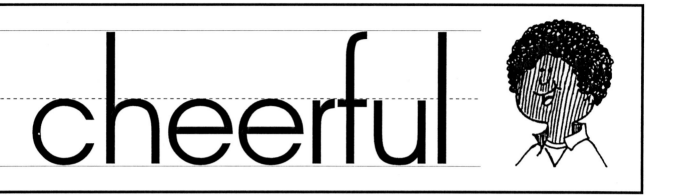

cheerful

determined

fair

fast

STRENGTH WORD CARD PAGE #3

Strength Word Cards (continued)

friendly

generous

hard worker

helpful

STRENGTH WORD CARD PAGE #4

Strength Word Cards (continued)

honest

kind

musical

organized

STRENGTH WORD CARD PAGE #5

Strength Word Cards (continued)

patient

sharing

strong

unselfish

STRENGTH WORD CARD PAGE #6

Strength Word Cards (continued)

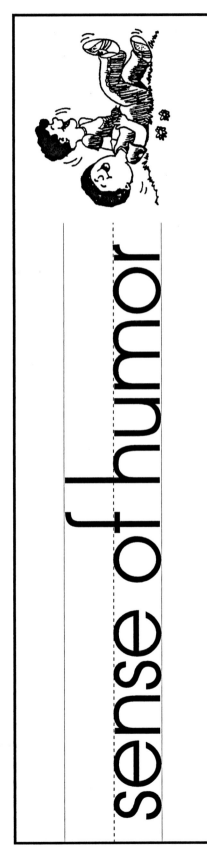

sense of humor

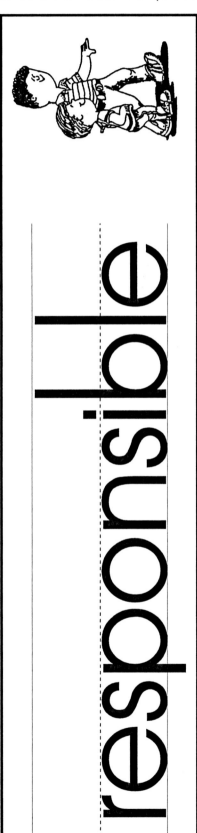

responsible

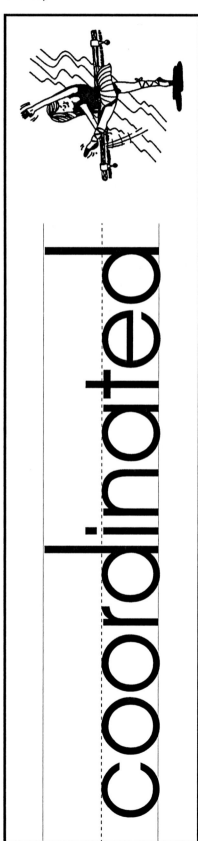

coordinated

STRENGTH WORD CARD PAGE #7

Strength Word Cards (continued)

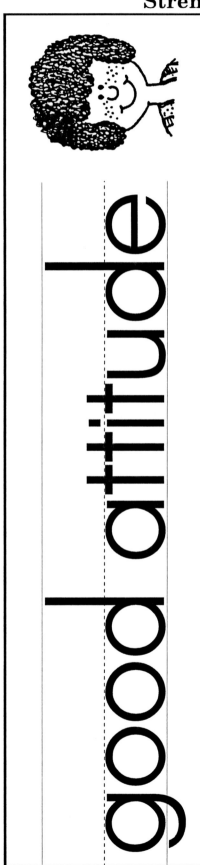

good attitude

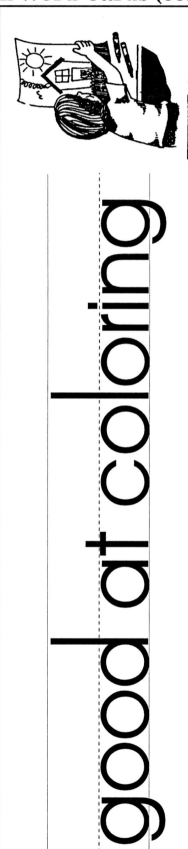

good at coloring

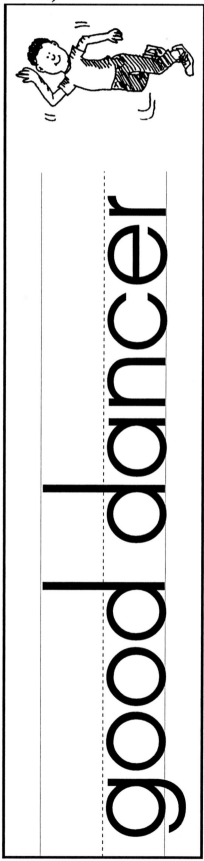

good dancer

STRENGTH WORD CARD PAGE #8

Strength Word Cards (continued)

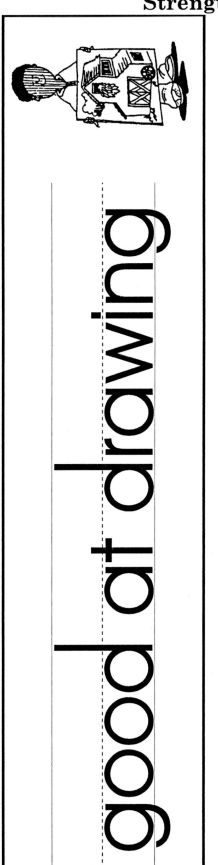

good at drawing

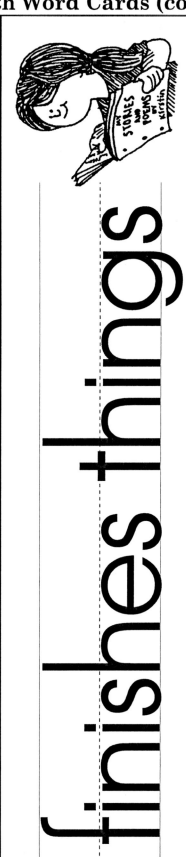

finishes things

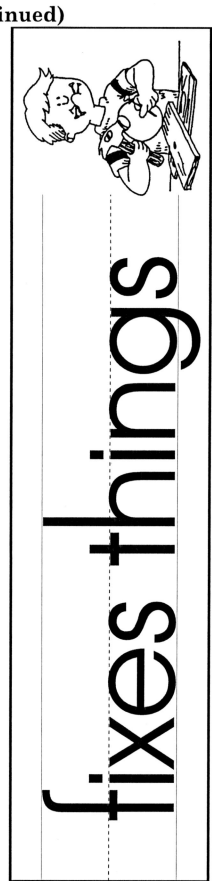

fixes things

STRENGTH WORD CARD PAGE #9

Strength Word Cards (continued)

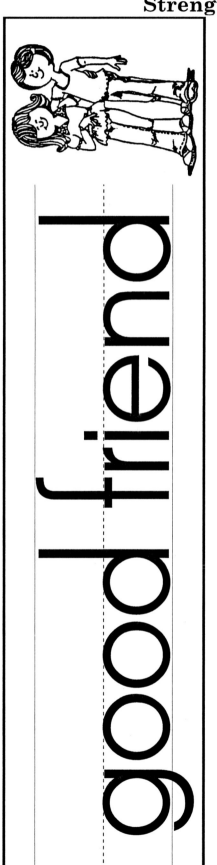

good friend

good imagination

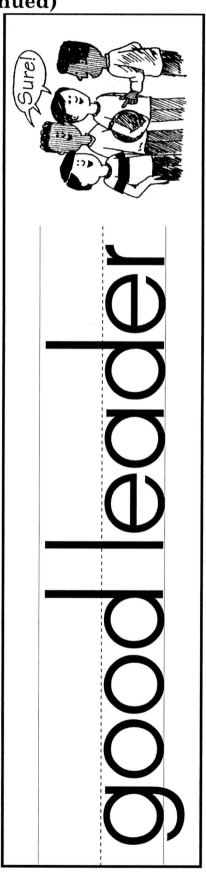

good leader

STRENGTH WORD CARD PAGE #10

Strength Word Cards (continued)

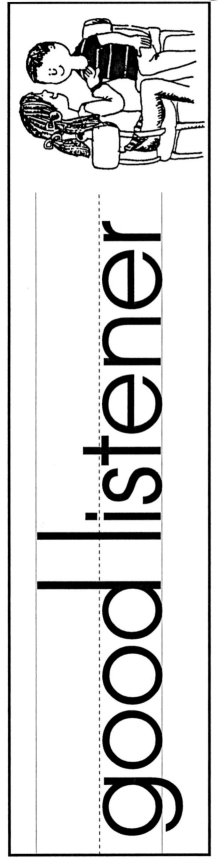

good listener

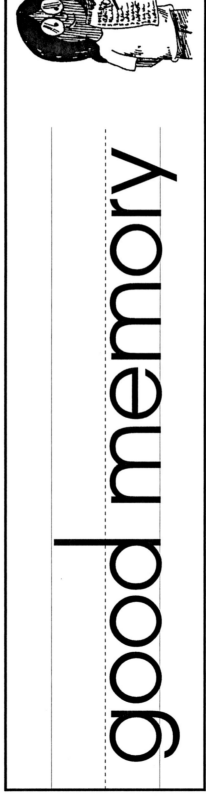

good memory

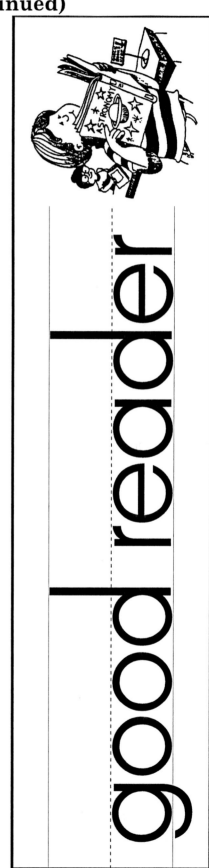

good reader

STRENGTH WORD CARD PAGE #11

Strength Word Cards (continued)

solves problems

good sport

good writer

Oh well, you can't win them all.

STRENGTH WORD CARD PAGE #12

Strength Word Cards (continued)

SUPPLEMENTARY ACTIVITY #1

I Wish I Were a Butterfly

Objective

Students will match characters from the story with their strengths or characteristics.

Materials

Children's book: Howe, J. (1987). *I wish I were a butterfly.* Orlando, FL: Harcourt Brace Jovanovich.

Supplementary Activity #1 Handout   -   "Can You Remember?"

Procedure

Tell the students that you're going to read them a story about a little cricket who thought that all the other creatures in the swamp had strengths but that he didn't.

Read the story to the class, stressing the strengths of each creature the littlest cricket admired. Lead the class in a discussion, asking questions such as the following:

- Why did the littlest cricket think he was ugly? *(The frog told him he was the ugliest creature that ever lived.)*

- The littlest cricket seemed to think that **looking wonderful** was a more important strength than **doing things well**. He admired creatures that he thought were beautiful. What did he admire about the glowworm? *(That the glowworm would someday be a beautiful lightning bug.)*

- What advice did the glowworm give the cricket? *("There's no use wishing for what can't be. Being a cricket seems fine enough for me.")*

- What did he admire about the ladybug? *(Her body was the "color of laughter.")*

- What advice did the ladybug give the cricket? *(Be satisfied with who you are.)*

- What did he admire about the dragonfly? *(It had whispery wings and a jewel-like body.)*

- What creature did the littlest cricket wish he could be? *(He wished he could be a butterfly.)*

- Who was the Old One? *(The Old One was a spider)*

- The Old One felt good about herself for reasons other than the way she looked. She felt good about herself because of her **strengths**. What two strengths was she proud of? *(She was proud of her strengths of waiting and spinning.)*

- What made the Old One feel beautiful? *(She felt beautiful because the littlest cricket thought she was beautiful.)*

- What did the Old One say she saw when they both looked at their reflections in the pond? *(She saw two beautiful friends.)*

- We can say that one of the littlest cricket's strengths was **being a good friend**. What was another strength that the Old One admired? *(The littlest cricket could make beautiful fiddling music.)*

- Who else admired the littlest cricket's fiddling? *(The butterfly admired the fiddling.)*

- What did the butterfly say when she flew by and heard the littlest cricket fiddling? *("I wish I were a cricket.")*

- How do you think the littlest cricket felt when he heard the butterfly say she wished she were a cricket? *(Allow for student response.)*

- Does everyone have some strengths? *(Yes!)*

Distribute copies of the handout "Can You Remember?" Instruct the students to draw lines to match each character from the story with that character's identifying descriptor.

Can You Remember?

Directions:

Draw a line from the words to the matching picture.

Which creature ...

1. Told some of the other creatures that they were ugly?

2. Was "the color of laughter?"

3. Would someday become a lightning bug?

4. Was able to make beautiful music?

5. Had whispery wings and a jewel-colored body?

6. Was wise and patient?

7. Wished she were a cricket so that she could make beautiful music?

SUPPLEMENTARY ACTIVITY #2

Cracking the Meaning of Strength Words

Objective   Students will practice identifying and explaining the meaning of words from their list of strength words.

Materials   Supplementary Activity #2 Strength Word List Pages #1-#3, cut apart into strips

Plastic eggs that come apart

Basket, egg carton, or other container for plastic eggs

Procedure   To prepare for the activity, place one strength word strip from the "Strength Word List" in each plastic egg and put the eggs into the basket or other container.

Call on the students to come to the basket and choose an egg. Knock the egg they select against a table as if to crack it, then open the egg. Have the student read the word on the strength word strip aloud. (Be sure to offer help if the student doesn't recognize the word.)

Ask the student, "What does (strength word) look like?" The student should describe a situation that demonstrates the strength word. Ask the other members of the class to hold up their thumbs if they agree. Then ask the student, "What does (strength word) sound like?" The student should then make up a sentence that a person using that strength might say. An example would be if the student said, "Would you like one of my cookies?" to demonstrate what **generosity** might "sound like." Again, ask the class members to hold up their thumbs if they agree.

Allow the student who has been responding to choose the next student to crack an egg.

SUPPLEMENTARY ACTIVITY #2 STRENGTH WORD LIST PAGE #1

determined

coordinated

brave

energetic

clever

patient

positive attitude

self-disciplined

finishes things

SUPPLEMENTARY ACTIVITY #2 STRENGTH WORD LIST PAGE #2

kind

optimistic

uses teamwork

cooperative

enthusiastic

gentle

honest

open-minded

tough

nice

SUPPLEMENTARY ACTIVITY #2 STRENGTH WORD LIST PAGE #3

considerate

organized

strong

artistic

thoughtful

understanding

graceful

responsible

flexible

SUPPLEMENTARY ACTIVITY #3

My Good Experience Pop-Up Page

Objective   Students will use two of their favorite good experiences to create a pop-up page.

Materials   Supplementary Activity #3 Handout #1 - "My Good Experience Pop-Up Page Strips," duplicated on tagboard or construction paper

Supplementary Activity #3 Handout #2 - "My Good Experience Pop-Up Page," duplicated on tagboard or construction paper

Scissors

Markers or colored pencils

Glue or tape

Procedure   Tell the students that they are going to make a pop-up page of two of their good experiences. (You may wish to relate this to the fact that their memories of good experiences are beginning to "pop up" since they've begun thinking about them.) It may help your students to visualize the finished product if you show them a completed model.

Distribute copies of the "My Good Experience Pop-Up Page Strips." Instruct the students to draw themselves having two of their good experiences in the large space on strips #1 and #2. After their drawings are complete, instruct the students to carefully cut out the two strips and fold them on the dotted lines. (You may wish to model holding a strip over the edge of a desk with the picture facing up; press a crease along the dotted line by folding the strip down against the edge.) Demonstrate for the students the "C-shaped" strip after it has been properly folded.

Distribute copies of the handout "My Good Experience Pop-Up Page" and instruct the students to write their names on the blank after the phrase "My name is _____." Instruct the students to fold this page in half on the dotted line. Demonstrate putting a thin layer of glue on the boxes labeled A and B on the page and carefully positioning Strip #1 so that the spaces labeled A and B are attached A to A and B to B. (These spaces must be well-aligned and the glue allowed to dry thoroughly if the pop-up is to function properly.) Strip #2 should be attached in the same way, C to C and D to D.

When dry, the pop-up page can be folded shut. When opened, the two strips should "pop up." If you like, have students close their pop-ups and write a title on the cover, such as "Good Experiences are Popping Up" by (name) or " (name)'s Good Experiences," and stack the pop-ups on a reading table for free time reading.

SUPPLEMENTARY ACTIVITY #3 HANDOUT #1

My Good Experience Pop-Up Page Strips

1.

On this strip, draw a good experience you had where you used your muscles to make the good experience happen.

STRIP #1

Glue
A

A good experience
I had using my
muscles.

Glue
B

2.

On this strip, draw a good experience you had where you did something for someone else.

STRIP #2

Glue
C

A good experience
I had doing something
for others.

Glue
D

SUPPLEMENTARY ACTIVITY #3 HANDOUT #2

My Good Experiences Pop-Up Page

My name is _____.

Glue
A

Glue
C

- -

Glue
B

Glue
D

Fun With Strength Words

Objective   Students will learn to recognize and use a number of new vocabulary words that describe personal strengths.

Students will continue to identify these strengths in themselves and others.

Materials   Blank transparency and pen

Strength Word Card Pages #1-#12 from Lesson 2

Handout #4 from Lesson 2   -   "Strength Word List" (made into a transparency)

Handouts #1A and #1B   -   "Strength Word Dictionary," stapled together

Transparency #1   -   "Looks Like—Sounds Like"

Handouts #2A and #2B   -   "Strength Flashcards," cut into card sets (one per student)

Handout #3   -   "Using My New Strength Words"

Handout #4   -   "Finding My Strengths in the Dictionary"

Children's book: Brett, J. (1992). *Fritz and the beautiful horses.* Boston, MA: Houghton Mifflin. (optional)

Standard pocket chart (available in educational supply stores)

To the Teacher   In this lesson students will build a sight and comprehension vocabulary of words that describe strengths. This expanded vocabulary will give them a larger bank of descriptors as they continue to look at good experiences and identify their own strengths and the strengths of their classmates. This lesson provides students with a "Strength Word Dictionary" and employs a game format for vocabulary drill that allows participation by students of varying verbal skill levels.

If you are able to locate the children's book, *Fritz and the Beautiful Horses* by J. Brett, gather your class around you and read this heartwarming story aloud. (Supplementary Activity #1 is also built on this story.) If you are unable to obtain this book, begin this lesson with a review of the "Strength Word Cards" from the previous lesson, focusing on sight recognition rather than comprehension.

The "Strength Word Dictionary" contains 16 descriptor words arranged alphabetically with definitions and/or synonyms; an example sentence using the strength word is included in each entry. Students are encouraged to have fun with their dictionaries, surprising others with the "big" words they know. The purpose of the dictionary is not for all students to master all the words, but for students to broaden their vocabularies of strength words according to their varying abilities.

After distribution of the "Strength Word Dictionaries," the students familiarize themselves with the vocabulary and layout by a word finding drill. When they are able to find most words with relative ease, they are ready to begin the task of learning the meanings of dictionary entries, using a game format.

In the "Stand Up, Sit Down Game," you will write a dictionary word on a transparency, and the students will look up the word and read its definition to themselves. You will then give them either a correct definition or an incorrect definition; the students will decide whether you've given the correct definition or not. When you say the signal, "Stand Up or Sit Down," the students will stand up if they think you've given the correct definition. The difficulty level of the exercise is increased as you begin saying the words instead of writing them on the transparency.

After students are familiar enough with the new vocabulary that they don't have to look up every word, they are ready for the "Cards Up Game." The "Cards Up Game" further adds to the difficulty of the task by requiring students to find the definitions, rather than the strength words. This game is played by pairs of Learning Partners, each of whom is assigned one of the two dictionary pages (Handout #1A or Handout #1B) to scan and given a set of "Strength Flashcards." (Grade level differences can be accommodated by playing with partial sets of cards.) In this game you will give the students a definition and they will scan their assigned dictionary page, find the word that matches the definition, and verify their choice with their Learning Partners. When you say the signal, "Cards Up," all the players will hold up their chosen "Strength Flashcard." (An additional use for the "Strength Flashcards" is suggested in Supplementary Activity #2 following this lesson.)

At the end of the lesson, the students will complete a cartoon page and demonstrate their comprehension of new strength vocabulary words in two ways: they will match strength words with pictures that demonstrate various strengths, and they will illustrate a good experience of their own and identify the strength they used to make the good experience happen. A homework page provides additional dictionary practice.

You may want to incorporate the strength vocabulary words presented in this lesson into your spelling word lists and creative writing activities.

Lesson Presentation

Book

FRITZ AND THE BEAUTIFUL HORSES

If you were able to obtain the children's book <u>Fritz and the Beautiful Horses</u> by J. Brett, tell the class that you're going to read them a story about a pony named Fritz who <u>used his strengths to have a good experience</u>. Gather the class around you and read the story aloud.

After reading the story, help students see the need for learning special "strength words" in order to describe their own and others' strengths. Say something like the following: **Fritz had a good experience, didn't he? He did something that turned out well, and he was proud of it. What strengths did Fritz have that made him able to create this good experience for himself?** *Allow for student response. Write students' responses on the chalkboard; be sure the list includes the words <u>kind</u>, <u>gentle</u>, <u>sure-footed</u>, and <u>dependable</u>.* **"Sure-footed" and "dependable" are interesting strength words, aren't they? Today you're going to learn some other interesting words that describe strengths.**

REVIEWING THE STRENGTH WORD CARDS

Strength Word Card Pages #1-#12

We've been looking for our strengths by remembering our good experiences. In our last lesson we started collecting a list of strength words. Some of these words are pretty hard words, but you've been doing a good job at starting to learn some of them. Let's see how many of these strength words we can remember. *Choose three to six of the "Strength Word Cards" and display them in a pocket chart. Drill students on sight recognition of the words by asking questions such as, "Can anyone find the word <u>cheerful</u>? It means <u>happy</u>. Which is the word* *cheerful?" The emphasis in this exercise is on sight vocabulary, rather than word meaning. Call on student volunteers to come up and identify the words. Then ask the class who they notice has the strength of being* cheerful. *Ask this question about each strength word identified. Give the appropriate cards to the students who are named as having each strength and ask them to write that strength word on the inside of their "Strengths Folders." (When they are generating the final list of their strengths, they may want to consider including these strengths on their lists.) As words are identified, replace them with new cards, mixing the cards up each time to lend an air of mystery. Review the identified cards with a flashcard drill.*

FINDING WORDS IN ALPHABETICAL ORDER

(You may wish to omit this next exercise for third grade students.)

Today we're going to get some special "Strength Word Dictionaries" so that you can use some really interesting words to name each others' strengths. But before we do, let's practice finding words in alphabetical order so you'll be able to use your new dictionaries well. Take out your "Strength Word Lists" from your "Strengths Folder." It looks like this:

Handout #4 from Lesson 2

Put the transparency copy of Handout #4 from Lesson 2, "Strength Word List," on the overhead and check to see that the students have taken out their copies of the same list. **I'm going to name some of these strength words, and I want you to find them on your list. The words are in alphabetical order on this list, so remember to listen to the first letter of the word to help you know whether to look at the beginning, the middle, or the end of the list. When you find the word, put your finger on it and raise your hand. Then I'll ask a volunteer to come up and draw a circle around the word with my colored pen.** *Call out words from the list, emphasizing the sound of the initial letter. It may be necessary to ask students to tell you what the initial letter is after you give phonic clues in order to keep less skillful* *readers on track. Call on volunteers to come up and circle the word after most of the class has raised their hands. Have students who pointed to the correct word clap once or pat themselves on the back. When finished, clean the transparency for further use.*

INTRODUCING THE STRENGTH WORD DICTIONARY

Handout #1A
Handout #1B

Good job! I think you're ready for your new dictionaries. *Distribute copies of Handouts #1A and 1B, "Strength Word Dictionary."* **You can have a lot of fun using these dictionaries impressing grown-ups with the big words you know. Instead of saying, "Coach, you're a happy guy," you can say "Coach, you have a <u>positive attitude</u>." Instead of saying, "My friend shares her things with me," you can say, "My friend is <u>generous</u>." As you grow older, it's important to have a more grown-up way of talking.**

We're going to play a game with our new dictionaries, but first let's practice finding the words, just like we did on our "Strength Word Lists." I'm going to put a mark by one of the words on the transparency, and I want you to find that word in your dictionaries. Remember to look at the first letter and decide whether the word comes at the beginning of the alphabet, the end of the alphabet, or somewhere in between. When you find the word in your dictionary, put your finger on it. I'll walk around and see how you're doing. *Put a mark by one of the words, ask a student to identify it aloud, and walk around the room as students find the word and put their fingers on it. Ask student volunteers to read the definition and example sentence from their dictionaries. Continue this drill until students seem to be comfortable with using their dictionaries.*

CLARIFYING THE MEANINGS OF DIFFICULT WORDS

Transp. #1

Some of these strength words are new to us and may be a little hard to understand at first. Let's look at some of them. *Write the word "organized" in the box at the top of Transparency #1,*

"Looks Like—Sounds Like,"and show it on the overhead. **Can anyone tell me what this word is?** *Call on a student volunteer to identify the word "organized."* **Organized! That's a pretty big word—a hard one, too. If someone had the strength of being organized, this is what it might look like.** *Write the following descriptive phrases under the heading "Looks like."* **Someone who was organized might <u>keep their room tidied up</u>; they might <u>clean out their desk often</u>; they might <u>keep all their papers in order in their folder</u>; <u>they might always have a pencil when they need it</u>. Does anyone else have an idea about what being organized might look like?** *Allow for student response and write appropriate phrases under the heading "Looks like."*

Good! I think you have a good idea about what the strength of being organized looks like. *Point to the "Sounds like" column on the transparency.* **Did you know that the strength of being organized also has a sound? This is what being organized might sound like if organized kids said their thinking out loud.** *Write the following phrases under the heading "Sounds like" on the transparency.* **"<u>I'll put my books on the shelves and my models in this box</u>." Or it might sound like this: "<u>I'll write down my assignment so I won't forget what I'm supposed to do</u>."Or it could sound like "<u>I keep my pencil in a place in my desk where it doesn't fall out</u>."Do any of you have any ideas about what being organized might sound like?** *Write student suggestions under the heading "Sounds like."*

Erase the transparency and write the strength word "<u>responsible</u>" in the box at the top. Ask students to tell what being responsible would "look like." Write appropriate responses on the transparency. Ask them what a responsible person might "sound like" and write those responses on the transparency also. Do the same exercise with the strength word "<u>positive attitude</u>," and any other words that prove difficult for your class.

THE STAND UP, SIT DOWN GAME

Blank Transp.

I think you're ready to play the Stand Up, Sit Down Game. This is how it's played. I'm going to write one of your strength words on the overhead, and you find it in your "Strength Word Dictionaries." When you find it, read the definition to yourself to find out what it means, but don't tell anyone! Then I will say the definition; I may say the <u>right</u> definition, and I may say the <u>wrong</u> definition. You decide, but still don't tell anyone! Then I'll say, "Stand Up or Sit Down." If you think I gave the right definition, you will <u>stand up</u>! If you think I gave the wrong definition, you'll <u>stay sitting down</u>. Then I'll ask someone to read the definition, and everyone will know if they got it right! *Choose words at random from the dictionary pages and write them one at a time on a blank transparency.*

If your class is doing well at recognizing this new vocabulary, increase the difficulty of the exercise by saying: **Let's make this a little bit harder. From now on I'm not going to write the words on the overhead; I'm just going to <u>say</u> them. You look for them and wait for me to tell you a definition just like before, and then I'll say "Stand Up or Sit Down."** *Continue playing this game until the class begins to gain mastery of the strength word vocabulary.*

THE CARDS UP GAME

This game increases the difficulty of the task of using the "Strength Word Dictionary" by requiring students to find <u>definitions</u>, rather than words. By this time they will have become familiar enough with the words that they may not need to look many of them up, however. Play this game with the whole class.

We're having so much fun playing games today, I thought we'd play one more! This is called the "Cards Up Game," and you'll play it with your Learning Partner. One of you

will be in charge of looking for words on page one of your dictionary; you'll be the Page One Captain. The other partner will be in charge of looking for words on page two—the Page Two Captain. I'll give everyone their own set of "Strength Flashcards," and you'll spread them out on your desks so you can see all of them. Then I'll tell you a definition or a sentence clue about one of your strength words. It will be <u>your</u> job to find that strength word. The Page One Captain will hunt for it on page one of the dictionary, and the Page Two Captain will search on page two. If you think you already know what the word is without looking it up, be sure to check to see if you are right so you and your Learning Partner won't miss it. When one of the Captains finds the word, you'll both talk about it and quietly decide if you've found the right word. Don't let anyone else hear you! Then when I say, "Cards Up!" everyone will hold up the "Strength Flashcard" they've decided on. When I tell you the right answer, everyone who is holding up the right card will jiggle their cards, like this. *Demonstrate holding up a word card and jiggling it back and forth.*

**Handout #2A
Handout #2B**

Distribute to every student Handouts #2A and #2B, "Strength Flashcards," cut apart into sets of cards. If a smaller selection of card options is more appropriate to your grade level, divide each set into several smaller sets. If this is the case, play the game for awhile with the first subset of cards, have the students put aside that subset, and then distribute another subset for play. Continue until all the cards in a full set have been played. (If you decide to divide the card sets, do so in advance to make sure that all students are playing with the same word cards at the same time.)

A WRITTEN EXERCISE

Handout #3

You've worked really hard playing these games today. I'm proud of how well you're learning these hard new words. I have a cartoon page for you now that I think you'll have fun with. *Distribute Handout #3, "Using My New Strength Words."*

You can tell by looking at the cartoons what these kids' strengths are. Find the strength word in your dictionaries and write it on the blank spaces. There are just exactly enough spaces for the right word to fit, so you'll know if you have the right strength word. In the last square make a cartoon about <u>yourself</u>! Think about some of the good experiences you've had and the strength you used to make them happen. Draw a picture of yourself using that strength and complete the sentence under the picture: *(student's own name)* is *(strength word)* . *When the students have finished this exercise, tell them to save it in their "Strengths Folders."*

USING THESE NEW WORDS IN THE FUTURE

All of your hard work learning these new strength words is going to pay off in the next few weeks. You're going to be helping your classmates discover their strengths, and you'll have a whole dictionary of new words to use when you do it. You'll also be able to use some of these great new words as you learn more and more about your OWN strengths.

HOMEWORK ASSIGNMENT

Handout #4

Distribute copies of Handout #4, "Finding My Strengths in the Dictionary," and instruct the students to choose two strength words from their "Strength Word Dictionaries" that they feel describe them especially well. Tell them to write each word in the small box labeled "strength" and then on the lines in the larger box describe a time they used that strength.

Supplementary Activity #1 Handout/Transp.

You may also wish to use as homework the Supplementary Activity #1 Handout, "Fritz and the Beautiful Horses," at the end of this lesson. Make a transparency of the handout and review the words listed next to the illustration of Fritz having his good experience, covering the bottom half. Read over and discuss the strength words listed at the bottom of the transparency and ask the students to *choose <u>one</u> that they feel best describes them. Distribute copies of the handout and instruct the students to circle their chosen strength word and draw themselves using that strength.*

SUPPLEMENTARY ACTIVITIES

Use the Supplementary Activities provided to reinforce the skills taught in this lesson:

- *"Fritz and the Beautiful Horses"*
   (Supplementary Activity #1)

- *"Strength Touchdown!"*
   (Supplementary Activity #2)

- *"Strength Baseball"*
   (Supplementary Activity #3)

- *"Strength 'Concentration'"*
   (Supplementary Activity #4)

- *"Strength Bingo"*
   (Supplementary Activity #5)

HANDOUT #1A

Strength Word Dictionary

athletic - <u>strong; active</u>
Carlos would rather play sports than do anything else; he is very **athletic**.

caring - **<u>interested in the feelings of others</u>**
Andy is a caring boy who looks out for little kids so no one hurts them.

cheerful - <u>happy</u>
Rosa is so **cheerful**, she makes everyone feel in a good mood.

cooperative - <u>works well with others</u>
Tim is **cooperative** with the people in his group.

coordinated - <u>has muscles that work well</u>
Ann is good at P.E. because she is so **coordinated**.

creative - <u>thinks up new ideas and new ways of doing things</u>
Joe is so **creative** he can always think of a new game to play.

dependable - <u>can be counted on</u>
Sue is **dependable**. She does what she says she will do.

determined - <u>sticks with something; doesn't give up easily</u>
Marcy is **determined** to learn to skateboard.

energetic - <u>likes to move</u>
Sitting still is hard for Pam because she is so **energetic**.

generous - <u>willing to share</u>
John is so **generous** he always shares his chips at lunch.

Strength Word Dictionary (continued)

imaginative - <u>thinks up new ideas</u>
Everyone wanted to see Jill's drawing because she is very **imaginative**.

organized - <u>does things in a neat and careful way</u>
Wong keeps his folder and desk neat and clean. He is very **organized**.

patient - <u>waits without getting upset</u>
Grandmother is **patient** with us when we're learning something new.

positive attitude - <u>thinks happy thoughts; thinks things will turn out well</u>
Mary is never grumpy. Her **positive attitude** helps our classroom to be a happy place.

problem solver - <u>works things out</u>
When Tom has a problem, he can always think of a way to work things out. He is a very good **problem solver**.

responsible - <u>can be trusted to do things that are important</u>
The teacher knew Jane would take good care of our pet rat during the winter holidays because Jane is **responsible**.

unselfish - <u>thinks about others</u>
Allen asked the new kid if he wanted to be first to use the ball. Allen is **unselfish**.

TRANSPARENCY #1

Looks Like—Sounds Like

Looks like:

Sounds like:

HANDOUT #2A

Strength Flashcards

determined	energetic	generous
cooperative	coordinated	creative
athletic	caring	cheerful

HANDOUT #2A

HANDOUT #2B

Strength Flashcards (continued)

imaginative		
problem solver	responsible	unselfish
organized	patient	positive attitude

HANDOUT #3

Using My New Strength Words

Directions:

Use both the pictures and the number of spaces for the letters to help you find the right word for each sentence.

Allen is _ _ _ _ _ _ _ _.

Jane is _ _ _ _ _ _ _.

Bill is _ _ _ _ _ _ _ _.

Matt is _ _ _ _ _ _ _ _ _.

Patty is _ _ _ _ _ _ _ _ _ _.

_____ is _____.
(your name)

HANDOUT #4

Finding My Strengths in the Dictionary

Directions:

Look through your Strength Word Dictionary to choose two strength words that describe you especially well. For each word, tell a time when you used that strength.

1. I was

(strength)

the time I . . .

2. I was

(strength)

the time I . . .

SUPPLEMENTARY ACTIVITY #1

Fritz and the Beautiful Horses

Objective
Students will understand that peoples' strengths are more important than their physical appearance and will draw a picture of themselves using one of their strengths.

Materials
Supplementary Activity #1 Handout/Transparency - "Fritz and the Beautiful Horses"

Children's book: Brett, J. (1992). *Fritz and the beautiful horses*. Boston, MA: Houghton Mifflin.

Procedure
Tell the students that it's common for kids to think that the way they look is really important. They may think it's better to be tall or better to be short, better to have long hair or short hair, or better to have blue eyes or brown eyes. If you haven't already read *Fritz and the Beautiful Horses* to students tell them you want to read them a story about a pony named Fritz, because how you look isn't the most important thing about who you are. Fritz wasn't as beautiful as other horses, but he became a favorite among the children in his village because of his strengths.

Read the story, emphasizing the strength words as you read them (kind, gentle, sure-footed, dependable). Show students the book's pictures as you read.

Put the transparency, "Fritz and the Beautiful Horses," on the overhead and relate Fritz's strengths to the story. Distribute copies of the handout. Help students choose one of their strengths from the words listed at the bottom of the page. Instruct them to circle that strength word and then draw a picture of themselves using that strength.

Allow students to color their picture if time permits.

SUPPLEMENTARY ACTIVITY #1 HANDOUT/TRANSPARENCY

Fritz and the Beautiful Horses

Here is Fritz using his strengths.

kind

gentle

sure-footed

dependable

Directions:

Circle a word that is one of the strengths **you** have.

artistic

athletic

brave

determined

generous

gentle

hard worker

musical

Draw yourself using that strength.

SUPPLEMENTARY ACTIVITY #2

Strength Touchdown!

Objective

Students will increase their recognition and/or understanding of strength vocabulary words using a game format.

Materials

Blank transparency and pen (optional)

"Strength Flashcards" from the lesson (for team or individual play)

Supplementary Activity #2

Handout/Transparency - "Touchdown!" (duplicated on green construction paper for each pair of Learning Partners; duplicated on a strip of green vinyl for individual play; as a transparency for teams play)

Football (from template provided at the end of this activity; either cut from transparency film colored brown, or cut out of brown felt, construction paper, or leather scraps)

Sack to hold flashcards

Procedure

This game can be played by the whole class divided into two teams, by the whole class with Learning Partners, or individually by two students during free choice time. Use this game initially to teach word recognition of the new strength vocabulary. You may wish to increase the difficulty by asking students to give an example of the strength or use the word in a sentence.

TEAMS—Divide the class into two teams of fairly equal ability. Name the teams "A" and "B." Place the "football field" transparency on the overhead and position the transparent "football" on the 50-yardline. Assign each team an end zone to "defend," and tell them that they can score by moving the football into their opponent's end zone. Flip a coin to decide which team will be "in possession" of the ball and go first.

Choose a player from that team to come up and draw a "Strength Flashcard" from the sack. If the player is able to correctly read the word for his or her team, move the football forward ten yards toward the opposing team's end zone. Play then goes to the opposing team and they have the opportunity to draw and read a "Strength Flashcard" in an attempt to move the football in the opposite direction. The first team to cross into the opposing end zone is the winner. For continued play, award six points and return the football to the 50-yardline. Allow the nonscoring team to "kick off" with the first turn of the new round. (You may wish to announce in advance whether the game will be played for a specified number of minutes, rounds, or points.)

LEARNING PARTNERS—Each pair of Learning Partners will need a green construction paper or vinyl "playing field" and a "football," positioned on the 50-yardline. Help the partners determine who will go first; then either say one of the strength words or write it on a blank transparency for the whole class to see. The student whose turn it is then tells his or her Learning Partner what the word is. Call on a student to read the word aloud for the class. Partners who correctly identified the word advance the football ten yards toward the opposite goal on their playing field.

When one partner moves the football into the opposite end zone and scores a touchdown, the football is repositioned on the 50-yardline for another kick off and continued play. Partners may want to keep score on a piece of scratch paper.

INDIVIDUAL—Two students will need a green vinyl or construction paper "playing field," a "football," and a stack of "Strength Flashcards." The football is positioned on the 50-yardline for the kick off. Students take turns drawing "Strength Flashcards" and reading the vocabulary word correctly. After a correct response, the student advances the football ten yards toward the opposite goal. The student whose football crosses into the opposing end zone first scores a touchdown and wins the game.

VARIATIONS

If the task of word recognition is not challenging enough and you find the football continuing to hover around the 50-yardline, you may wish to impose a time limit of three seconds for responses. You may also ask students to give an example of the strength word they have drawn or to use it in a sentence.

A student can be designated to act as "Referee" or "Umpire" and be charged with the responsibility of deciding whether a response is correct. (This may be especially useful when two students are playing independently.) To add interest, you may wish to give the "Ref" or "Ump" a yellow bandana to toss up as a "flag on the play" when an incorrect response has been given. This variation is more effective when students are giving examples of the strength word or using it in a sentence.

Before the initial "kick off" you may wish to announce that you will play four 5-minute quarters, two 10-minute halves, etc. Appoint a Timekeeper to watch the clock and perhaps give a countdown during the last ten seconds of each playing period. When the clock "runs out," return the football to the 50-yardline for another kick off, regardless of its previous position.

For more advanced students, you may offer an "extra point" after a touchdown if they can spell a word you draw from the sack.

A simplified version of the game can be played with two "footballs," one for each team, placed in opposing end zones. Each team or student takes turns drawing "Strength Flashcards" and either reading, defining, or using the strength word in a sentence. After each correct response, the team or student advances his or her football ten yards down the field toward the advances his or her football ten yards down the field toward the opposite end zone. The first team or student to move his or her football 100 yards down the field and into the opposing end zone scores a touchdown and wins the game.

FOOTBALL TEMPLATES

SUPPLEMENTARY ACTIVITY #2 HANDOUT/TRANSPARENCY

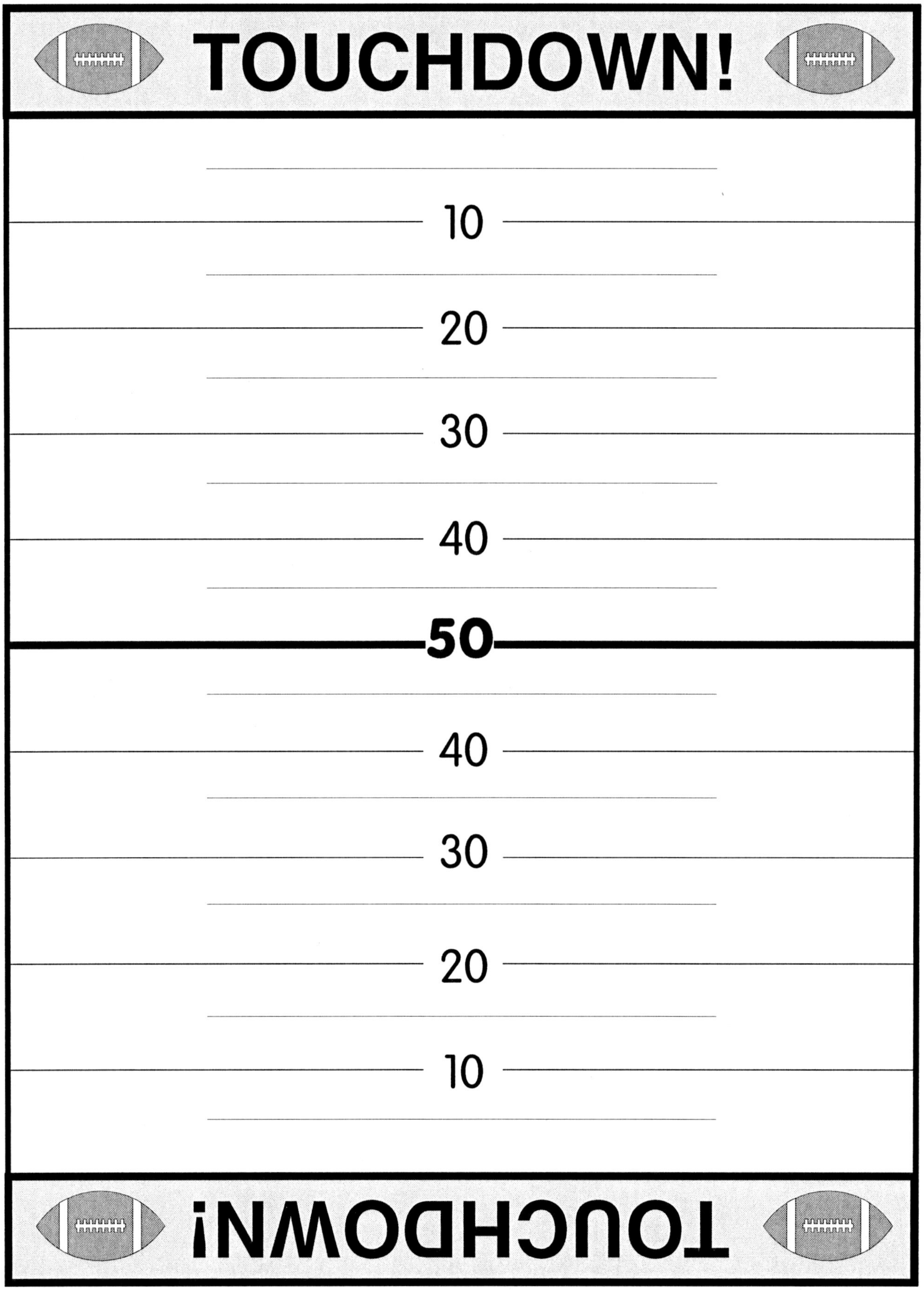

TOUCHDOWN!

10

20

30

40

50

40

30

20

10

TOUCHDOWN!

SUPPLEMENTARY ACTIVITY #3

Strength Baseball

Objective   Students will review the spelling and meaning of a variety of strength words.

Materials   Handout #4 from Lesson 2   -   "Strength Word List"
Markers for four bases

Procedure   Explain to students that they will play "indoor baseball" as they practice the spelling and/or meaning of strength words. Determine where home plate and the three bases will be placed in the room. Students will need to be able to walk to each base. Divide students into two equal teams and decide who will be at bat first. Sit or stand near home plate.

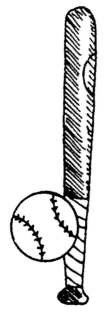

VARIATION 1—Strength Spelling Baseball

As you call, "batter up," a student comes up to home plate. Ask that student to spell one of the strength words on the "Strength Word List." If he or she does so correctly, the student may proceed to first base. Ask the next student on that team to spell another strength word; if he or she does so correctly, that student goes to first base and the student on first moves to second base. Continue in this fashion. When a student is moved to home plate by a successful teammate, a home run is scored. Any student who cannot spell a word "strikes out." After three outs the next team is up.

VARIATION 2—Strength Definition Baseball

This game is the same as above except that students must give the definition of a strength word and use it correctly in a sentence in order to move to first base.

VARIATION 3—Strength Spelling and Definition Baseball

Students who can spell the strength word can go to first base. If they can then give the definition of the strength and use it in a sentence, they can proceed to second base.

Important: When students are not up to bat, they should **all** be diligently studying how to spell the words on their strength word list or studying the definitions of strength words.

Strength "Concentration"

Objective   Students will increase their familiarity with strength vocabulary words.

Materials   Supplementary Activity #4 Card Pages #1-#4   -   "Strength 'Concentration' Cards"

Procedure   This activity works like the regular "Concentration" card game, except that here students will be matching "strength words."

Most students will be familiar with the "Concentration" game. For those who are not, explain that in this game all the cards are placed face down on a table and mixed around. Each student playing gets to turn two cards face up. If the cards are a match, then the student removes them and gets to play again. If they are not a match, the cards are turned back over. Players are challenged to remember where particular cards are so that they can create matches. Play continues until all the cards have been matched, and the player with the most matches wins the game.

Divide the class into small groups of two or three students. (The game can be played with four students, but only if the students have long attention spans or above-average memory skills.) Give each group a deck of "Strength Concentration Cards." Have the shortest student in each group go first and the tallest go last, and then proceed in that order of play.

The "Strength Concentration Cards" should be copied on heavy paper, so that the printing on them cannot be seen through the cards' backs. The number of cards in each deck determines the difficulty level of the game; to make the game less difficult, remove some of the matching pairs from the deck. If you wish to make the game more difficult or more specific to your students' needs, simply use this same format to create new matches and add these to the deck.

This game can be used as a free time activity or when two or more students have finished a class assignment before their classmates.

SUPPLEMENTARY ACTIVITY #4 CARD PAGE #1

Strength "Concentration" Cards

ARTISTIC	ARTISTIC	ATHLETIC
COORDINATED	COORDINATED	ATHLETIC
BRAVE	BRAVE	*DETERMINED*

SUPPLEMENTARY ACTIVITY #4 CARD PAGE #2

Strength "Concentration" Cards (continued)

ENERGETIC	*ENERGETIC*	FAST
FINISHES THINGS	*FINISHES THINGS*	FAST
GOOD MEMORY	GOOD MEMORY	*DETERMINED*

SUPPLEMENTARY ACTIVITY #4 CARD PAGE #3

Strength "Concentration" Cards (continued)

GOOD THINKER	**GOOD THINKER**	**GOOD WITH WORDS**
HARD WORKER	**HARD WORKER**	**GOOD WITH WORDS**
IMAGINATIVE	*IMAGINATIVE*	*MUSICAL*

SUPPLEMENTARY ACTIVITY #4 CARD PAGE #4

Strength "Concentration" Cards (continued)

ORGANIZED	**ORGANIZED**	**STRONG**
PROBLEM SOLVER	*PROBLEM SOLVER*	**STRONG**
RESPONSIBLE	**RESPONSIBLE**	*MUSICAL*

SUPPLEMENTARY ACTIVITY #5

Strength Bingo

Objective   Students will name possible strengths that could have been used to create a good experience.

Materials   Handout #4 from Lesson 2 - "Strength Word List"

Handouts #3A and #3B from Lesson 2 - "Possible Good Experiences"

Supplementary Activity #5 Handout - "Strength Bingo Grids"

Procedure   Have students number two grids randomly from one to nine (e.g., see illustration below). Each grid should be numbered in a different order. Describe a good experience (refer to Handouts #3A and #3B from Lesson 2 for ideas). Now ask students to think of a strength that could have been used to create the good experience you just described. They can refer to their "Strength Word Lists" Handout #4 from Lesson 2 for ideas. Then give the good experience a number from 1 to 9. The students should write the strength word they choose in the box of their grid that has the same number as the one you just told them. Continue in this fashion, numbering the good experiences you describe. If a student writes three strength words in a row in any direction on the grid he or she calls "Bingo." Compare the strength words the student selected with the good experience scenarios you described. If you feel the student selected appropriate words, you can reward him or her with a reinforcer of your choice. All students then proceed with a new grid and a new game is started.

7	1	3
2	5	4
6	8	9

Strength Bingo Grids

Remembering Good Experiences in Nonphysical Areas

Objective

Students will practice looking in areas other than kinesthetic when identifying their strengths.

Materials

Transparency #1 - *"No one* is good at *everything*. *Everyone* is good at *something*."

Transparencies #2A-#2D - "Have You Had Good Experiences in Any of These Ways?"

Transparency #3 - "Good Experiences Other Than Physical"

Handout #1 - "My 'Good Experience Channel'"

Handout #2 - "Think of a Good Experience You've Had in One or Two of These Areas"

Children's book: McPhail, D. *Something special.* Boston, MA: Little, Brown & Company. (optional)

To the Teacher

Since a major developmental task of elementary-age students is physical mastery, students tend to overuse examples of physical feats when asked to relate their good experiences. The purpose of this lesson is to facilitate students' ability to remember their good experiences in nonkinesthetic areas.

If you can obtain a copy of the children's book *Something Special* by David McPhail, gather your class around you in a circle and read it as a wonderful anticipatory set. The book does a good job of identifying strengths in areas other than athletics. (If the book is not available at your school, begin the lesson at the heading "Looking for Good Experiences in Areas Other Than Physical.")

In this lesson, students are encouraged to recall experiences where they used words or math, did art or music activities, acted responsibly or helped others, and engaged in various other positive classroom behaviors. A homework assignment is used to further encourage students to look for good experiences that were not kinesthetic. Supplementary Activity #1 ("Something Special") can be used as a homework assignment for younger, nonreading students.

Transparency #1, *"No one* is good at *everything*. *Everyone* is good at *something*.", can be enlarged to provide a poster to hang in your classroom.

SOMETHING SPECIAL

Book

Gather your class around you and say: **I'd like to read you a story about a little raccoon who had a hard time discovering that he had some strengths. It seemed to him that everyone else had strengths but him. Then one day he had a good experience—something that turned out well for him. He did something that went the way he wanted it to and he was proud of it. It was then that the little raccoon realized that he had strengths too! Listen to the story and be thinking about what his special strength might be.**

Transp. #1

Read <u>Something Special</u> *by David McPhail. At the conclusion of the story, say:* **Everybody has something they can do well.** *Show Transparency #1, "No one is good at <u>everything</u>. <u>Everyone</u> is good at something.", and read it to the students.* **You don't have to be perfect at something to be proud of it or feel you're good at it.**

Are there any of you who are good at art like the little raccoon in our story? *Allow for student response.* **How many of you are good at sports like the little raccoon's sister?** *Allow for student response. Respond to the raised hands by saying:* **A lot of you are good at sports and at doing physical things!**

LOOKING FOR GOOD EXPERIENCES IN AREAS OTHER THAN PHYSICAL

Today we're going to look at good experiences you might have had in areas other than sports. I know that most of you have things other than physical activities in which you've worked hard and finally been able to do them well. All of you have other things besides sports to feel proud of. These may be things you've forgotten about up to now, but we'll spend this lesson helping you remember!

Transp. #2A
Transp. #2B
Transp. #2C
Transp. #2D

Show Transparencies #2A-#2D, "Have You Had Good Experiences in Any of These Ways?" beginning with "Art or Making Things" on #2A. Cover the bottom of each transparency until you are ready to refer to it.

Some of you may remember a time when you drew something that turned out just the way you wanted it to, and you felt really proud of it, or maybe you put together a model that looked especially good when you were finished. Can anyone remember a good experience you had with <u>art or making something</u>? *Allow for student response.*

Others of you may have had an experience with <u>words</u> that you felt proud of. There are three kinds of experiences you may have had with words. Perhaps you <u>read</u> a really hard book or a book that was very long. Maybe you <u>wrote</u> a story that you liked a lot, or you studied hard for a <u>spelling</u> test and did really well. Has anyone had a good experience with words—either reading them, writing them, or spelling them? *Allow for student response.*

Some of you may have had a good experience in <u>math</u>. Maybe you learned your number facts quickly or got good grades on your assignments. Maybe you're able to solve hard math problems. Has anyone had good experiences with math? *Allow for student response.*

It could be that some of you may have had some good experiences with <u>music</u>. Maybe you learned all the words to a song and could sing it well, or perhaps you practiced and practiced on a musical instrument until you could play a piece just right. Do any of you remember a time when you did something in the area of music that made you feel proud? *Allow for student response.*

Maybe you remember doing something for someone else that made you feel good. *Point to the top left side of the* *transparency.* **Perhaps you taught someone how to do something—a little brother or sister or a friend.** *Point to the top right side of the transparency.* **Maybe you did something nice for someone and said, "I did this just for you!" What do you think this girl who is pointing at something might have done for someone?** *Allow for student response.* **Have any of you ever had a good experience <u>helping another person</u>?** *Allow for student response.*

Some of you may remember a time when you did something or remembered to do something <u>all by yourself</u> without an adult having to ask you over and over to do it. Maybe you took care of a pet without being reminded or you cleaned up the house or apartment without being asked. Has anyone ever felt proud of themselves for <u>being responsible</u>?

I bet you can remember a time when you were a <u>hard worker</u>. You've all had times when you stuck with a big job even though it took a lot of work to finish it. I can think of lots of times when I've seen people in our class being <u>hard workers</u>.

Some of you may have felt good about yourself when you were able to be <u>patient</u>. Have you ever shown someone how to do something when it took them a long time to catch on? Or do you remember a time when you were proud of yourself for being able to wait 'till later for something instead of having to have it RIGHT NOW? *Allow for student response.*

Perhaps you can remember a time when you showed a lot of <u>self-control</u> and you felt good about it. Maybe you saved your allowance instead of spending it on candy or you didn't say anything when you felt like giving someone a put-down. Who can remember a time when you felt good about using <u>self-control</u>? *Allow for student response.*

"GOOD EXPERIENCE CHANNEL" PAGES

Transp. #3

Today I'd like you to do another "Good Experience Channel" page, but this time I want you to try to draw or write about something other than sports or doing something physical. *Show Transparency #3, "Good Experiences Other Than Physical." Point to each of the categories on the TV screen as you say:* **This time your drawing should be about a time you did something you felt proud of in the area of art, music, math, using or reading words, helping others, using self-control, or being responsible, patient, or a hard worker. Maybe you'll remember something you did you felt good about but had forgotten!**

Handout #1

Distribute copies of Handout #1, "My 'Good Experience Channel,'" and again instruct the students to try to think of a good experience they have had in <u>one</u> of the areas written at the bottom of the screen.

LESSON SUMMARY, HOMEWORK, AND PREVIEW OF NEXT LESSON

Summarize the lesson by having students respond verbally to one of the following sentence stems:

- *I liked . . . .*

- *I was surprised . . . .*

- *I learned . . . .*

- *This lesson would have been better if . . . .*

Handout #2

For homework, give the students a copy of Handout #2, "Think of a Good Experience You've Had in One or Two of These Areas," asking them to try to remember a time when, in one or two of the areas shown on the page, they tried hard or worked at something and things turned out the way they wanted them to.

Tell the students that they'll have more chances in the following days to share their good experiences and find out more of their strengths.

SUPPLEMENTARY ACTIVITIES

Use the Supplementary Activities to provide additional practice with lesson concepts:

- *"Something Special"*
  (Supplementary Activity #1)

- *"Strength Bracelet"*
  (Supplementary Activity #2)

- *"Strength Word Letter Search"*
  (Supplementary Activity #3)

TRANSPARENCY #1

No one is good at _everything_.

Everyone is good at something.

TRANSPARENCY #2A

Have You Had Good Experiences in Any of These Ways?

ART or MAKING THINGS

Have you been proud of something you've **drawn, colored,** or **put together?**

WORDS

Maybe you're proud of a time you were a **good reader,** a time you **wrote a good story,** or a time you **did well in spelling.**

Have You Had Good Experiences in Any of These Ways? (continued)

MATH

Have you done something you were proud of **using numbers** or **solving problems**?

MUSIC

Maybe you're proud of a time you **remembered a song** or **played an instrument**.

Have You Had Good Experiences in Any of These Ways? (continued)

TRANSPARENCY #2D

Have You Had Good Experiences in Any of These Ways? (continued)

HARD WORKER

Maybe you're proud of a time you were **hard worker**.

PATIENT

Maybe you're proud of a time you were **patient**.

SELF-CONTROL

Maybe you're proud of a time you used good **self-control**.

TRANSPARENCY #3

Good Experiences Other Than Physical

HANDOUT #1

My "Good Experience Channel"

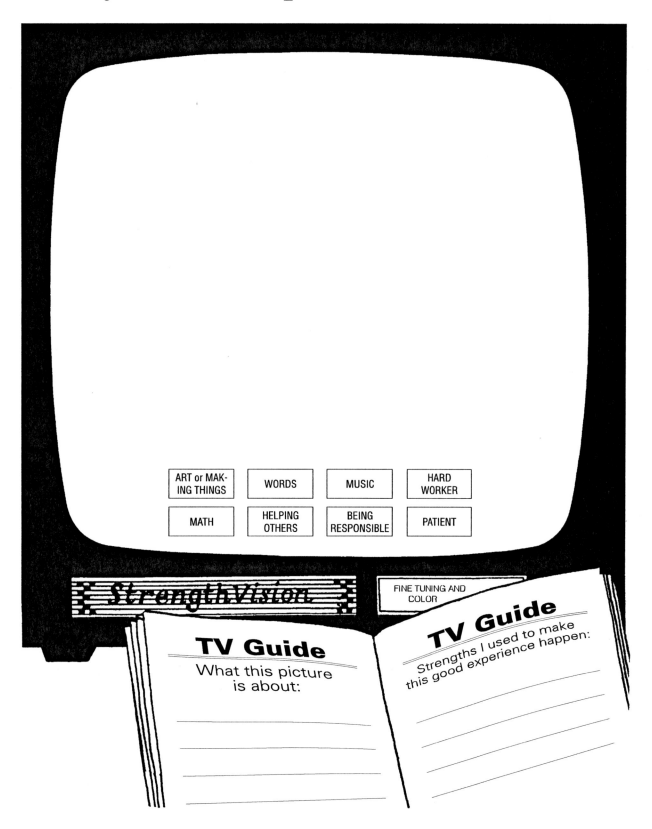

HANDOUT #2

Think of a Good Experience You've Had in One or Two of These Areas

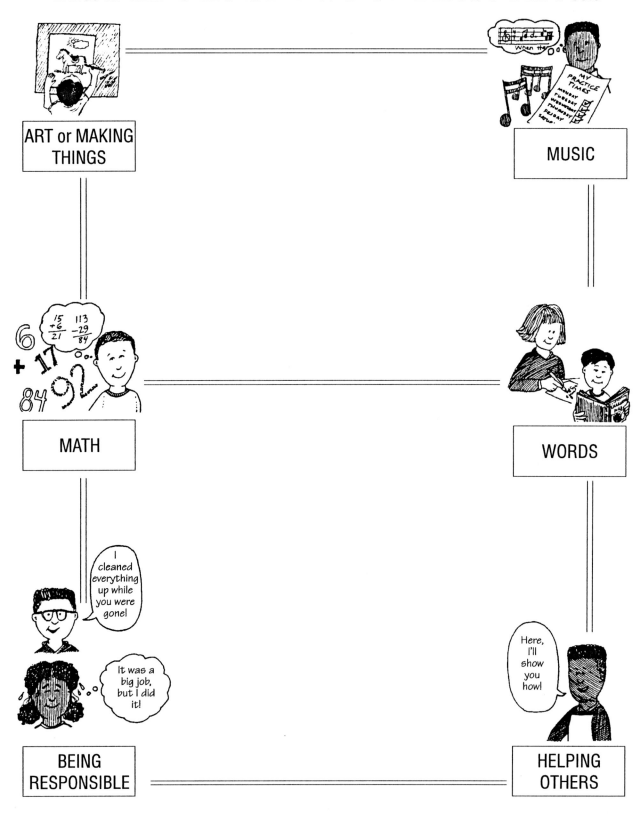

Something Special

Objective

Students will recognize that, although they may not have the same strengths as others around them, they have special strengths of their own.

Materials

Supplementary Activity #2 Handouts #1A and #1B - "Something Special"

Children's book: McPhail, D. *Something special*. Boston, MA: Little, Brown & Company.

Procedure

Talk to students about the fact that many times people look around at others' strengths and don't notice their own. They may think that because they don't have the same strengths as others, they don't have any strengths at all. If you read the book *Something Special* at the beginning of the lesson, remind students of the little raccoon who thought he had no special strengths. If you haven't read the story to students yet do so, showing the pictures of the characters.

Then give students the handout, "Special Strengths." Ask them to draw lines connecting each of the characters with his or her special strength (represented by the pictures on the righthand side of the page). At the bottom of Handout #1B, the students are to draw a picture of themselves in the lefthand box; in the righthand box they are to draw something that represents their own "special strength."

SUPPLEMENTARY ACTIVITY #1 HANDOUT #1A

Something Special

Directions:

Draw lines that connect the characters to their strengths.

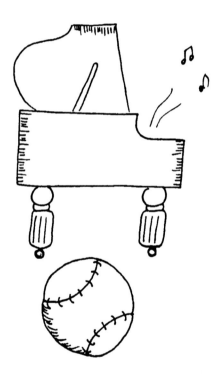

SUPPLEMENTARY ACTIVITY #1 HANDOUT #1B

Something Special (continued)

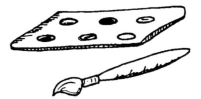

Draw yourself.

Draw one of your strengths.

SUPPLEMENTARY ACTIVITY #2

Strength Bracelet

Objective   Students will express legitimate pride in their strengths and accomplishments.

Materials   Construction paper
Miscellaneous art supplies

Procedure   When students accomplish something which they feel proud of, have them give you a strip of their favorite color of construction paper. Write the strength that underlies their accomplishment and/or the accomplishment itself on the strip of paper. Let them decorate it any way they wish, then tape it at the ends to fashion a "bracelet" which they can wear with pride at school and at home that day.

SUPPLEMENTARY ACTIVITY #3

Strength Word Letter Search

Objective   Students will guess the letters in a word that describes a classmate's strength.

Materials   None

Procedure

This activity works like the "Wheel of Fortune" game show. It reinforces students' awareness of different strength words and how they are spelled.

Explain to students that the class will be playing a game where they guess the letters in a word that describes one of their classmate's strengths. Ask for a volunteer who is willing to have others try to guess his or her strength. This student will whisper the word to you and how it is spelled. He or she can refer to his or her copy of the "Strength Word List" (Handout #4 from Lesson 2), if necessary. The student volunteer will then draw on the chalkboard a long rectangle divided into the same number of boxes as there are letters in his or her strength word. (Check this for accuracy.)

That student then calls on classmates to try to guess the letters in the word and, as soon as they are able, to guess the word itself. As students guess correct letters, these are written in the appropriate boxes. If a letter is repeated in the word, all the repetitions are filled in when the letter is first guessed. Incorrect letters are written outside the rectangle to help students remember which letters have already been guessed. When the word is guessed, the student who claimed it as a strength then gives an example of a time he or she used this strength to create a good experience.

VARIATIONS

To familiarize students with more difficult or less frequently used strength words, you may choose to be the one writing the strength words on the chalkboard. In this variation, to win the game a student who guesses the word must also be able to give an example of how this strength could be used to create a good experience in general. An even better response would be if the student could relate a time he or she actually used this strength.

If you are confident of students' accuracy in being the person spelling the word at the chalkboard, this activity can also be done in smaller groups. In this format, each student takes a turn at asking other group members to guess his or her strength.

Becoming Strength Spies

Objective

Students will further develop their ability to detect strengths in others and in themselves.

Materials

Transparency #1 - "Two Spies"

Transparency #2 - "Spy Reports—Examples"

Handout #1 - "Spy Reports"

Handout #2 - "Other Ways to Show Strengths"

Handout #3 - "Letter to Family Member"

Handout #4 - "Your Child Has Many Strengths"

"Spy Box" (a shoebox with a slit cut in the top for students to deposit their "Spy Reports")

For Beginning First Grade Students:

Handout #5 - "Spy On the Good Things Others Do"

Plastic wrap, cellophane, or transparency film: one 5" square
for each student

Construction paper

Scissors, glue, or paste

To the Teacher

The purpose of this lesson is to encourage students to focus on one another's strengths. Encouraging students to notice what is positive in others is a "win/win" exchange, as it builds the self-esteem not only of the one whose attribute is noticed, but of the one who notices it as well. When students identify each others' strengths, the classroom becomes a more nurturing environment for all.

After reviewing with your students the concepts taught in the previous lessons, you will read a story, "Two Spies," to the class. This story portrays the difference between watching for positive attributes in classmates as opposed to focusing on negative behaviors. Students learn to be "Strength Spies" who secretly watch for positive behaviors in their classmates. They learn to fill out special "Spy Reports" which they will put into a "Spy Box." The lesson suggests several ways that these reports can be used to reinforce positive behaviors in the classroom. To further help students identify strengths in their classmates, you will also give students a list of other ways strengths can be demonstrated.

Younger spies who are not yet able to write can tell the teacher or another designated adult who they saw doing what, as well as what strength they think was used. This information can then be written down for them on a "Spy Report." Alternately, spies can verbally give their reports in the classroom on a daily basis. (If you use this latter option, have each student draw a name in the morning. After lunch or at the end of the day, you can ask if anyone has noticed any strengths in his or her "subject" and is ready to make a report.) The lesson also provides an alternative "Spyglass" activity that can be used in place of written spy reports for younger, nonreading students.

Completed "Spy Reports" and "Spy Glasses" can be used to create an "I Spied a Strength" bulletin board.

This lesson includes two handouts to send home to family members. One is a letter that suggests ways the family can support the child as he or she learns to recognize and identify his or her strengths. The second handout asks a family member to identify strengths observed at home and cite examples. This handout should be returned to school and kept in the student's "Strengths Folder."

Lesson Presentation

REVIEW OF CONCEPTS

Say or paraphrase: **We've had some fun these last few weeks thinking of good experiences and finding strengths in ourselves and in each other. Who can tell me why we're taking the time to do this?** *Allow for student response. Make sure that students are aware of the following concepts: (1) remembering our good experiences helps us to feel good about ourselves; (2) thinking about our good experiences helps us realize we have certain strengths; (3) thinking about our strengths can help us do better at the things we're working on; and (4) helping each other find the strengths hidden in good experiences is something nice we can do for each other and can help us appreciate each other more.*

SPYING ON ONE ANOTHER TO NOTICE STRENGTHS

Today we're going to look for strengths in each other in a new way. We're going to <u>spy</u> on each other! We're going to try to catch others doing good things when they don't know

we're looking. Before I teach you how to be a good "Strength Spy," though, I want to tell you a story called "Two Spies."

THE STORY OF "TWO SPIES"

Transp. #1

Show Transparency #1, "Two Spies," covering the bottom half. Say:

This story is about two animal kids just about your age who lived in a forest far, far away from here. These kids' names were Rodney Raccoon and Helen Hedgehog. Rodney and Helen loved to watch spy movies on TV, and they both thought it might be fun to be spies when they grew up.

One day Rodney Raccoon decided that he was going to practice being a spy while he was still a little raccoon so he would be very good at it when he grew up. "A good spy takes notes," Rodney thought. And so he found a yellow pencil and a little black notebook and wrote "Rodney's Spy Notes" on the front page.

At recess Rodney took his little notebook and pencil and found a small bush where he could sit quietly and spy on his classmates. He could see them, but they couldn't see Rodney. After only a few minutes of watching Rodney saw Corinda Cat ask Reggie Rat if he wanted to use her jump rope. Rodney wrote, "Corinda asked Reggie if he wanted to use her jump rope. Corinda sure is <u>generous</u>!" "This is fun!" thought Rodney.

Every day after that Rodney sat quietly behind the small bush during recess and spied on the other kids in his class as they played. Rodney would watch a little and then write a little. Then he'd watch a little more and he'd write a little more. At the end of each recess, Rodney read his spy notes. They said things like this:

<u>Monday</u>—Tommy Turtle swam into the pond to get the soccer ball for Bobby Bobcat; Tommy's strength is being <u>helpful</u>.

<u>Tuesday</u>—Billy Bear decided to stay inside and finish his math assignment; Billy's strength is being a <u>hard worker</u>.

<u>Wednesday</u>—Winnie Wolf offered to pick up all the trash on the playground today; Winnie's strength is that she is <u>responsible</u>.

(continued)

As Rodney read his spy notes, he thought it would be fun to show them to Mrs. Badger, the teacher. Since he was practicing being a spy, he folded the notes up and put them on Mrs. Badger's desk when Mrs. Badger wasn't looking.

When Mrs. Badger found Rodney's spy notes, a big smile spread over her face. She complimented Corinda Cat, Billy Bear, Tommy Turtle, and Winnie Wolf. She said, "I'm a lucky teacher to have such a wonderful class!" Rodney's spy notes put Mrs. Badger in a <u>very</u> good mood!

Every Friday after that Rodney secretly folded his spy notes and put them on Mrs. Badger's desk. The other kids were really surprised to find out that someone was watching when they did something helpful, and you can imagine how good they each felt when Mrs. Badger read the spy notes about them.

Now I'll tell you about Helen Hedgehog. *Uncover Helen Hedgehog on the transparency; cover Rodney Raccoon.* She also liked the idea of being a spy—remember? She watched her classmates, too.

On Wednesday she noticed that Karen Kangaroo didn't finish her homework. On Thursday she saw Wally Woodpecker peck a hole in Millie Mouse's bag of potato chips. On Friday Sammy Squirrel wouldn't let Ricky Rabbit have a turn on the computer. "What a bunch of creeps!" Helen thought to herself. "I'm going to tell the teacher!"

Helen began to tell Mrs. Badger whenever she saw these kinds of things happen. "They should get in trouble!" she thought to herself. Pretty soon she was running up to tattle to Mrs. Badger several times a day. Since she was always looking for things others did wrong, Helen was usually in a bad mood. The kids didn't like it, and soon no one wanted to play with Helen.

Mrs. Badger didn't like the tattling either. She tried to ignore it. She finally told Helen in a firm voice, "Helen, please don't tell on the other kids unless someone is likely to get hurt."

Discuss the story with the class, asking questions like the following:

- **What kind of things did Rodney Raccoon watch for in his class?**
- **What kind of things did Helen Hedgehog watch for?**

- How did the teacher feel about the kind of spying Rodney did?
- How did the teacher feel about the kind of spying Helen did?

- How did the kids in the class feel about the kind of spying Rodney did?
- How did the kids in the class feel about the kind of spying Helen did?

- How did Rodney's spying make him feel?
- How did Helen's spying make her feel?
- What kind of advice would you give Helen so she would be a happier little hedgehog?

BEING STRENGTH SPIES

Today we're going to practice being spies. But we're not going to be like Helen Hedgehog was, with our eyes darting around trying to catch someone doing something wrong so we can tattle on them. *Pantomime with hunched shoulders, eyes darting around the room.* We're going to practice being a "Strength Spy" like Rodney Raccoon was. We're going to quietly watch for kids being kind and helpful to each other, for kids finishing their work and taking turns, for kids doing helpful things like picking up trash or cleaning up the room, and for kids sticking with something even when it's hard.

MODELING HOW TO FILL OUT A "SPY REPORT"

NOTE: If you are teaching beginning first grade students, before continuing further please review the "Variation for Beginning First Grade Students" found near the end of this lesson.

Transp. #2

Instead of using a little notebook like Rodney did, I've made some special "Spy Reports" for you to use instead. This is what they look like. *Put Transparency #2, "Spy Reports—Examples," on the overhead and read the first example to the class. Then fill in the bottom "Spy Report" with an example of a positive behavior of a student in the classroom.*

Say or paraphrase: **Now, if I were going to secretly fill out a "Spy Report" on a student in our class—let's say __(student)__ — the first thing I'd do is write his** *(her)* **name here.** *Write the student's name in the top blank of the sample report.* **Then I'd write down what I saw happening.** *Paraphrase the good experience or good behavior and write it on the next lines.* **Next, I'd think to myself, "What strength do I think __(student)__ used when he** *(she)* **did this?"** *Ask for suggestions from the class.* **Good! I think that's it!** *Write the strength word on the transparency. (If students suggest more than one strength, help them decide on the best one.)* **Finally, the last thing to do is for me to write down the name of the spy—that's me!** *Write your name on the name blank.*

Spy Box

After I've finished my "Spy Report," I'll secretly fold it and put it in this special box we're going to call our "Spy Box." *Show the class the "Spy Box."*

STUDENT PRACTICE IN FILLING OUT SPY REPORTS

Let's practice that again. I'll tell you something else I saw in our room the other day. Then I'll call on some of you to help me fill out a "Spy Report." *Wipe off the previous example you wrote on the transparency. Recount another example of a student (or students) who had a good experience or engaged in a positive behavior. Call on students other than the ones involved in the example to tell you what to write on each line of the "Spy Report." Offer assistance if needed as students attempt to identify the strength used by the student in the example.*

If you wish to provide more examples, clean off the transparency and continue giving new examples or ask for student volunteers to give examples or allow them to fill out the "Spy Report" on the transparency one line at a time.

Handout #1

If you feel your students need even more practice filling out "Spy Reports," give each student a copy of Handout #1, "Spy Reports." Suggest a positive behavior you observed in a class member. Lead the class through the first report on the handout, having them fill it out themselves. Walk around the room to see if students are able to fill out the report. Give assistance as needed. Suggest that students cut out the other three "Spy Reports" on the handout and complete them over the next few days and put them in the "Spy Box."

USING THE SPY BOX

That was fun! I think there are going to be some good "Strength Spies" in this class. I'll put the "Spy Box" up here with a stack of "Spy Reports" next to it. You keep your "spy-eye" open just like Rodney Raccoon did. You can spy on kids in the classroom, in the lunchroom, and on the playground. It's best if you just write "Spy Reports" for kids in our room—every time you see someone in our room doing something positive, you can fill out a "Spy Report" on them and put it in the "Spy Box."

From time to time, we'll open the "Spy Box" and read the reports. If the report is about something YOU did, then you get to put it in your "Strengths Folder!" *Put a stack of extra "Spy Reports" next to the "Spy Box."*

Handout #2

Distribute copies of Handout #2, "Other Ways to Show Strengths." Here is a list of things you can watch for while you're spying. See if you can catch kids in our class doing any of these things. You can also use this list to help you with your spelling when you fill out your "Spy Report." You may want to use your Strength Word List *(Handout #4 from Lesson 2)* to help you with your spelling, too.

VARIATIONS FOR USING SPY REPORTS

You can adapt the writing of "Spy Reports" for your students by using any of these variations:

- *Have each student draw a name of a classmate in the morning and ask them to "spy on" this classmate secretly during the day. At then end of the day, allow student volunteers to read their reports. Have all the "Strength Spies" give their "Spy Reports" to the student they spied on so those students can put the reports in their "Strengths Folders."*

- *Select a particular behavior for a day and ask the "Strength Spies" to notice students doing this behavior. For example, the spies could be asked to watch for anyone being a good sport, a good listener, a good worker, showing some form of kindness, etc. Doing this will reinforce the particular behavior(s) you with the students to work on.*

HOMEWORK AND LESSON SUMMARY

Tell students that their homework assignment for this lesson is to fill out a "Spy Report" on one of their parents or another family member. Explain that you have some homework for their parents to do, too!

Handout #3
Handout #4

Give students a copy of Handout #3, "Letter to Family Member," and Handout #4, "Your Child Has Many Strengths." Tell students that their family member knows their strengths better than anyone, and that the second handout asks the family member to list two of their strengths and times when they used them. Explain to the students that the completed handout will be shared during the next lesson with a small group of classmates who will be helping the students determine their list of top strengths. They'll need to have the completed handout to prepare their strength list for the "Celebration of Strengths Party," yet to come.

(The first handout to take home is a letter to a family member which explains what the family member is to do.)

VARIATION FOR BEGINNING FIRST GRADE STUDENTS

Handout #5

For beginning first grade students only: After reading the story, "Two Spies," substitute the following activity for the section "Modeling How to Fill Out a 'Spy Report.'" Give students Handout #5, "Spy On the Good Things Others Do." Using the handout as a pattern, have students cut two "Spy Glasses" from colored construction paper, discarding the center circle labeled "cut out." (You may need to demonstrate for the students how to cut out the center circle without cutting through the "Spy Glass" sides.)

Give each student a 6" square of plastic wrap, cellophane, or transparency film and demonstrate how to glue or paste the two "Spy Glasses" together, sandwiching the plastic wrap between the two pieces of construction paper. Once glued, the students should trim off the corners of the plastic wrap. Have students write their names on the handles of their "Spy Glasses."

Use these "Spy Glasses" during "Spy Time," when you ask students to identify classmates who demonstrated strengths or positive behaviors. You may specify a specific strength by asking, "Has anyone spied someone being (helpful/kind/patient/a hard worker/etc.)?" A student volunteer can take his or her "Spy Glass" over to another classmate, pretend to "spy" through it, and describe the time he or she saw the student performing a positive behavior. Before ending "Spy Time," ask if any students have spied on someone not yet mentioned who did something positive they want to report about.

You can also create a bulletin board using the "Spy Glasses." Have each student write his or her name on the handle. Attach these to a bulletin board at a height where the students can reach them. Each time students "spy" a classmate doing something good, they can draw a little eye or star on the rim or handle of that student's "Spy Glass."

Proceed with the rest of the lesson as presented, adapting suggested variations as necessary.

LESSON SUMMARY AND PREVIEW OF NEXT LESSON

Summarize the lesson by having the students respond verbally to one of the following sentence stems:

- *I liked . . . .*

- *I was surprised . . . .*

- *I learned . . . .*

- *This lesson would have been better if . . . .*

Tell students that they'll have more chances in the following days to share their good experiences and find out more of their strengths. Then they will each decide, with the help of their classmates, what their top strengths are, and the whole class will have a "Celebration of Strengths Party."

SUPPLEMENTARY ACTIVITIES

Use the Supplementary Activities to provide additional practice with lesson concepts:

- *"Who Do You Think of When You Hear the Word . . . "*
    (Supplementary Activity #1)

- *"Strength Mobiles"*
    (Supplementary Activity #2)

- *"Give Yourself a Pat on the Back!"*
    (Supplementary Activity #3)

TRANSPARENCY #1

Two Spies

TRANSPARENCY #2

Spy Reports—Examples

S P Y   R E P O R T

Person I spied on: _____Monica_____

What I saw: _She lent her colored markers_
___to Susan._____

_____

Strength I think he or she was using: __generous_____

_____

My name: _Jack_____

S P Y   R E P O R T

Person I spied on: _____

What I saw: _____

_____

_____

Strength I think he or she was using: _____

_____

My name: _____

HANDOUT #1

Spy Reports

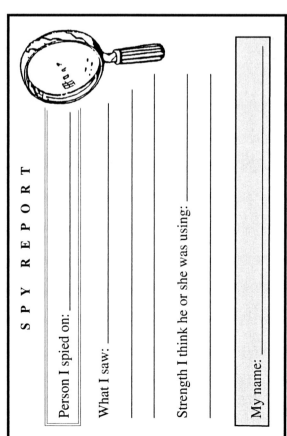

SPY REPORT

Person I spied on: _____

What I saw: _____

Strength I think he or she was using: _____

My name: _____

SPY REPORT

Person I spied on: _____

What I saw: _____

Strength I think he or she was using: _____

My name: _____

SPY REPORT

Person I spied on: _____

What I saw: _____

Strength I think he or she was using: _____

My name: _____

SPY REPORT

Person I spied on: _____

What I saw: _____

Strength I think he or she was using: _____

My name: _____

HANDOUT #2

Other Ways to Show Strengths

Good attitude

Good at coloring

Good dancer

Good at drawing

Good friend

Good imagination

Good leader

Good listener

Good memory

Good reader

Good sport

Good writer

HANDOUT #3

Letter to Family Member

Dear Family Member,

I am currently teaching some lessons in which students are learning ways to identify their strengths. While not overlooking students' needs to overcome their weaknesses, there is much to be gained from helping children understand and appreciate their talents and abilities.

Students are learning to identify their unique combination of strengths by examining their good experiences. They are encouraged to think about and share events of which they are proud. Then they are helped to find the strengths they used to create these good experiences.

By communicating the strengths you see in your child, you can help build self- confidence and increase his or her motivation to improve. A good way to help your child believe in his or her strengths is to point out specific times when you saw these strengths being used. The attached sheet provides space for you to do this. If you will fill this out, we will use the strengths you identify, along with those identified by classmates and adults at school, to help your child create a list of his or her top strengths.

Use any of the following categories to spark ideas about your child's strengths: school subjects or activities; sports; creative, artistic, or musical activities; friendships; family life; work or chores; hobbies. Here are some examples of comments other parents have made:

Strength: Good Sport
A time it was used: I heard you say "Good game!" to the other team even though you felt bad about losing.

Strength: Sense of Humor
A time it was used: You have a great way of getting us all laughing—like you did last night about the burnt broccoli.

Strength: Good With Your Hands
A time it was used: I'm amazed at the way you can fix things. You put that broken model together and it looks like new.

You might want to set aside regular times for focusing on the strengths or positive qualities of all your family members. These times can be during family dinners or on birthdays or holidays. After experiencing having their strengths pointed out to them, children are usually able to name strengths of others.

Thank you for helping remind your child that you honor his or her diverse talents and skills.

Sincerely,

HANDOUT #4

Your Child Has Many Strengths

Of the many strengths you have observed in your child, please choose two and write them in the stars below, describing a time when you saw your child use each strength.

Strength

Time I saw it being used:

Strength

Time I saw it being used:

HANDOUT #5

Spy On the Good Things Others Do

Who Do You Think of When You Hear the Word . . .

Objective
Students will name classmates who they think demonstrate specific strengths.

Materials
Supplementary Activity #1 Transparency - "Strength Word List"

Procedure
Place the transparency on the overhead with all the words covered. Uncover each word, one at a time, and read it aloud. For each word, ask questions such as the following:

- "Who can think of someone in our class who is **caring**?"
- "Who in our class is nearly always **cheerful**?"
- "Who do you think of when you hear the word **fair**?"
- "Who in here is very **dependable**—when they say they'll do something, they do it."
- "Who do you think is a very **forgiving** person in this room—someone who doesn't hold a grudge?"
- "Who in here is a **good listener**? Think of someone who doesn't interrupt you when you're talking to them, and who is interested in what you say."

Call on the students who raise their hands; ask a student to look at the person he or she thinks has the quality you've just named. Have the student say that person's name out loud for all to hear.

As you go through the list, ask the students to listen carefully so they can try to name classmates who **haven't been mentioned yet**.

SUPPLEMENTARY ACTIVITY #1 TRANSPARENCY

Strength Word List

artistic

athletic

brave

caring

cheerful

cooperative

coordinated

creative

determined

energetic

fair

fast

friendly

generous

good memory

hard worker

helpful

honest

imaginative

kind

musical

organized

patient

positive attitude

problem solver

responsible

sense of humor

sharing

strong

unselfish

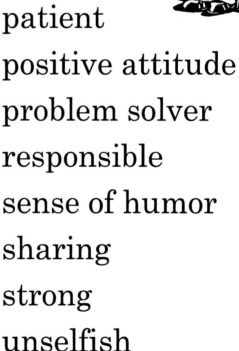

SUPPLEMENTARY ACTIVITY #2

Strength Mobiles

Objective

Students will determine two strength words they think describe them best.

Students will name one another's strengths.

Students will appreciate the diversity of strengths represented in their class.

Materials

Strength Word Card Pages #1-#12 from Lesson 2, copied onto construction paper or tagboard with the illustrations cut off

Differently-colored construction paper, four equal size squares for each student

Colored yarn

Glue

Procedure

Choose 10-12 "Strength Word Cards" from Lesson 2 that name strengths you think your students will identify with. Give each student four squares of construction paper. Have students write their first name in large letters on one side of all four squares. (These cards will be glued back to back, so the students will each end up having only two name cards.) Tell the students that you will read some strength words aloud, and they should listen carefully to decide which **two** strengths sound **the most like them**. Slowly read the strength words (from the "Strength Word Cards"), laying them out on a long table as you do so.

Have students all come up to the table and lay down two of their name cards next to each of their two top strength words. If a student can't decide on his or her top two strengths, ask the class which strengths they observe the student often using. Add your own opinions regarding which of the strengths you observe most often, then let the student choose from these suggestions.

When all students are satisfied with their choices, help them to assemble mobiles. For each strength word that was chosen by any of the students, glue yarn between the name cards of all the students who chose it, with the strength word itself at the top of this "list" (see illustration). Suspend each strength word mobile from the ceiling or from string fastened across the room like a clothesline. Point out the diversity of strengths represented in the class and comment upon how fortunate students are to have so many different talents in their classroom.

There are a variety of ways you can extend this activity. During the days that follow, you may pick one or two of the strength word mobiles and ask each student on that mobile to tell about a time he or she used that strength. Alternately, you may wish to refer to the mobile and point out instances of strengths yourself, saying something like, "Jim has the strength of determination. I know that's true because Jim works really hard to do his math assignment, even when it's something difficult." You might also ask members of the class to volunteer times when they have seen students using their strengths.

This activity can also provide a springboard for a discussion of the diversity of strengths in the classroom and the value of this diversity.

VARIATION

Rather than making mobiles, you can post the "Strength Word Cards" on a bulletin board and pin the students' name cards under their identified strengths.

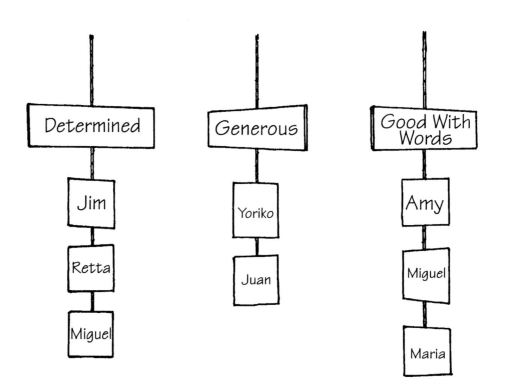

SUPPLEMENTARY ACTIVITY #3

Give Yourself a Pat on the Back!

Objective   Students will feel acknowledged for their strengths.

Students will begin to recognize their strengths by hearing them pointed out by others.

Materials   Supplementary Activity #3 Poster   -   "Give Yourself a Pat on the Back!"

Procedure   Hang up the poster in the classroom. Whenever you see a student exercising a strength, point it out and then invite the student to go over and lean against the poster to receive a "pat on the back" for using his or her strength.

VARIATION

At the end of the day, invite the class to name classmates they saw using a strength and describe the strength used. Acknowledged students then use the poster to give themselves pats on the back. (You will want to offer acknowledgments yourself to those students who tend to be overlooked.)

SUPPLEMENTARY ACTIVITY #3 POSTER

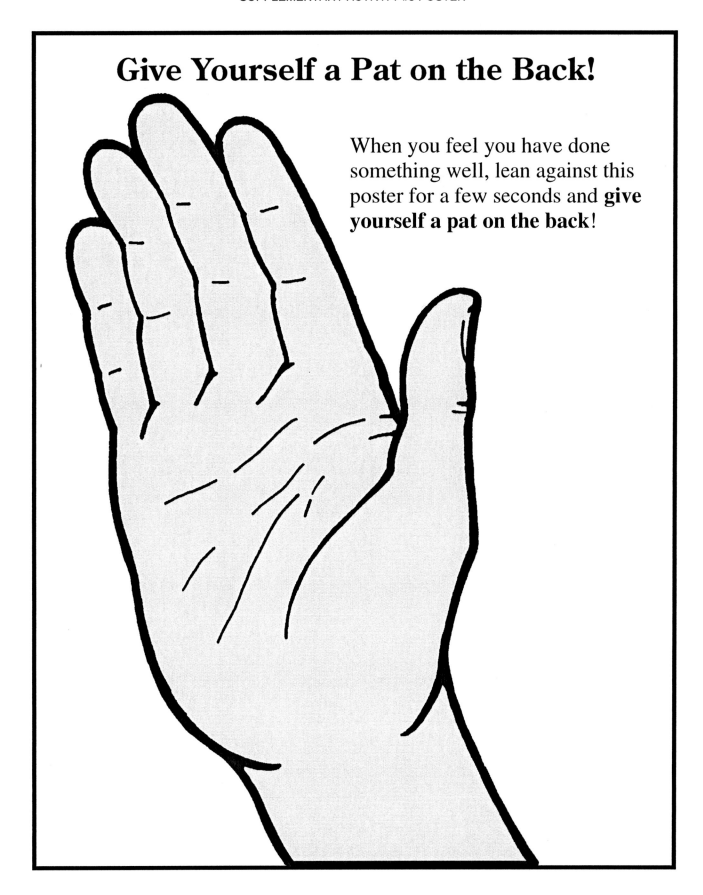

Give Yourself a Pat on the Back!

When you feel you have done something well, lean against this poster for a few seconds and **give yourself a pat on the back!**

Preparing Strength Reports

Objective

Students will use information from their previous activity sheets to construct a list of their particular strengths.

Materials

Handout #4 from Lesson 5 - "Your Child Has Many Strengths" (one completed copy from each student's family member)

Transparency #1/Handout #1 - "My Strengths"

Strengths Folders (all students')

To the Teacher

In this lesson students meet with you and their peers in small groups. With your help and the help of the other members of the group, each student will generate a list of his or her top strengths. This list will be drawn from all the exercises the student has done so far and has been keeping in his or her "Strengths Folder." After all the students have made a list, they are asked to choose one strength and think of a time in the future when they will use that strength to create a good experience for themselves.

The small groups should consist of six to eight students. If you have a parent helper or an aide, you may have that individual facilitate a group as well. The parent or aide will need instruction and/or modeling on how to lead the group, based on the guidelines given in this lesson.

If possible, meet with the small groups one at a time in a circle near a chalkboard or chart. The rest of the class can work at their desks either on activities you've selected from the Supplementary Activities that follow this lesson, or on assignments from the content areas.

Lesson Presentation

OVERVIEW OF THE ACTIVITY

To the class: **You've been working really hard these past few weeks remembering your good experiences and looking for the strengths you used to make these experiences happen. You've asked your family to help you find your strengths, and you and your classmates have helped each other by** writing reports about the strengths you've seen others using.

Transp. #1

Now we're going to use all these things you've done to help you decide what your special strengths are. When we're done, each of you will be able to write your <u>top strengths</u> on this special strength page. *Show Transparency #1, "My Strengths."*

Handout #4 from Lesson 5

You'll be working on your strength list in small groups. I'll work with one small group at a time. When I call for your group to meet with me, you'll need to bring with you your "Strengths Folders" with all the handouts you've done, like all your "TV channel pages," any "Spy Reports" other kids have written about you, and the page with the stars that a member of your family filled out. *(Hold up a copy of the handout "Your Child Has Many Strengths.")* When I'm meeting with a small group I'd like the rest of you to work quietly at your seat. Here are some activities for you to work on. *Hand out copies of the Supplementary Activity handouts you've selected from those found at the end of this lesson or assign work from the content areas. Explain or model how to do the activities, if necessary.*

SMALL GROUP ACTIVITY

In the small group, explain that you'll review each student's "Strength Folder," reading the strengths listed on the "Your Child Has Many Strengths" handout filled out by the student's family member, the "TV channel pages," and the "Spy Reports." Then everyone will work together to help each group member determine his or her top strengths. Within the small group, discuss each student's positive qualities in a manner similar to the following:

Refer to the "Your Child Has Many Strengths" handout. **Listen to the strengths that someone in Mary's family noticed in her.** *Read the strengths listed on the stars on the handout.* **Since Mary's family knows her so well and they say that these are**

her strengths, let's list these two strengths here. *Print the two strength words from the stars on the chalkboard or chart for all the group members to see.*

Strengths Folders

Take Mary's "TV channel pages" (there should be three pages for good experiences) out of her "Strengths Folder." Review the pages with the small group, asking Mary for clarification on items as necessary. If Mary has filled in the strength boxes at the bottom of the pages, say for each: **Mary says she used the strength of** _____ **to create this good experience for herself.** *(If Mary hasn't filled in the boxes, ask the group for each:* **What strength do you think Mary used to create this good experience?** *Ask Mary if she agrees with the group's assessment of her strengths.) Help Mary choose two strength words that she thinks fit her the best, and write these words on Mary's strengths list on the chalkboard or chart.*

Next, go over any "Spy Reports" that may be in Mary's "Strengths Folder." Review what she was seen doing, and what strength the "spy" noticed. Say: **Mary, it looks like your classmates have noticed some more strengths of yours that we should add! Let's add these to your list.** *Help Mary choose one or two of those strengths mentioned on the "Spy Reports" which she feels are the "most like her." Add these to her list on the chalkboard or chart.*

Finally, ask the group members if there are any strengths not yet on the list which they have noticed that Mary uses a lot. The students will often mention one or two more strengths.

Handout #1

Say: **Now, Mary, I want you to decide which three or four of these strengths you feel are your very top strengths. I'll write down the ones you tell me to on this handout.** *Use Handout #1, "My Strengths." (If a student feels he or she can't narrow the list down to three or four strengths, simply allow that student to claim up to five.) After you have written the student's name and his or her strengths on the handout, give it to the student and ask him or her to put it in his or her "Strengths Folder."*

Repeat this procedure for the rest of the students in the small group.

The bottom section of the "My Strengths" handout is designed to be a simple goal-setting exercise. The students are asked to choose one of their strengths and pick a specific time they will deliberately use this strength to create a new good experience for themselves. The students should dictate to you how and when they will use their strength in the future so you can complete this portion of their handout for them.

When you've finished with all the students in the group, say: **I have something fun to tell you! In the next few days we're going to plan a party—we'll call it our "Celebration of Strengths Party." We're going to celebrate because we have so many neat kids with so many important strengths in our class!**

As part of getting ready for the party, we're all going to make a video. You'll each be on the video saying your name and reading the list of your top strengths that we just made and when you will use one of your strengths. Don't worry or be nervous about doing this, because you'll get a chance to practice before we make the video, and I'll be there to help you with the words when we do the real tape.

At our "Celebration of Strengths Party" we'll eat treats and watch our video. It'll be fun to see all of you on TV—and this time it won't be imaginary TV in our heads, it'll be <u>real</u> TV!

Dismiss students to their seats. Remind them that they need to work quietly on the activities you handed out at the beginning of the lesson. (They may also color the border of their "My Strengths" handout if they like.)

Call up the next small group and continue these procedures until all the students have developed a list of their top strengths.

SUPPLEMENTARY ACTIVITIES

Use the Supplementary Activities to keep the students occupied during the small group meetings or to provide additional practice with lesson concepts:

- *"Strength Kid"*
  (Supplementary Activity #1)

- *"My Strengths T-Shirt"*
  (Supplementary Activity #2

- *"A Scroll of Strengths"*
  (Supplementary Activity #3)

- *"An Accordion Book of Strengths"*
  (Supplementary Activity #4)

TRANSPARENCY #1/HANDOUT #1

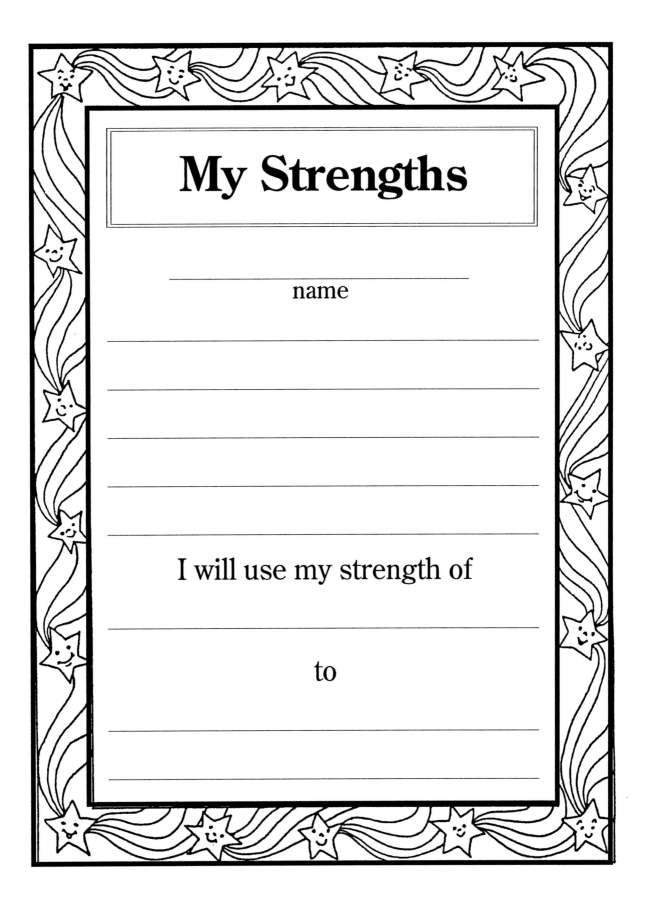

My Strengths

_____
name

I will use my strength of

to

SUPPLEMENTARY ACTIVITY #1

Strength Kid

Objective Students will guess the letters in a word that describes a partner's strength.

Materials Pencils and paper

Procedure This activity is a variation of the popular "Hangman" game. Explain to the students that they will be playing a game with a partner where they guess the letters in a word which describes one of their partner's strengths. Divide the participating students into pairs. Have the taller partner of each pair go first. This partner will think of a word which describes one of his or her strengths, referring to the "Strength Word List" (Handout #4 from Lesson 2) as necessary. He or she will then draw a "Strength Kid" stand and put an underlined space for each letter in the strength word, as illustrated.

As in "Hangman," the other student will try to guess the letters in the word and, as soon as he or she is able, to guess the word itself. As the student guesses correct letters, these are filled into the appropriate spaces. If the letter is repeated in the word, all the repetitions are filled in when the letter is first guessed. Incorrect letters are written down on the paper, to help the students remember which letters have already been guessed. If the word is guessed, the first student then gives an example of how he or she could use (or has used) this strength to create a good experience.

For each incorrect letter, a new body part of the "Strength Kid" is drawn in, as illustrated. If the drawing is completed before the word is guessed, the guessing student loses. In this case, the first student will tell what the word was and an example of a time he or she used this strength to create a good experience.

After this first game is completed, the players switch roles and continue play.

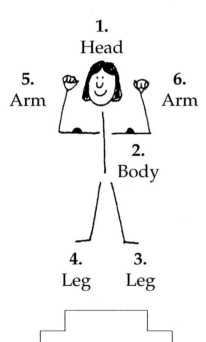

SUPPLEMENTARY ACTIVITY #2

My Strengths T-Shirt

Directions:

Design a T-shirt showing one of your strengths with words or drawings!

SUPPLEMENTARY ACTIVITY #3

A Scroll of Strengths

This is a fun way to show how you've used your strengths.

1. Get a strip of paper several feet long from your teacher.

2. Draw pictures of yourself using your strengths. Under each picture, write what you are doing and identify at least one or two of the strengths the picture shows you using.

3. Roll the paper up into a scroll and tie a ribbon around it.

4. On the outside of the scroll, write your name and what a few of your strengths are. Trade scrolls with a friend and look at each others' or give the scroll to a family member to read.

SUPPLEMENTARY ACTIVITY #4

An Accordion Book of Strengths

Use this book to tell the story of your strengths. You can draw pictures of yourself using your strengths now or at times in the past, or you can make up a story and show yourself using your strengths as the story unfolds. If you make up a story, try to show at least one of your strengths being used on each page. You can make this book as long as you want.

To make your Accordion Book:

1. Make a title page for your book.

2. On pieces of paper that are all the same size as the title page, draw pictures of yourself using your strengths. Write below each picture what the strength or strengths are that you're showing on the page, and how you're using them.

3. Put the pages into the order you like, or that tells your story.

4. Using transparent tape, tape the pages together like the illustration below, so that they will fold up like an accordion.

5. Turn over the entire set of pages and tape the back sides, then fold up your book.

6. Pass the book around the class for others to unfold and look at, or display the book on a table in the classroom.

Celebrating Your Strengths

Objective

Students will understand that saying their strengths aloud is not bragging, and will demonstrate this understanding by being videotaped saying their strengths.

Students will learn ways to help themselves believe in their strengths.

Students will celebrate their strengths by watching the videotape of their strengths and having a "Celebration of Strengths Party."

Materials

For Videotaping:

• Video Title Page - "We Have Many Strengths!"

• Transparency #1 - "Things We Say to Ourselves That Stop Us From Believing in Our Strengths

• Transparency #2/Handout #1 - "Strengths Badge"

• Handout #1 from Lesson 6 - "My Strengths" (a completed copy for each student)

• VCR and videotape

• Video camera/camcorder and tripod (and camera batteries as necessary)

• Masking tape or a sheet of paper to mark the spot on the floor where the students are to stand when being videotaped

• Post-It Notes

For "Celebration Of Strengths Party":

• Transparency #3/Handout #2 - "Sharing Our Strengths"

• Handout #3 - "Strengths Award"

• Completed "Strengths Badges" (Handout #1)

• Strength Word Card Pages #1-#12 from Lesson 2

• The completed strengths videotape of all the students in the class.

• Children's book: Pfister, M. (1992). *The rainbow fish*. New York: North-South Books.

- Tape or pins

- Colored markers or crayons

- Scissors

- Snacks (to be provided by parents)

- Aluminum foil and/or metallic markers or glitter (optional)

- Plastic wrap (optional)

- Gold stars for attaching to the "Strengths Awards" (Handout #3) (optional)

To the Teacher

This lesson is the culmination of the strengths discovery process for primary age students. The students will have the opportunity to be videotaped telling their strengths, then will watch the video at a "Celebration of Strengths Party." At the end of the party they will be encouraged to find ways to share their strengths with others. Finally, students will be reminded that as they get older they will continue to discover in themselves new strengths.

Because this lesson includes a number of different activities, it could take several days to complete. Specifically, you may find you prefer to do the videotaping component over several days, rather than trying to do it all in one day.

The lesson begins by reminding students that talking about one's strengths isn't bragging, as long as it's not being done in a way that puts others down. The students are then led to understand that a person can have a strength even if it is not used all the time or if someone else can do it better. With this preparation, the students are then videotaped reading their strengths and their goal on the "My Strengths" handout you helped them complete in Lesson 6.

For many students, seeing themselves on video is a fun and rewarding experience. At the "Celebration of Strengths Party," each student is also rewarded for exploring his or her strengths by wearing a special "Strengths Badge" and by being given a "Strengths Award."

The book *The Rainbow Fish* by Marcus Pfister is used at the end of the party to encourage students to see that strengths can be shared with others, to the benefit of both the student who shares and the person who receives. Students will make a bulletin board which identifies strengths they would like to share with others.

Lesson Presentation

Video Title Page

BEFORE YOU BEGIN

Color the Video Title Page ("We Have Many Strengths!"), and prepare a final ending credit for the videotape by writing "The End" on another sheet of paper. You may also wish to create "credits" for the video by listing the class members' names on additional sheets of paper which will be shot at the conclusion of the videotape. Hang these pages on the wall or a bulletin board so that you can easily film the title page as a lead-in at the beginning of the video and the "The End" and credits pages at the video's conclusion. (When filming all these pages, be sure to hold the camera on each page for at least eight to ten seconds or the students won't have time to read them when viewing the videotape.)

Determine where you want the students to stand when they read for the video camera and mark the floor with an "X" made of masking tape or with a sheet of paper.

INTRODUCING THE ACTIVITY

Say or paraphrase: **Today we're going to start taping our movie for our "Celebration of Strengths Party." Everyone will get a chance over the next few days to stand up here on the "X" (** *or paper***) and read their strengths from their "My Strengths" pages. You all worked hard to find out your best strengths. Now it's time to see yourself on video proudly saying what your strengths are!**

READING OUR STRENGTHS IS NOT BRAGGING

How many of you think you might feel a little embarrassed standing up in front of a camera and saying some nice things about yourself? Does anyone think they might feel like they're bragging? *Allow the students to raise their thumbs in response.*

We may often wonder if it's bragging when we say something nice about ourselves. It's NOT bragging to say positive and true things about yourself, especially if you're not trying to make yourself seem better than someone else. The main reason I'd like you to say your strengths out loud is so you'll remember them the next time you're feeling down or discouraged. Seeing yourself saying your strengths is a powerful way for you to remember them.

SOMETIMES WE SAY THINGS THAT STOP US FROM BELIEVING IN OUR STRENGTHS

Finding our strengths can be fun—but did you know that it's hard for some kids to do? Even though they're very good at some things, some kids say things to keep themselves from believing in their strengths. Let me show you one of the things they say to themselves.

ERROR #1: "I DON'T DO IT WELL EVERY TIME, SO IT'S NOT A REAL STRENGTH"

Transp. #1

Use Post-It Notes or paper squares to cover the "thought bubbles," then show Transparency #1, "Things We Say to Ourselves That Stop Us from Believing in Our Strengths." Point to "Seth." This is Seth. One day during math he lent his Learning Partner one of his new pencils because she didn't have one. The teacher noticed and said, "That's very <u>generous</u> of you Seth. I've seen you share before, and I think being generous is one of your strengths. We're lucky to have someone like you who shares with others in our class!"

You would think Seth would feel pretty good about that, wouldn't you? But, no! He didn't! Seth said something to himself that kept him from <u>believing</u> that he was <u>generous</u>. This is what Seth said to himself. *Uncover the top left thought bubble and read:* "<u>I'm not that way ALL the time.</u>" Seth thought to himself, "Sometimes I'm selfish. I hate sharing my dessert at lunch! I'm not ALWAYS generous, so it can't be one of my strengths!"

How many of you have ever done what Seth just did—told yourself you really weren't good at something just because you weren't good at it every single time? *Ask students to raise their thumbs if they've had a similar experience. (If you like, share an experience of your own before you invite the students to share times they have kept themselves from believing in their strengths in this way.)*

The truth is that you can have a strength even though you don't use it every time you could. Let's say that one of your strengths is that you're brave. Even though you're usually willing to try new things, there's one time you keep remembering when you were afraid to try something. Does that one time mean you can't say that one of your strengths is being brave? *Allow for student response.*

What if you're usually a good friend to your classmates, but every once in awhile you forget and give someone a put-down? Does that mean that you can't say that one of your strengths is being <u>kind</u> or <u>caring</u>? Of course not!

So if Seth finds himself thinking, "I'm not that way ALL the time," what could he think instead to help him believe in his strength? *Uncover the top right thought bubble and read:* **"<u>I don't have to be perfect ALL the time!</u>" This can help Seth believe in his strength. Saying this might help you, too, if you have a hard time believing in one of your strengths because you don't use it all the time.**

<hr>

ERROR #2: "IF I'M NOT THE BEST AT IT, IT'S NOT A REAL STRENGTH"

<hr>

We found a way to help Seth believe in his strength. Now let's see if we can help Rikki. *Point to Rikki on the transparency.*

Rikki likes art and is quite good at it. She always looks forward to art time, and the other kids often ask her for ideas. You would think Rikki would feel good about her strength in art, wouldn't you? But Rikki <u>doesn't</u> believe in her strength! This is what she tells herself. *Uncover the bottom left though bubble and read:* "He's BETTER at it than I am." That's right! There <u>are</u> two or three kids in Rikki's class who are even better at art than she is. Just because they're better at art than Rikki, she thinks her art strength doesn't count!

Raise your thumb if you've ever stopped yourself from believing you were good at something just because some others were better at it than you were. Maybe they could run faster or were better at sports than you were. Would anyone want to share a time they thought their strength didn't count just because someone else was better at it? *Allow for student response.*

What can Rikki say to herself to help herself believe in her own strength, even though someone else is better at it than she is? *Remove the bottom right tab and read:* She could say, "<u>Just because HE's good at it, that doesn't mean it's not MY strength, too!</u>" There will <u>always</u> be people who are better than you at some things! It's not necessary to compare yourself with others. Just be proud of your own strength!

So remember as you go to say your strengths out loud or as you listen to others tell their strengths, that a person can have something as a strength even if he or she doesn't use it every time it could be used and it can be a strength even if someone else might be better at it than that person is.

INSTRUCTIONS FOR THE VIDEOTAPING

In just a few minutes, we're going to be reading our list of strengths in front of the video camera. This is how we'll do it. *Model for the class as you give the following instructions:* When it's your turn to read, you'll stand in front of the camera here on the "x." When you talk, be careful not to hold your paper in front of your face, because we want to see you in our movie!

When I give you a nod like this *(demonstrate)* you'll say, "Hi! My name is ____, and my strengths are _____." You'll have to speak very slowly, as if you're moving . . . in . . . slow . . . motion! Kids who don't speak slowly often end up sounding like the fast forward on the VCR! After you've named three or four of your strengths, you can add this if you like: "The strength I like to use the most is _____."

You should also speak very LOUDLY—as if your words were a ball and you're throwing them ALL THE WAY TO THE BACK OF THE ROOM! If you don't speak loudly, you won't be able to hear yourself in our movie. Remember, it's <u>not bragging</u> to say your strengths.

Remember, too, what we talked about today—that you don't have to be PERFECT every time and that you don't have to be the VERY BEST at something for it to be your strength! You're simply saying that the strengths you've discovered were ones you used when you created good experiences for yourself. They are also strengths your parents or classmates have seen you use a lot. So say them proudly in a loud, strong voice.

When we're videotaping one of us saying his or her strengths, everyone else will have to be very quiet. Please don't whisper, move your chair, or rustle your papers. While you're waiting for your turn and when your turn is done, you can work quietly at your desk. We'll take a few wiggle-breaks now and then for you to get things out of your desk or move around a bit to take a stretch.

Everyone will get a practice run before I turn on the camera, and I'll help you with the words, if you like, so there's no need to worry that you'll mess up. This is just going to be a fun video about our strengths! It's not something that has to be serious or perfect!

MAKING STRENGTH BADGES FOR THE PARTY

While we're making our video, you can be working on a special badge to wear at our "Celebration of Strengths Party." You may have time to do some other fun activity pages, too. *(You can provide students with handouts from some of the Supplementary Activities at end of this lesson.)*

Transp. #2

Put Transparency #2, "Strengths Badge," on the overhead and use colored transparency markers to demonstrate how to fill it out. If you think it will be helpful, you may also wish to duplicate a copy of the badge to demonstrate cutting it out.

First you'll write your name on the bottom line. Then you'll write two or three of your top strengths on your badge. When you've done that, you can color your badge. You can color the fringe in rainbow colors, if you want.

When you're done coloring, cut out your badge. If you want, you can cut carefully on the lines at the bottom to make fringe on your badge. You can curl the fringe around a pencil or leave it straight.

You can pin this badge on during our "Celebration of Strengths Party" to remind you and your classmates that you're the kind of person who is ____ and ____, or ____, ____, and ____. *Fill in the blanks on the transparency with various strength words.* **Be sure to choose the words from your "My Strengths" page.**

Handout #1

Distribute copies of Handout #1, "Strengths Badge," and begin videotaping the students saying their strengths. During the time you're taping the students, the rest of the class can work on the activities provided from the Supplementary Activities, or they may do assignments from the other curriculum areas.

THE "CELEBRATION OF STRENGTHS PARTY"

After you've finished videotaping each student in your class, schedule a convenient time for a "Celebration of Strengths Party." If you like, add to the festive mood by asking students to bring treats from home to share during the party. Emphasize that the purpose of the party is to celebrate the fact that each one of them has special strengths.

As the party gets underway, affix students' "Strength Badges" with pins or tape. Distribute the refreshments and allow the students to eat them while watching the video.

SHARING OUR STRENGTHS: THE RAINBOW FISH STORY

storybook

After watching the video together, have the class gather around you to listen to the story The Rainbow Fish *by Marcus Pfister. Say or paraphrase:* **I'm going to read you a story about a special fish who learned to share something that was very important to him. At the end of the story, I'm going to see if you can guess what I'd like YOU to share with others.** *Read the story aloud, showing the illustrations.*

Next, lead the following discussion: **Why was the Rainbow Fish so happy at the end of the story?** *Allow for student response, then say or paraphrase:* **Even when it's hard to do, sharing makes us feel good and often brings us friends. What are some things you already share?** *Allow for student response.*

What are some things you could share? *Allow for student response.*

I'm not going to ask you to share your most precious possession like the Rainbow Fish did, but I would like you to share something important that each of you have. Can anyone guess what that might be? *Allow for student response.* **Right! I'm asking you to share your strengths. Who can suggest how a person might share a strength?** *Allow for student response, then give the following examples.*

Often in order to share your strength means you'll also be sharing your <u>time</u> with someone. If you have the strength of being <u>athletic</u>, for example, you might teach a younger person how to be better in a certain sport or game. If you have the strength of being <u>organized</u>, you might help a classmate clean out his or her desk and, if they ask, show them a good way to store things so their desk looks neat. You might help them organize their papers in their folder or notebook, if they would like you to.

If you have the strength of being <u>artistic</u>, you might teach someone how to draw something, if that's something they'd like. If you have the strength of being good at <u>spelling</u>, you might show a friend some tricks you know for remembering how to spell certain words. If you have the strength of having a <u>good memory</u>, you could help someone who has forgotten directions.

There are hundreds of ways you can share your strengths. Before you offer to do something for someone, though, you should always ask them if they'd like you to share it. You should only share if the other person wants you to.

Strength Word Card Pages #1-#12 from Lesson 2

Do any of you have any ideas about how you could share one of your strengths? *Allow for student response. At this point you might wish to name strengths you feel particular students could* *share well. As you name these strengths, you can place on the appropriate students' desks the corresponding "Strength Word Card" from Lesson 2. This can add to the acknowledgment of these students' strengths, as well as help with the students' spelling.*

Here are a few examples. You might say:

- *"Molly, you could share your strength of being artistic by helping someone to draw horses. You do that so well!" and then place the card "artistic" on Molly's desk.*

- *"Rolando, I heard that you are really good at jumping over puddles with your bike. Maybe you could share your strength of being coordinated by teaching someone else how to do that. Here's the word "coordinated" to help you spell this strength, if it's one that you want to share."*

- *"Ramesh, you're really good at coloring. Maybe someone might like you to color something for them." Provide the "good at coloring" card.*

- *"Chiang-shin, you are really good at organizing things. Maybe you could help someone clean out their desk and organize their papers." Provide the "organized" card.*

- *"Nels, you're a good writer. Maybe you could share this strength by finding someone who'd like help improving a story they've written." Provide the "good writer" card.*

- *"Dory, one of your strengths is being caring or kind. You could remember someone's birthday and surprise them or you could help a new student feel like they belong." Provide the "kind" card.*

I'd like for each one of you to try to think of one strength that you could share with others in our class or with someone at home or that you know. I have a handout that you can color like the Rainbow Fish, and you can write the

strength you'll share on it. When you're all done, we'll hang up all the handouts for everyone to see. This way you'll get to know what people in this class want to share, and you can let each other know if you want help with a certain thing.

Handout #2

Distribute copies of Handout #2, "Sharing Our Strengths." Ask the students to each write their name on the tail and the strength they're going to share on the top fin. Allow the students to color the scales so they "shine brilliantly." To add more sparkle to the Rainbow Fish's scales, you may wish to give the students some aluminum foil to cut and paste on, or to provide metallic markers or glitter (silver and gold work best).

Have the students cut out their fish. You can create a "School of Strengths" bulletin board display by fastening the fish cut-outs to a blue bulletin board and covering them with smooth pieces of plastic wrap or transparent bags (e.g., from a dry cleaners), making sure the strengths are still legible through the plastic "water." Use the bulletin board in the weeks following this unit to remind students of their strengths and continue to ask them to give examples of how they are sharing them.

DISTRIBUTING THE AWARDS

Watching that video made me appreciate each one of you. The kids in this class have a lot of different strengths. We have kids who are ____, ____, ____. *List several strength words.* Each one of you has strengths you can be proud of.

Handout #3

Hold up Handout #3, "Strengths Award." I have an award I'd like to give each of you. This award says you've worked hard and discovered many things about yourself and your classmates. You may want to put this award in a special place at home. This is what it says. *Read the award aloud. You may wish to hand out the awards one at a time (diploma-style) or you can call up groups of four or five students to accept their awards as a group.*

UNDISCOVERED STRENGTHS

Because you've discovered a lot about yourselves, you may think you already know all the things you do well. But who knows what strengths you'll discover you have when you're in middle school or high school! Who knows what strengths you'll have discovered you have when you're 25-years or 30-years old! You still have many strengths tucked away inside you like hidden treasures. When you get in the right situation at the right time, they'll come out.

The important thing is to remember that you have many strengths, and that <u>you can make good experiences for yourselves by using them</u>!

Extend this "discovery of strengths" process for as long as you want. Throughout the year the students can continue to identify good experiences and the strengths they used to create them, writing these in journals or on additional "TV channel" handouts. At the end of the year, the students will take home a complete "Strengths Folder" to serve as a reminder of their special skills and abilities.

SUPPLEMENTARY ACTIVITIES

Use the Supplementary Activities to keep the students occupied during the videotaping or to provide additional practice with lesson concepts:

- *"I'm Made Up of Many Strengths"*
  (Supplementary Activity #1)

- *"Classroom Book of Strengths"*
  (Supplementary Activity #2)

- *"Strengths That Keep Me Moving"*
  (Supplementary Activity #3)

- *"A See-Through Strength Card"*
  (Supplementary Activity #4)

VIDEO TITLE PAGE

We Have Many Strengths!

TRANSPARENCY #1

Things We Say to Ourselves That Stop Us From Believing in Our Strengths

1. SETH

2. RICKI

Strengths Badge

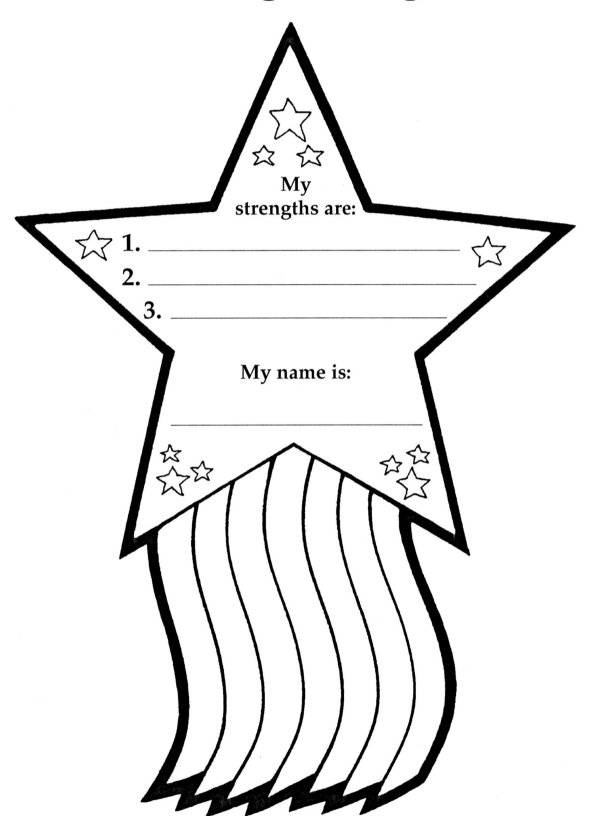

My
strengths are:

1. _____

2. _____

3. _____

My name is:

_____

TRANSPARENCY #3/HANDOUT #2

Sharing Our Strengths

HANDOUT #3

Strengths Award

Presented to

for

• Sharing many of your good experiences
• Learning about your strengths
• Helping others discover their strengths

Signed: _____

Date: _____

CONGRATULATIONS!

SUPPLEMENTARY ACTIVITY #1

I'm Made Up of Many Strengths

Objective   Students will identify four strengths they feel are "most like them" and then reinforce this awareness through an art project.

Materials   Supplementary Activity #1 Handout - "I'm Made Up of Many Strengths," duplicated on heavy paper

Crayons, markers, colored pencils

Scissors

For Variation 1:

- Four small brads for each student

For Variation 2:

- Glue or paste and an additional sheet of paper for each student

Procedure   Distribute a copy of the handout "I'm Made up of Many Strengths" to each student. Have them write four strength words which they feel are the "most like them," one on each of the arms and legs of the paper cut-out. Have the students write their name on the trunk of the cut-out. Have them draw on hair that looks like their own, or, alternately, use the hair as drawn on the handout, allowing boys to cut off the lower, long hair on the head of the figure and girls to add barrettes, ribbons, etc. as they wish.

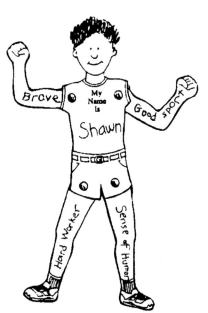

Students will next color the cut-out, being careful not to obscure the strength words or their name. After coloring, have them cut out the five pieces. Then choose one of the following procedures.

VARIATION 1

To create a movable jointed figure, the students should then use their pencils to **carefully** punch holes on the little X's. Next they will lay the arms and legs **under** the trunk, aligning the punched holes.

Brads are then pushed through the holes, front-to-back, to form movable limbs on the figure.

VARIATION 2

To create a figure pasted on a page, the students should place the cut out parts on a second sheet of paper, arranging the arms and legs into the position they wish (with the ends of the arm and leg pieces fitting under the trunk). Once the students have an arrangement they like, they should glue or paste the pieces to the page. If time allows, you may let them color in a background for the figure using the rest of the page.

The completed figures can be posted on each student's desk or put up on a class bulletin board.

I'm Made Up of Many Strengths

Directions:

On each of the arms and legs write a different strength word which
describes a strength that is the most like you.
Write your name on the figure's body.

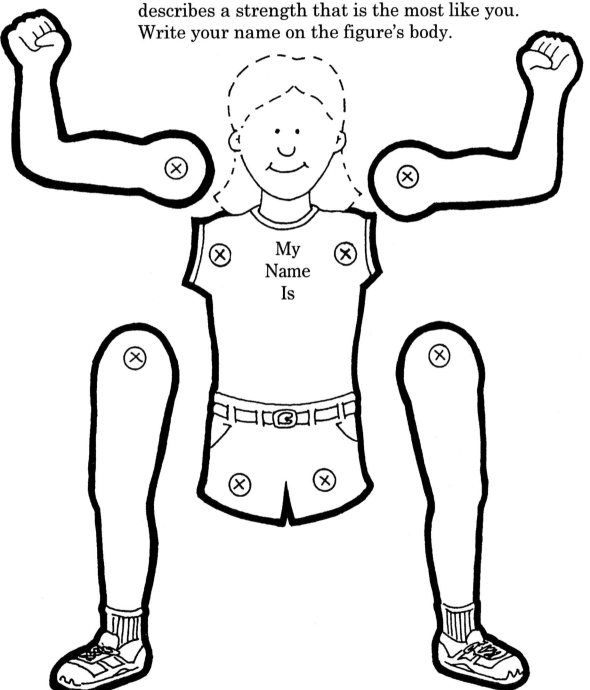

SUPPLEMENTARY ACTIVITY #2

Classroom Book of Strengths

Objective   Students will draw a picture of themselves using their favorite strength and add it to a "Classroom Book of Strengths"

Materials   Handout #1 from Lesson 6   -   "My Strengths"

A piece of construction paper or tagboard for each student, with a line drawn about two inches from the bottom and hole-punched to fit a three-ring binder

Three-hole punch

Three-ring binder with a decorative cover labeled "Our Classroom Book of Strengths"

Crayons or markers

Procedure   Tell the students they will be making a book for the classroom which will have in it examples of each student's strengths.

Distribute to each student one of the construction paper book pages you have prepared as indicated above. Before the students begin working, make sure they position this paper so that the line is near the **bottom** of the page. Have the students choose one of their favorite strengths from their "My Strengths" handouts they completed in Lesson 6. Ask them to draw and color a picture of themselves using that strength in the large space at the top of their strength book page. Encourage students to do their best work, because this page will be part of a class book that will be placed in a special place in the classroom.

Call students to your desk when their drawings are completed and ask them to tell you what strength they chose to illustrate. Print the word for this strength on the line. Help each student think of a sentence that uses his or her strength word and describes the illustration, then write this sentence in the space below the illustration. To

complete the page, print the student's name in the top right-hand corner.

Compile these pages in the three-ring binder (or in another manner you prefer) and place the "book" on a table for classmates to look at during free time.

ACTIVITY EXTENSION IDEAS

1. Read parts of the finished "Our Classroom Book of Strengths" during story time, showing pages to the class as you describe the pictures and making supportive comments about the students' strengths.

2. Allow each student to show to the class his or her page in the book, describing the illustration and "reading" the descriptive sentence to the class.

3. Randomly turn to a page in the book. Read the sentence and describe the illustration. Show the illustration to the class, but cover the student's name at the top of the page as you do so. Allow the class two guesses as to the "author" of the page, then have that student stand up. Doing this at random times during the day or week will help the students to be aware of their own strengths and to remember to use them, and will also help the students learn about the strengths of others.

SUPPLEMENTARY ACTIVITY #3

Strengths That Keep Me Moving

Directions:

Write three of your top strengths on the lines on this critter! Then color him in.

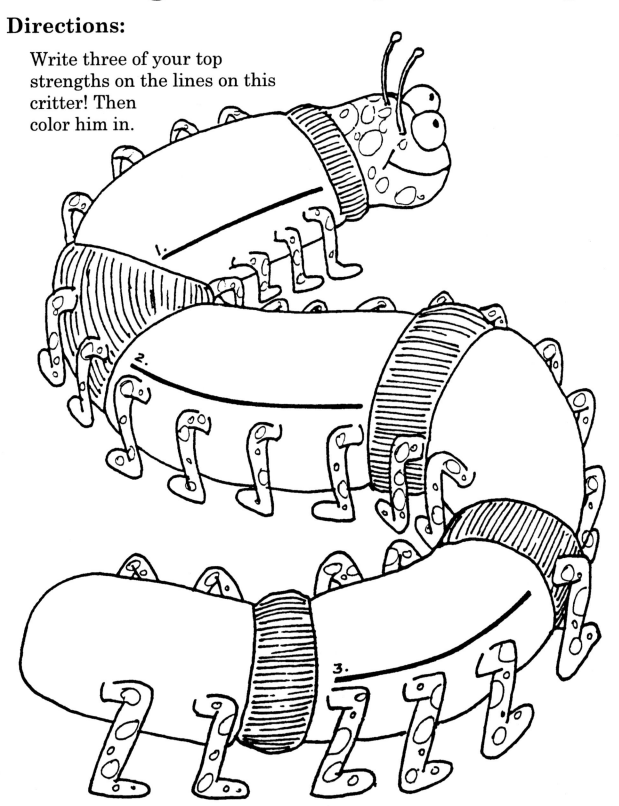

SUPPLEMENTARY ACTIVITY #4

A See-Through Strength Card

This makes a fun guessing game for you and your friends.

Directions:

1. Draw a picture of yourself using one of your strengths or find a picture in a magazine or newspaper that shows your strength. Write the name of your strength on the bottom of the picture.

2. Paste your picture on a piece of paper.

3. Cut a small hole out of another piece of paper, so that when this sheet is laid over the first sheet only a small part of the picture can be seen through the hole.

4. On the top piece of paper, write what one of your **good experiences** was where you used this strength. Attach this sheet to the bottom sheet at the top or at one side.

5. Cut out a paper flap big enough to cover the description of your good experience and attach it to the top sheet.

6. Now ask other students to try to guess what the strength is in the picture on the bottom sheet. Have them guess first just by looking at the drawing they can see through the small hole. If they need more help, let them lift the flap to read about the good experience you've described.

7. Make up one of these see-through cards for at least four of your strengths.

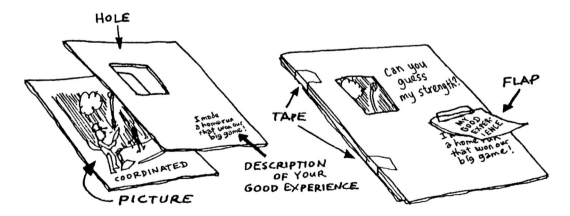

A UNIT FOR
INTERMEDIATE GRADES

Looking at Good Experiences to Discover Particular Strengths

Objective

Students will understand that they are a mix of strengths and areas that need improving.

Students will understand that they can discover their strengths by remembering their good experiences.

Students will feel comfortable focusing on and sharing their good experiences.

Materials

Transparency #1 - "Can You Describe Your Strengths?"

Transparency #2 - "Everyone Is a Mix of Strengths and Things That Could Be Improved"

Transparency #3 - "Do You See Yourself Like This?"

Transparencies #4A, #4B, and #4C - "Which Park Would You Rather Play In?"

Transparency #5 - "We Can Discover Our Strengths by Thinking About Our Good Experiences"

Transparency #6 - "The Definition of a Good Experience"

Handout #1 - "My Trail of Good Experiences"

Transparency #7 - "My Trail of Good Experiences—An Example"

Handout #2 - "Good Experiences Other Kids Have Shared"

Handout #3 - "Memory Triggers for Good Experiences"

Transparency #8 - "Memory Triggers for Good Experiences—Examples Others Remembered"

Chart of large, ruled paper   (for creating a "Strength Word Bank")

Construction paper and brads

File folders or small report notebooks for students to create "Strengths Folders"

To the Teacher

In this lesson students learn that they are multifaceted, a mix of strengths and areas that may need improvement. They are cautioned about making generalizations about their negative traits and about using only these traits to measure their worth. Their deficits are not denied, but the benefits of focusing instead upon their strengths are emphasized.

Students learn that they can gain a clearer picture of their particular strengths by taking a close look at the good experiences in their lives. Students will learn the definition of a good experience: something they feel they did well; they were proud of it. With the help of their teacher, parent, or classmates, students can "tease out" the core strengths which helped them create these good experiences.

Many students are hesitant to tell about a good experience or to express pride in an achievement for fear of being seen as a braggart. In this lesson students discuss the difference between bragging and showing appropriate pride in their strengths.

While teaching this lesson, it is important to be aware that whenever students share a good experience in the classroom, they take a risk of someone putting them down or making a comment which negates that good experience. This can rob a child of a valuable and happy memory. Therefore, an atmosphere of safety must be established in the class before students are asked to share any memories of the experiences they have had that they are proud of. An effort is made in this lesson to establish a "safety net" against put-downs, and to make it a class norm that students will be safe when verbalizing their good experiences or their perceived strengths.

In this lesson the major task for students is to generate a list of a variety of their good experiences, starting with their earliest memories. They will also begin to look for strengths that underlie these experiences. To help them in this process, prepare a large chart on ruled chart paper and title it "Strength Word Bank" for listing strength words as they are introduced.

When defining a "good experience" for students, give only as many examples of good experiences as they need to clearly understand the definition. It is best to have students try to remember their own good experiences without becoming too influenced by the examples of others. Whenever examples are given, some students will latch onto these and repeat them, rather than searching their memory banks for good experiences which might be richer and more meaningful to them. If some students are having great difficulty remembering their good experiences, however, go ahead and provide these students with the list of examples other students have generated (Handout #2). After students have completed Handout #1 where they create their "trail of good experiences," you may then provide them with the lesson handouts which are designed to trigger more of their memories, if you wish.

Students should have the option of writing or drawing their experiences, honoring their preferred style of expression. If their drawing is not clear to an observer, they can jot down a few words to explain it.

Give students folders or construction paper so they can each make a "Strengths Folder." During this unit, they should keep all the handouts you give them in this folder, as they will refer to these handouts on several occasions.

Lesson Presentation

LESSON OVERVIEW

Say or paraphrase: **Each one of you has certain strengths or skills that you can be proud of. Today we're going to begin a unit in which I'll show you ways to discover what you're good at—the things that are your strengths. By the end of this unit you'll be able to name several of your particular strengths and even prove that you have them.**

STUDENTS ARE CHALLENGED TO NAME THEIR STRENGTHS

Transp. #1

Show Transparency #1, "Can You Describe Your Strengths?" **Just for fun, let's pretend that the manager of an amusement park called "DizzyWorld" have decided to hire several kids to help them come up with some new rides and a new idea for a theme park for the place. They think that kids would have lots of fresh ideas and enthusiasm. They're looking for some clever kids who have enough good qualities to do the job. Let's also say this job will be a lot of fun and will pay a lot of money.**

Are there any of you who can name five strengths you have that might convince this manager that you would be the right person for the job? Who can tell me five good reasons why you should be the one they hire? Don't tell me what you would do once you get the job—just tell me strengths you already have that make you special. *Generally, none of the students will be able to do this. If some do identify five strengths, tell* *them to describe some evidence that shows they have these strengths. Rarely can a student produce this <u>evidence</u>.*

Say or paraphrase: **Very few people can describe their strengths well. By the time we're finished with this unit, you'll be able to list your strengths. You'll be able to write a letter of application for the DizzyWorld job that will convince the manager that you're just the right kid he should hire. You'll even be able to do this without bragging or sounding conceited!**

EVERYONE IS MULTIFACETED

Transp. #2

Show Transparency #2 "Everyone Is a Mix of Strengths and Things That Could Be Improved." **Every person is a mix of strengths and weaknesses. Every person alive has pluses and minuses—things about them that are great and things that need improving. For instance, we might say that someone has the strength of making friends easily or is good at math.** *On the transparency, write "Making friends easily" on line #1 and "Good at math" on line #2 of the plus category.* **What are some other strengths kids might have?** *Write these student suggestions on the other four blank lines for this category.* **Good. We usually think of these positive characteristics people have as "strengths."**

Now, what about the "weaknesses," the areas that could use some improvement? These might be things like not knowing how to keep friends or not being good at reading. *Write these examples on lines #1 and #2 of the minus category.* **What are some other characteristics we could think of as "minuses," or areas that could use some improvement?** *Write student suggestions on the other four lines provided.*

Transp. #3

Many kids see themselves the way this kid does. *Show Transparency #3, "Do You See Yourself Like This?"* **They mainly notice the faults in themselves and feel they should be better.**

They might admit they have a few strengths here and there, but they don't let themselves feel good about them. For example, a kid may be able to draw well, but all he thinks about is how badly he did on the math test. Another kid might only think of how she is a klutz in sports, and ignore the fact that other kids really like how dependable she is as a friend.

THE "I'M NOT O.K." PARKS

Transp. #4A

Let's imagine there are special parks which are the only places kids who think like this are allowed to play. Let's see what it might be like to be in each of these parks. *Show Transparency #4A, "Which Park Would You Rather Play In?"* In this first park, all the kids think they're not O.K. or not good enough. They don't think other kids are good enough either. They only notice each others' faults or weaknesses. They don't notice any strengths or plus points about themselves or others at all.

Begin in the foreground and point to the children on the transparency as you say: For instance, here's Maria. She's thinking, "What a bunch of losers these creeps are! If I weren't such a klutz around people, I'd get out of here." Over here is Erwin—he's wearing his "Big City Losers" sweatshirt. That's the name of his soccer team, because they all know they'll <u>never</u> be any good at soccer.

Look at Randall moping on the park bench. What could he be thinking? *Allow for student response.* Now, look at Walter; he just failed his science test yesterday. He told his teacher "Science is stupid!" but really what Walter is thinking is that <u>he</u> is stupid. Back here is "Bad Luck Betty." What's happened to her? *Allow for student response. Continue to point out other characteristics of the park—upside-down birds, dead flowers, etc.*

Imagine what it would be like to think you're not O.K., and not to feel good about anything about yourself. How happy would you say these kids are? Who could imitate how a kid in this park might look or what kinds of things the kid might say? *Allow for student response. Just for fun, you might suggest that all students spend a few seconds imitating the kids in this park.*

Transp.#4B

Show Transparency #4B, "Which Park Would You Rather Play In?"

Let's look at a different park. This is the park for kids who think they're no good and who think other people are <u>better</u> than they are. As in the first park, these kids also only look at their weaknesses. Guess what they look at in others? That's right—their strengths or good points. *As you did for the first park, use the figures on the transparency to make up typical statements that the kids in this park might be saying to themselves. After you have done this for a few of the characters, ask students to participate in this process, as with Transparency #4A.*

Imagine what it would feel like to be one of the kids in this park. How happy do you think these kids are? Who could imitate the kids in this park? How would they stand? What might they do or say? *Allow for student response as before.*

THE "I'M O.K. AND YOU'RE O.K., TOO" PARK

Transp. #4C

When we focus our thoughts on our weaknesses, we're spending our time in one of these "I'm Not O.K." parks. We don't have to do this, though, because there's another park we can choose to be in. This is the "I'm O.K. and You're O.K., Too" park. *Show Transparency #4C, "Which Park Would You Rather Play In?"*

In this park all the kids think that they're O.K. and they think others are O.K., too. They can see that everyone is a mix of strengths and weaknesses, but they don't feel they always have to think about the weaknesses. In fact, they pay more attention to the good things in themselves and others.

Beginning in the foreground, point to each of the figures on the transparency as you describe them. Here's Eric. He's glad he's found a lot of kids who are so friendly. Over here is Marvin—he's thinking, "Wow, only two kilometers to go and I'm still keeping up my pace! This is my best race ever!" On the sideline is Hai-Chang. What could he be thinking as he cheers for Marvin? *Allow for student response.* Standing over here are Marla and Michelle. Marla is saying, "And then Mrs. Bedichek told me I'd really improved in playing the piano." What do you think Michelle might be thinking? *Allow for student response.*

Imagine what it would be like to be in this park. How happy do you think these kids are? Why? How much fun do you think they have? Why? Who can imitate what these kids might be like? *Allow for student response.*

Which of the three parks do you think would be the most fun to be in? Where do you think the kids are the happiest? *Allow for student response.* I'd like to invite you all to stay in the "I'm O.K. and You're O.K., Too" park while we're working on finding our strengths.

STUDENTS WILL FIND THEIR STRENGTHS BY LOOKING AT THEIR GOOD EXPERIENCES

Transp. #5

Who can guess what the first step is in finding out what your particular strengths are? *Allow for student response. Now show Transparency #5, "We Can Discover Our Strengths by Thinking About Our Good Experiences."* You can use your good experiences to help you discover your strengths. By remember- ing things you did well and had fun doing, you can get some clues as to what your strengths are. I'm going to be asking you to remember some of your good experiences.

After you share these, we'll help each other discover the strengths that helped create them.

Transp. #6 *Show Transparency #6, "The Definition of a Good Experience." Read it to students.* By remembering things that we did well and feel proud of, we can get some clues as to what our strengths are.

THE DIFFERENCE BETWEEN BRAGGING AND FOCUSING ON STRENGTHS

Some kids feel that saying they are proud about something is bragging. Before we start remembering our good experiences, I want to make sure you know the difference between bragging and feeling happy about something that went well for you.

When people brag, they act like they are better than others. You can sometimes tell the difference between bragging and being happy that things turned out well by listening to a person's tone of voice. Braggers talk about themselves in a way that puts other people down and makes the bragger look like a big shot.

Let me show you what I mean. *Use the following script or make up one of your own:*

> Here, look at MY picture! See how I drew my dog and cat? It's perfect! It's WAY better than yours is. Want me to do yours over for you?

Now, what did I say that made it sound like I thought I was a big shot? What did I say that put the other person down? *Allow for student response.*

Now, I'll try talking about my picture again. I'll still be proud of what I drew, but this time I'll talk about it without bragging:

Look at this picture I drew of my dog and cat. I think it's the best one I've ever done! Sometimes I have trouble and I get the head too big for the body, but this time I got it just right. The picture turned out just the way I wanted!

What did I do differently? *Allow for student response.* **Would someone like to show us another example of what bragging sounds like?** *Select a student volunteer. After he or she has finished, brainstorm with the class ways that the volunteer could have talked about his or her subject without bragging. Repeat this process until you feel students have an understanding of the difference between bragging and making an honest statement of pride.*

So, it seems that we <u>**can**</u> **talk about the things we're proud of. We can say these things in a way that shows we're happy or excited that something good has happened to us or that we've done something well. We can also say it in a way that doesn't make other people feel that they're not as good as we are.**

Model for the students saying something about yourself that you feel pleased about. Then ask some students to volunteer to do the same. Say or paraphrase the following: **It's O.K. to talk about things that have turned out well for you or things you've accomplished. It doesn't mean you think you're better than others. It just means you notice you have some strengths or neat things about you. It means you can let others be proud of their strengths and accomplishments, too.**

MAKING THE CLASSROOM SAFE FOR OTHERS TO SHARE THEIR GOOD EXPERIENCES

I want our classroom to be a place like the "I'm O.K. and You're O.K., Too" park when we share our good experiences. If someone shared something they were proud of and somebody near them made some comment like, "What's so good about that?" or "Oh, brother" or "Big deal"—or even if they just rolled their eyes or made some face—what could

that do to the person's good experience?" *Allow for student response.* It could ruin it, couldn't it! Besides hurting the person's feelings, they might no longer be proud about something they used to feel good about. We have to be very careful we don't ruin someone's good experience with a comment or even a look. Someone else's good experience may not seem like a big deal to you, but it may have been a great moment for the other person when it happened.

Do you think it will be possible to keep our classroom a safe place for people to share their good experiences? *Allow for student response. Discuss any concerns students may bring up and try to reach agreement on a "no put-downs" rule.*

STUDENTS REMEMBER THEIR OWN GOOD EXPERIENCES

We're going to play a remembering game now. I'd like you to think back to when you were little, before you started school. Try to think of something you were proud of and you enjoyed doing. *Pause.* If you think of your mind as a computer, you can give it a command to retrieve some memories of your early good experiences. Close your eyes and watch the memories or pictures that come to you. *Pause.* Think about a time when you were much younger—maybe you learned to do something new. *Pause.* Maybe you did something better than you had ever done it before. *Pause.* Maybe you did something that made you feel good inside. *Pause.*

Handout #1

I'm going to give you a handout so you can write or draw about some of those early good experiences. *Give students Handout #1, "My Trail of Good Experiences," and have them fill in the bubbles with words or pictures.*

If your students generally work in cooperative learning groups, it is likely that they will spontaneously share some of their memories, thus triggering memories for each other. However, if some students have difficulty remembering their good experiences, you may want to use one of the following strategies:

Transp. #7

- *Show Transparency #7, "My Trail of Good Experiences—An Example," and discuss some of the experiences other students have remembered. Ask students not to use these same examples, if possible.*

Handout #2

- *For those few students who continue to draw a blank, run off a few copies of Handout #2, "Good Experiences Other Kids Have Shared," and quietly place them on their desks. If the majority of the class is having difficulty, read a few of these examples aloud to the class.*

- *Share some of your own good experiences, past and present.*

MODELING SHARING A GOOD EXPERIENCE AND FINDING UNDERLYING STRENGTHS

It's now time to share some of the good experiences we've remembered and see if we can guess what strengths we used to make these good experiences happen. Let me show you what I mean by sharing one of mine. You listen and then see if you can figure out what I did to make this good experience happen. *Share an experience that would lend itself to identification of underlying strengths.*

Chart

After you have described the experience ask: **What do you think I did to make this good experience happen?** *Allow for student response. If they identify any skills or strengths that did help you, write them on a "Strength Word Bank" chart you've previously prepared for noting strength words. Then mention some other skills, qualities, or strengths that you feel helped you have the good experience, if any, and write them on the chart as well.*

STUDENT VOLUNTEERS SHARE GOOD EXPERIENCES WHILE THE REST OF THE CLASS LISTENS FOR STRENGTHS

Now I'd like to hear some of <u>your</u> good experiences. Will someone volunteer to share one of the good experiences you put on <u>your</u> "trail"? *After the volunteer has shared, ask the class:* **What did he** *(she)* **do that made this good experience happen? What skills or strengths did he** *(she)* **use that helped him** *(her)* **have this experience?** *List appropriate student responses on the chart.*

Continue this strength finding procedure for the students who wish to volunteer, while at the same time building up the "Strength Word Bank" on the chart.

You may find it necessary to assist with this strength identification process by saying: **That good experience tells me something else about your strengths.** *If a student describes some physical feat, you could say:* **That tells me you're "coordinated"!** *You might ask the student if the experience he or she described took lots of practice or re-attempts. If so, you can say,* **That tells me you're "determined"!** *Write "coordinated" and "determined" on the chart.*

Continue this process until you feel students have a sense of how to deduce strengths from good experiences. Ask students to select the strength words from the chart which fit their own good experiences and then write these words on their handouts next to the description of their experiences.

MAKING "STRENGTHS FOLDERS"

I have some materials for everyone to make a special "Strengths Folder." You'll be keeping all your handouts from this unit in this folder. You'll put your "My Trail of Good Experiences" handout in this folder, as well as the homework assignment I'm going to give you. *Give students* *materials to make the "Strengths Folders." They can decorate them in their spare time.*

LESSON REVIEW AND PREVIEW OF NEXT LESSON

Say or paraphrase: **A good experience is like a little story in which several strengths are hidden. Many of you have shared your good experiences with us today. And many of you have listened and helped others find the strengths hidden in their good experiences. Those of you who didn't have a chance to share or to help someone find their strengths will have other opportunities to do both during the next couple of weeks. I want everyone to save this very important "My Trail of Good Experiences" handout because you're going to need them for something special we'll be doing later.**

In the days ahead you'll be sharing more of your good experiences and learning some new words that describe strengths. The important thing now is to remember <u>as many good experiences as you can</u>. The page you'll be getting for homework will help you remember them.

Let's make sure all of you know exactly what we mean by a <u>good experience</u>. Take a piece of scratch paper or a page of your "think pad" and see if you can write down the definition of a good experience. Turn it over when you're done. When I give the signal, I want you to all hold them up in front of your chest so I can see them. *As students show their work, walk around the room and make encouraging comments.*

I'm glad to see so many of you remembering. I'd like you to give me a little feedback now as we review what we've learned. *Ask students to respond to the following sentence stems to give you feedback regarding their understanding of lesson concepts:*

- *I learned . . . .*

- *I liked . . . .*

- *I'm confused about . . . .*

- *I was surprised . . . .*

HOMEWORK ASSIGNMENT

**Handout #3
Transp. #8**

Give students Handout #3, "Memory Triggers for Good Experiences." **This homework assignment will help you remember more good experiences. We'll use this page in our next lesson and put it in our "Strengths Folders."** *Show students Transparency #8, "Memory Triggers for Good Experiences— Examples Others Remembered," to give them a sense of how to complete the handout.*

SUPPLEMENTARY ACTIVITIES

Use the Supplementary Activities at the end of this lesson to provide additional information or practice regarding the lesson concepts:

- *"A Good Experiences Checklist"*
  (Supplementary Activity #1)

- *"Our Good Experiences—A Bulletin Board"*
  (Supplementary Activity #2)

- *"More Possibilities for Finding Good Experiences"*
  (Supplementary Activity #3)

TRANSPARENCY #1

Can You Describe Your Strengths?

TRANSPARENCY #2

Everyone Is a Mix of Strengths and Things That Could Be Improved

+

1. _____
2. _____
3. _____
4. _____
5. _____
6. _____

–

1. _____
2. _____
3. _____
4. _____
5. _____
6. _____

We can choose to focus on our strengths or on our weaknesses!

TRANSPARENCY #3

Do You See Yourself Like This?

A lot of kids think that they have more weaknesses
than strengths, even though this isn't true.

TRANSPARENCY #4A

Which Park Would You Rather Play In?
Three Different Ways People Think

TRANSPARENCY #4B

Which Park Would You Rather Play In? (continued)
Three Different Ways People Think

TRANSPARENCY #4c

Which Park Would You Rather Play In? (continued)
Three Different Ways People Think

TRANSPARENCY #5

We Can Discover Our Strengths by Thinking About Our Good Experiences

TRANSPARENCY #6

The Definition of a Good Experience

Something that you feel you did well.

You were proud of it!

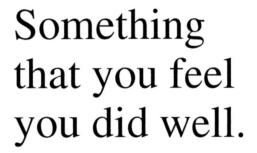

FOOD BANK

HANDOUT #1

My Trail of Good Experiences

TRANSPARENCY #7

My Trail of Good Experiences—An Example

The time I got to be so good in gymnastics!

The time I did Ballet.

I cared about someone in my class when nobody else did.

I caught my fish in winter through an ice hole.

first

ice

Babysitting a baby.

I learned my fractions in about five days.

$\frac{1}{2}$ $\frac{2}{4}$ $\frac{4}{8}$

I learned to play the violin. I can play about 12 songs.

HANDOUT #2

Good Experiences Others Kids Have Shared

- "I dug a three-foot hole in the sandbox when I was in preschool."

- "I finally learned to color in the lines."

- "The time I caught my first fish."

- "I learned to whistle."

- "I saved a mouse by opening my aunt's cat's mouth and taking the mouse out."

- "I was nice to a new student and he became my friend."

- "I learned to dribble with my left hand."

- "I wrote my first report in school."

- "I made a gift for a person in a nursing home."

- "I gave my sister a present for no reason at all."

- "I learned to play 'Chop Sticks' on the piano."

HANDOUT #3

Memory Triggers for Good Experiences

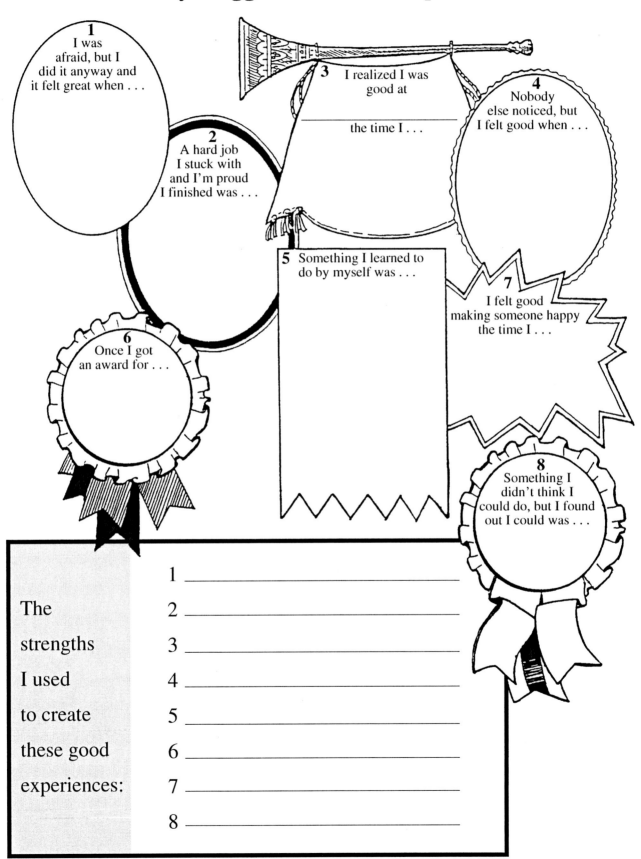

1 I was afraid, but I did it anyway and it felt great when . . .

2 A hard job I stuck with and I'm proud I finished was . . .

3 I realized I was good at _____ the time I . . .

4 Nobody else noticed, but I felt good when . . .

5 Something I learned to do by myself was . . .

6 Once I got an award for . . .

7 I felt good making someone happy the time I . . .

8 Something I didn't think I could do, but I found out I could was . . .

The strengths I used to create these good experiences:

1 _____
2 _____
3 _____
4 _____
5 _____
6 _____
7 _____
8 _____

TRANSPARENCY #8

Memory Triggers for Good Experiences—
Examples Others Remembered

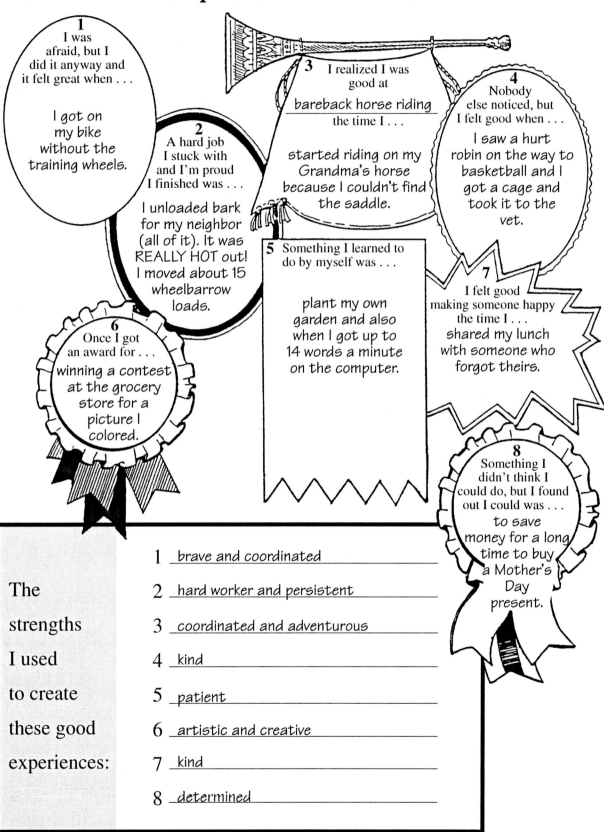

1 I was afraid, but I did it anyway and it felt great when . . .

I got on my bike without the training wheels.

2 A hard job I stuck with and I'm proud I finished was . . .

I unloaded bark for my neighbor (all of it). It was REALLY HOT out! I moved about 15 wheelbarrow loads.

3 I realized I was good at bareback horse riding the time I . . .

started riding on my Grandma's horse because I couldn't find the saddle.

4 Nobody else noticed, but I felt good when . . .

I saw a hurt robin on the way to basketball and I got a cage and took it to the vet.

5 Something I learned to do by myself was . . .

plant my own garden and also when I got up to 14 words a minute on the computer.

6 Once I got an award for . . .

winning a contest at the grocery store for a picture I colored.

7 I felt good making someone happy the time I . . . shared my lunch with someone who forgot theirs.

8 Something I didn't think I could do, but I found out I could was . . . to save money for a long time to buy a Mother's Day present.

The strengths I used to create these good experiences:

1 brave and coordinated

2 hard worker and persistent

3 coordinated and adventurous

4 kind

5 patient

6 artistic and creative

7 kind

8 determined

A Good Experiences Checklist

Objective

Students will use a checklist to help them recall their good experiences and will then write a brief description of each.

Materials

Supplementary Activity #1 Handouts #1A and #1B - "My Good Experiences Checklist"

Procedure

Distribute the handout. Have students read through the checklist, putting a check mark in the box if they recall having had a similar experience. For items they check, students should write a brief description on the line provided.

Following this individual work, you can debrief this exercise as a group activity if you wish. To do so, read various checklist items and ask students to hold up their hands if they checked that experience. Call on two or three students to share their specific experiences for each. If you notice some students are not participating, you may involve them by asking questions such as, "Johnny, tell us about an experience **you** checked," and then have classmates raise their hands if they checked the same experience as "Johnny."

Another option is to take a "class inventory," reading several of the items and asking those who checked that experience to stand. Count and record the number of students for each item to discover the most commonly shared types of experiences in the class.

SUPPLEMENTARY ACTIVITY #1 HANDOUT #1A

My Good Experiences Checklist

Directions:
Put a check in the box for each good experience you have had.

❑ Did my best in a spelling bee.

❑ Showed improvement on my report card.

❑ Learned to write in cursive.

❑ Learned my times tables.

❑ Helped someone with his or her homework.

❑ Shared something of mine I liked a lot with someone else.

❑ Stood up to a bully.

❑ Stuck up for someone when others made fun of him or her.

❑ Saved an animal's life.

❑ Helped someone who was hurt.

❑ Did an especially good job on an art project.

❑ Built something all by myself.

❑ Learned to play an instrument.

❑ Memorized my first music piece.

❑ Played in a recital.

❑ Taught my little brother or sister something.

❑ Beat an adult at a game.

❑ Made an especially good play in a sport.

❑ Helped someone who was younger than I am.

SUPPLEMENTARY ACTIVITY #1 HANDOUT #1B

My Good Experiences Checklist (continued)

❑ Made a good grade on a hard assignment.

_____

❑ Drew something that looked exactly right.

_____

❑ Got an award.

_____

❑ Learned to swim or dive.

_____

❑ Made someone in my family proud of me.

_____

❑ Babysat myself.

_____

❑ Taught an animal a trick.

_____

❑ Saved my money and bought something special for someone.

_____

❑ Felt scared about something and did it anyway.

_____

❑ Cooked something that tasted good.

_____

❑ Got myself out of a jam all by myself.

_____

❑ Make someone sad feel better.

_____

❑ Acted in a play.

_____

❑ Made my friend laugh.

_____

❑ Controlled my temper when I was really mad.

_____

❑ Stuck to a hard job until I finished it.

_____

❑ Surprised myself at how well I did at something.

_____

❑ Made someone else happy.

_____

❑ Learned to do something I thought I could never do.

_____

SUPPLEMENTARY ACTIVITY #2

Our Good Experiences—A Bulletin Board

Objective   Students will identify strengths in the good experiences of their
                        classmates.

Materials   Supplementary Activity #2 Transparencies #1A and
                        #1B - "Good Experience Examples"

                        Supplementary Activity #2 Handout   -   "One of My Good
                        Experiences"

Procedure   Tell students that they are going to make a class bulletin board
                        about their good experiences and that you want them to take a
                        minute to remember their all-time favorite good experience.

                        Show Transparencies #1A and #1B, "Good Experience Examples,"
                        and discuss the drawings and descriptive paragraphs written by
                        other students.

                        Distribute the Handout, "One of My Good Experiences," and tell
                        students they're going to create a page of their own like the two
                        they've just seen, only it will reflect **their** good experience. Tell
                        them to do their best work because it will be part of a bulletin
                        board.

                        They are to leave the box at the bottom **blank**. Have the students
                        write their paragraphs and draw their pictures. They may want to
                        color them. Display these "One of My Good Experiences" pages on a
                        bulletin board at the students' eye level.

                        After you have taught the concept of deducing strengths from good
                        experiences and provided students with strength word lists in Les-
                        son 2, students can write strength words they used to create their
                        good experiences in the boxes provided on their handouts. You may
                        wish to encourage students to read classmates' completed hand-
                        outs and write strengths they think may have been used in the
                        boxes.

SUPPLEMENTARY ACTIVITY #2 TRANSPARENCY #1A

Good Experience Examples

Draw your good experience below.

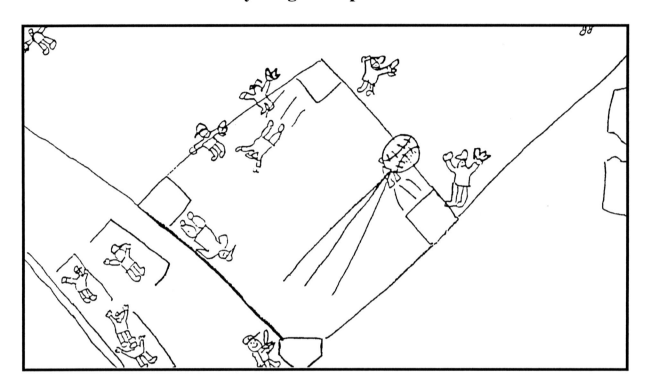

Describe below what you drew. Tell why you were proud of it.

There were two outs the top of the 6th. It was 10-3 in favor of

the other team. We would have lost by 7 points but I was

determined to either win or lose honorably, so I stepped up to

the plate, bases loaded, and hit a GRAND SLAM!

SUPPLEMENTARY ACTIVITY #2 TRANSPARENCY #1B

Good Experience Examples (continued)

Draw your good experience below.

Describe below what you drew. Tell why you were proud of it.

I trained a horse by myself. I was proud

because it was hard but I kept doing it and

I did a GOOD job!

SUPPLEMENTARY ACTIVITY #2 HANDOUT

One of My Good Experiences
Draw your good experience below.

Describe below what you drew. Tell why you were proud of it.

_____

_____

_____

_____

Strengths Used to Create This Good Experience

SUPPLEMENTARY ACTIVITY #3

More Possibilities for Finding Good Experiences

Directions:

Choose **three** of the categories below and write a short paragraph describing a time you did something in each of those categories that you are proud of.

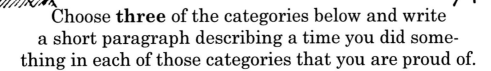

1. **Helping or caring for people:** being sensitive to other peoples' feelings; making things for others; being a good friend; being a helpful family member; doing things for others; visiting an old person.

2. **Helping or caring for animals:** daily care; training; showing.

3. **Creative activities:** making things of all kinds; coming up with new ideas for things people or animals can use; building; making models; artistic work or crafts.

4. **Teaching experiences:** showing people or animals how to do things.

5. **Gardening:** taking care of plants indoors or outdoors; creating a garden.

6. **Taking care of the environment:** all types of recycling; picking up trash on the playground or elsewhere; using recyclable materials; being energy conscious by turning off lights, etc.; not wasting paper.

7. **Using tools, equipment, or machines:** using computers; kitchen appliances; knitting needles or sewing machines; using shop tools, yard tools, or lawn mowers; art equipment.

8. **Reaching a goal:** successfully completing something; improving your ability to do things, for example learning times tables; making a team; etc.

9. **School learning experiences:** doing research or reports; learning something new; doing class presentations or plays; contributing to class discussions; learning to be a good listener.

Learning to Be a Strength Detective

Objectives

Students will identify and share good experiences.

Students will listen for and identify strengths demonstrated in one another's good experiences.

Students will build a vocabulary of words that describe strengths.

Materials

Blank transparency and pen

Transparency #6 from Lesson 1 - "The Definition of a Good Experience"

Handout #3 from Lesson 1 - "Memory Triggers for Good Experiences" (completed homework)

Transparency #1/Handout #1 - "Self Strengths (Short Version)"

Transparency #2/Handout #2 - "People Strengths (Short Version)"

Transparency #3 - "Memory Triggers for Good Experiences"

Handout #3 - "Good Experiences I'd Forgotten About Until Now"

Handout #4 - "Strength Detective Reports" (cut apart and stacked)

Transparency #4 - "Strength Detective Reports—An Example"

Transparency #5/Handout #5 - "Some Phrases That Describe Strengths"

Scratch pad (or evenly-cut quarter sheets of typing paper)

Open box or basket

"Strength Word Bank" chart from Lesson 1 (displayed)

Students' "Strengths Folders" from Lesson 1, with completed handouts

"Strength Detective Box" (a covered shoebox with a slot cut in the top)

Opaque container containing a paper name slip for each student in the class

To the Teacher

In this lesson students will become "Strength Detectives" for their classmates. They will also continue to expand their vocabulary of strength words, and are given two new lists of words which describe strengths. The first list contains strengths that can be used in situations and activities involving individual attributes. These are referred to as "self strengths." The second list contains strength words that refer to qualities found mostly in social situations. These are termed "people strengths." You will be adding the words from these two lists to the "Strength Word Bank" chart, which you should keep displayed in the classroom for easy reference during this unit.

You can strengthen the concepts in this lesson by incorporating them into the vocabulary building and spelling portions of your language arts program. This will allow students to become more familiar with these words and to be able to use them in context more easily. Supplementary Activity #2 that follows this lesson can also assist students with vocabulary building.

During this lesson students will share good experiences from their Lesson 1 homework sheet, "Memory Triggers for Good Experiences," as well as look for the strengths behind other students' experiences. They may refer to their strength word lists ("people strengths" and "self strengths") as necessary.

The concept of being a "Strength Detective" is introduced with a "Strength Detective Box." Students will watch for strengths in their classmates, then fill out "Strength Detective Reports" which they will put in the box. When you then read some of these reports in class, it motivates and reinforces students to watch for the strengths in others.

It usually works best to read some of the "Strength Detective Reports" aloud over the next several days, rather than trying to read them all at the beginning of Lesson 3. Acknowledge both the student who displayed the strength and the "Strength Detective" who identified it. Choose several "Strength Detective Reports" to be posted on a special bulletin board, later returning them to the students who displayed the strengths to keep in their "Strengths Folders." They will need them in Lesson 6 when they prepare a summary of their strengths.

In this lesson students will continue to generate additional examples of good experiences, both during class time and as a homework assignment for the next lesson. A list of example phrases that describe strengths is provided for those students who may have trouble remembering their good experiences.

When teaching this lesson, you may find the following suggestion helpful. At the end of each day, ask students if they have had any good experiences during the day, then help them find some of the strengths which they used to create each of these experiences. You may also ask students if they've done anything during the day in which they used one of their strengths.

Students should keep all their handouts from this lesson in their "Strengths Folders."

Lesson Presentation

REVIEW OF PREVIOUS LESSON

In the last lesson you learned that you can look at the good experiences you've had to discover your own special skills and strengths. Today you'll be sharing some of your good experiences with the rest of us. Each of you will also practice "detecting" the strengths behind your classmates' good experiences. We'll call this being a "Strength Detective."

Transp. #6 from Lesson 1

REVIEW OF THE DEFINITION OF A GOOD EXPERIENCE

Who remembers the definition of a good experience? *Allow for student response; then show Transparency #6 from Lesson 1, "The Definition of a Good Experience." Emphasize the fact that a good experience is something people <u>do</u>, not something that just happens to them. Say:* **Getting a new bike or a puppy isn't what we mean by this kind of a "good experience," because those are things that just happened to you. The kind of good experience we're talking about today is one that you had because <u>you did something to help make it happen</u>.**

For instance, although just getting a bike isn't what we would choose, trying again and again to gain the balance needed to <u>ride</u> a bike—and finally even learning to ride with no hands—could be something you feel you did well and are proud of, so it would then qualify as a good experience. Being given a puppy wouldn't count, but the experience of taking good care of a puppy or training it could, if you feel you did it well and you're proud of it. The kinds of good experiences we want to look at are the ones where you did something to make them happen.

THE "X-RAY TRICK"

Now that everyone understands what we mean when we say the words "good experience," we're ready to start using good experiences to be "Strength Detectives." But first I'm going to show you what a good "Strength Detective" I am. I'm so good at it, you might even say it's magic! You'll each need a sheet of paper and a pen or pencil for this amazing demonstration—for the magic to work you can't use markers.

Give each student a sheet off a scratch pad or another small sheet of paper. These pieces of paper must be identical in shape, size, and color. Say: **On your sheet of paper I want you to write down a good experience—something you did that you're proud of and where you like the way it turned out. If you have trouble thinking of something, you may take out your "Memory Triggers for Good Experiences" homework page for an idea.** *Pause while students write down their good experiences.* **Now, fold your paper in half twice, like this.** *Demonstrate this process, so that students' sheets will all look identical when folded. Collect the folded papers in an open box or basket.*

Now watch carefully. I will "X-ray" each of your good experiences and tell you what they say without even unfolding your papers! We won't have time to do this for all of the papers, but I'll do enough for you to get a real demonstration of my marvelous skill and talent.

I've got it! this person's good experience was . . . learning to swim!

Pick up the first slip of paper and hold it to your forehead without unfolding it. Make it appear that you are concentrating hard. Tell your "audience" that the slip says, "I learned to do a headstand." Ask who wrote it. No one will be able to claim this good experience, because you made it up. Unfold the slip of paper and nod your head as though you have guessed correctly, while you memorize the actual words of the good experience written on the slip of paper you've just opened. Announce to the students that they must admit it from now on when you say what they wrote on their paper. Leave the paper unfolded and put it back in the box or basket.

Pick up the next folded slip of paper, hold it to your forehead, and pretend to concentrate. Tell the class <u>the good experience you just memorized from the previous piece of paper</u>, the one you already opened and set back in the box or basket. Ask the person who wrote this to raise his or her hand. Since this is a real answer, a student will be able to claim it as his or her own. Congratulate the student on his or her good experience, as you open the slip of paper and read it, as if to check to see if you were right. Actually, what you are doing is once again reading what to say when you place the <u>next</u> slip of paper on your forehead. Continue in this way until most of the slips are read.

To lend extra credibility to your trick, comment at times upon the color of ink used, whether some words were hard to read, the size of the writing, etc. You may also use this type of commentary if the good experience was too illegible or confusing to understand. For this trick to work, it is important that you stand back from the class far enough so students can't see what's actually written on the slips as you're reading them. You must also be sure to stop before you "X-ray" all the slips, or you'll be one short (because the first "answer" was a fictitious one).

Conclude the trick by saying: **So, what do you think about my X-ray abilities? Pretty amazing, right? Of course, this is all a trick and not really X-ray vision. If all of you pay really close attention to the lesson today, I'll show you how to do this magic trick when the lesson is over!**

SELF STRENGTHS AND PEOPLE STRENGTHS WORD LISTS

Transp. #1
Handout #1
Handout #2

Now it's <u>your</u> turn to practice being "Strength Detectives." Before we begin, I want to give you a tool that'll help you uncover the hidden strengths in each others' good experiences. I'm going to give you two strength word lists. These

will make your job as a "Strength Detective" easier. Since it may be hard for you to see our "Strength Word Bank" chart when you're sharing with your classmates, this will give you your own list of words to refer to. *Show the students Transparency #1, "Self Strengths (Short Version)" and give them Handout #1, "Self Strengths (Short Version)," and Handout #2, "People Strengths (Short Version)." The two handouts should be stapled together.*

Read through the "self strengths" list with students. Make sure students can read each word. Define and give examples of all unfamiliar words. Say: **These are descriptions of strengths you might use in any situation.**

Transp. #2

Have students turn to Handout #2. Show students Transparency #2, "People Strengths (Short Version)" and say: **All of** <u>these</u> **strengths have to do with getting along with others.** *Read through the list, defining and giving examples of any words students may not know.*

USING THE STRENGTH LISTS

Now I'm going to give you some examples of good experiences and I want you to tell me if you'd look at the strength words on the "self" or the "people" strength list. *For the following examples, have students write a large "S" or a "P" on a piece of paper and hold it up as you read each example, or have them hold up one finger for the "self strength" word list and two fingers for the "people strength" word list.*

Let's say your classmate's good experience was pitching a no-hitter game. He didn't miss a single practice during the whole baseball season and practiced at home on weekends with his uncle. Which list of strengths would you look at to find some good words to describe strengths that might have helped your classmate have this good experience? Would you look at the "self strengths" list or the "people

strengths" list? *Pause while students hold up an "S" or a "P" to indicate their choice.*

If you guessed "self strengths," you were a sharp "Strength Detective"! What are some words on the "self strengths" list that might describe strengths that helped your classmate have this good experience? *Students could suggest athletic, coordinated, determined, energetic, fast, or strong.*

Now let's say a girl in our class had a good experience sticking up for another girl when some other kids were making fun of her. Later she and the girl became good friends. Which list would you look on first to find strength words to describe her? *Pause while students indicate their choice.* Right! This would be a "people strength," because this good experience had to do mainly with another person. What are some words on the "people strengths" list that might describe strengths that helped the girl have this good experience of sticking up for someone else? *Students could say caring, considerate, friendly, helpful, kind, or nice.*

Sometimes you'll find that there are strengths on <u>both</u> lists that helped create the good experience. Let's say someone in the class got all the kids in the neighborhood together and then led them in creating a play for the neighborhood adults. The adults loved it and gave the kids an ice cream party afterwards. What strengths might have helped your classmate have the good experience of making this neighborhood play happen? *If students don't mention them, suggest the words friendly, helpful, organized, good with words, and imaginative. Emphasize that in this case the words come from <u>both</u> lists.*

If you think students need more practice in knowing which list to refer to when looking for strength words, create a few more scenarios of your own and continue these procedures.

USING THE HOMEWORK TO SHARE GOOD EXPERIENCES AND LOOK FOR STRENGTHS

Now it's <u>your</u> turn to practice being "Strength Detectives." Who would like to share one of the good experiences they wrote about on their "Memory Triggers for Good Experiences" homework? I need a volunteer to share so the rest of us can practice our strength detecting. Let's all remember our agreement to make our class a safe place to share so that everyone will feel O.K. when they are sharing.

Transp. #3

Put Transparency # 3, "Memory Triggers for Good Experiences," on the overhead. Point to and read one of the sentence stems on the transparency. Call on a student volunteer to complete this sentence stem with a good experience from his or her homework sheet. Write this response in the space on the transparency.

That experience does sound like one someone would feel good about. Now, let's see if we can "detect" the strength you used in creating that good experience. O.K., class—what kinds of strengths did he *(she)* use to create this experience? Should we look on the "self strengths" list or the "people strengths" list? *Call on a volunteer or have students hold up their "S" or "P" sheets.* Good! Now we know which list to look at to find the strengths.

Blank Transp.

Who can find some strength words that <u>(student's name)</u> may have used to create his *(her)* experience? *Call on student volunteers to suggest strength words from the appropriate list. Write these on the chalkboard or on a blank transparency. Ask the student who shared the experience:* Do any of these strength words sound like strengths you think you used to create your good experience? *Have the student choose the strength word that sounds <u>the most</u> like him or her. Have the student write this word on the numbered blank that corresponds with his or her experience at the bottom of his or her homework sheet.*

Call on several other volunteers to share in the same manner and lead the class through the process of finding strength words for each of these experiences. In all cases, ask the volunteer if he or she agrees about the strengths the others suggest. As before, have the volunteer write the strength word that sounds the most like him or her in the appropriate numbered blank on his or her homework sheet.

Handout #3

Give students copies of Handout # 3, "Good Experiences I'd Forgotten About Until Now." Tell them they can use this handout to jot down memories of good experiences which may be triggered by the sharing of their classmates. Continue reading sentence stems from Transparency #3 and asking for volunteers. Be sure to let students offer their ideas about strengths before you make suggestions. This will prevent students from becoming dependent on your observations for this process. Add your ideas only after members of the class have had ample opportunity to name qualities and strengths without prompting, and emphasize that there will be more than one right answer when making these strength detections.

VARIATIONS FOR USING THE HOMEWORK SHEET TO DETECT STRENGTHS

- *Circulate around the room, reading aloud experiences from various students' homework sheets in order to include students who are too shy to volunteer. Follow the previous procedures.*

- *Help students gain further practice learning which list of words to use by asking for a student volunteer to give an experience which specifically used either a "self strength" or a "people strength." Discuss with the class whether the volunteer correctly identified his or her experience as requiring a "self" or a "people strength" (it may have used both). Ask the class to guess which strengths on the appropriate list the volunteer may have used. Then follow the previous procedure of asking the volunteer to choose the strength word that most describes him or her and writing this on his or her homework sheet.*

- *Toss a beanbag to a student and have that student read one of his or her good experiences. Follow the initial procedure. After he or she has decided on the strength word that sounds the most like him or her, have the student throw the beanbag to another student and then write the "most like me" word on his or her homework sheet.*

- *Read a strength word from one of the lists and ask for a volunteer to read a good experience in which that particular strength was used. Have him or her write it on his or her homework sheet.*

INTRODUCING THE "STRENGTH DETECTIVE REPORTS"

**Handout #4
Transp. #4**

During the next week or so we're going to continue practicing being good "Strength Detectives." I'm going to put a special stack of "Strength Detective Reports" up here at the front of the room for you. *Show students the stack of "Strength Detective Reports" (Handout #4 cut apart).* **Here is what these reports look like.** *Show Transparency #4, "Strength Detective Reports—An Example."*

To fill out these reports you'll be doing an "undercover" detective job. Each of you will draw the name of a classmate to "put under observation." That classmate will be your "target person" for the day. As you go through the day, silently observe your "target person" and be on the lookout for strengths you see him or her using.

**Strength Detective
Box**

When you spy your "target person" using a strength to create a good experience, fill out a "Strength Detective Report." Here's how to do that. *Demonstrate filling out the example "Strength Detective Report" on the transparency.* **You can put your completed "Strength Detective Report" into our "Strength Detective Box."** *Show the class the box.*

After you've written a good "Strength Detective Report" about the student whose name you drew, you can also keep

a sharp eye out for anyone <u>else</u> in the class you spy using a strength. Any time you spy someone using a strength to create a good experience, just secretly fill out a "Strength Detective Report" and put it in the "Strength Detective Box." From time to time I'll open the "Strength Detective Box" and read some of the "Strength Detective Reports" to the class. Later, I'll give you the "Strength Detective Reports" that your classmates filled out about you, so you can put them in your "Strengths Folders."

A LIST OF STRENGTH PHRASES

**Handout #5
Transp. #5**

I'm going to give each one of you a copy of some strength phrases you can use along with your "people strengths" and "self strengths" handouts when you're doing your strength detecting. Usually it's best to describe someone's strength with a single word, and you'll probably find your classmate's hidden strength on either the "self" or "people strengths" list. But, if you just can't find a word that fits the strength you noticed, you can look at this handout called "Some Phrases That Describe Strengths." *Distribute Handout #5, "Some Phrases That Describe Strengths," and show the corresponding transparency (Transparency #5).*

To make it easier to find the phrase you need, these phrases are grouped into categories that are like the things we do in school. There's the "Language Strengths" category, and that has to do with the ability to use words well. *Read or ask a student volunteer to read the phrases in the language category.* There's the "Math and Science Strengths" category. *Read or have a student volunteer read some of the math and science phrases.*

Review the "Art," "Music," and "Physical Strengths" categories in a similar fashion. Point out to students that physical strengths can refer to small muscle coordination equally as well as to whole body abilities.

You don't have to read everything on these pages to find a phrase you want—just ask yourself which area the person's experience seems to fit in. That will be your "clue." Then you'll look at the strength phrases under that category and choose one that you think fits your "target person."

Here are some examples. Let's say you overheard me talking about a good experience I'd had when I'd been a singer in a talent show. Which strength category would you look under to find a strength phrase to describe my experience? *Allow for student response. Point to "Music Strengths" on the transparency.* What are some words to describe a strength you might have detected when I told you about singing in the talent show? *Allow for student response.*

Here's another example. What if you knew I was good at math, and you saw me helping someone else with a math problem? Here's a hint: Look for <u>two</u> different kinds of strength categories. *Allow for student response. Point out that students could look at phrases under "Math and Science Strengths" <u>or</u> they could look on their "people strengths" list.* As you can see, you can use ALL the word lists to help you decide what to write on your "Strength Detective Report." I'm hoping to have <u>lots</u> of "Strength Detective Reports" in our "Strength Detective Box"!

DRAWING NAMES

Remind students that part of keeping the classroom a safe place is showing good sportsmanship and that you don't want to hear any groaning or negative comments when they draw a particular name as their "target person." Have students draw names and remind them that the name they've drawn is to remain a secret until you read the report to the class or hang it up on the bulletin board and their "target person" receives it. During the course of the week, you may want to fill out extra "Strength Detective Reports" on students whose strengths are not as readily apparent or who tend to be over-looked by their classmates.

PRACTICING AT HOME

Being a "Strength Detective" can be a lot of fun. Here's a way you can practice your strength detecting when you go home tonight: Ask the person who takes care of you to re-member a good experience and share it with you. See if you can tell them a strength they must have used to make that good experience happen.

REWARDING GOOD ATTENTION

As you promised previously, reward the students' good attention during the lesson by explaining how the "X-ray" trick works.

LESSON REVIEW

Have students complete one of the following sentence stems:

- *I learned . . . .*

- *I liked . . . .*

- *I was surprised . . . .*

- *I remember . . . .*

- *I'm confused about . . . .*

SUPPLEMENTARY ACTIVITIES

Use the Supplementary Activities to reinforce the skills taught in this lesson:

- *"Remembering Good Experiences"*
   (Supplementary Activity #1)

- *"Who Do You Think of When You Hear the Strength Word . . . "*
   (Supplementary Activity #2)

- *"Looking for a Partner's Strengths"*
   (Supplementary Activity #3)

- *"Detecting Your Own Strengths"*
   (Supplementary Activity #4)

TRANSPARENCY #1/HANDOUT #1

Self Strengths
(Short Version)

artistic	good thinker
athletic	good with words
brave	hard worker
coordinated	imaginative
determined	musical
energetic	organized
fast	problem solver
finishes things	responsible
good memory	strong

TRANSPARENCY #2/HANDOUT #2

People Strengths
(Short Version)

caring	helpful
considerate	kind
fair	nice
friendly	patient
generous	unselfish

TRANSPARENCY #3

Memory Triggers for Good Experiences

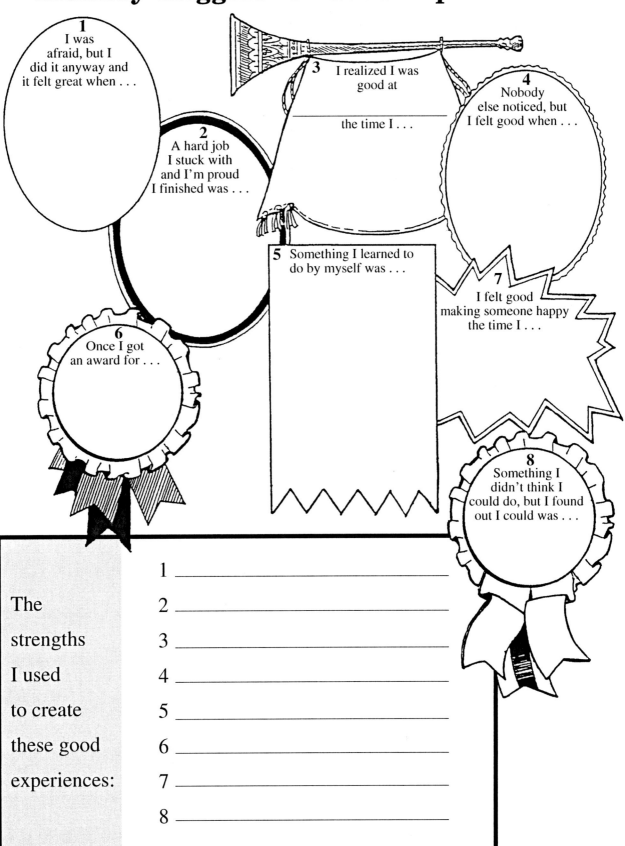

1 I was afraid, but I did it anyway and it felt great when . . .

2 A hard job I stuck with and I'm proud I finished was . . .

3 I realized I was good at _____ the time I . . .

4 Nobody else noticed, but I felt good when . . .

5 Something I learned to do by myself was . . .

6 Once I got an award for . . .

7 I felt good making someone happy the time I . . .

8 Something I didn't think I could do, but I found out I could was . . .

The strengths I used to create these good experiences:

1 _____
2 _____
3 _____
4 _____
5 _____
6 _____
7 _____
8 _____

HANDOUT #3

Good Experiences I'd Forgotten About Until Now

HANDOUT #4

Strength Detective Reports

STRENGTH DETECTIVE REPORT

Person I observed: _____

What I saw him or her doing: _____
_____
_____

Strength I think he or she was using: _____
_____
_____

My Name _____

STRENGTH DETECTIVE REPORT

Person I observed: _____

What I saw him or her doing: _____
_____
_____

Strength I think he or she was using: _____
_____
_____

My Name _____

STRENGTH DETECTIVE REPORT

Person I observed: _____

What I saw him or her doing: _____
_____
_____

Strength I think he or she was using: _____
_____
_____

My Name _____

STRENGTH DETECTIVE REPORT

Person I observed: _____

What I saw him or her doing: _____
_____
_____

Strength I think he or she was using: _____
_____
_____

My Name _____

TRANSPARENCY #4

Strength Detective Reports—An Example

STRENGTH DETECTIVE REPORT

Person I observed: _Jason_

What I saw him or her doing: _He shared_
his lunch when Tom forgot his.
_____
_____

Strength I think he or she was using: _____
kind
generous
_____

_____Brad_____
My Name

STRENGTH DETECTIVE REPORT

Person I observed: _____

What I saw him or her doing: _____
_____
_____

Strength I think he or she was using: _____
_____

_____
My Name

TRANSPARENCY #5/HANDOUT #5

Some Phrases That Describe Strengths

LANGUAGE STRENGTHS

good with words

expresses ideas well

good at writing stories, poems, reports, or letters

good at telling stories

comfortable speaking in front of groups

good reader

MATH AND SCIENCE STRENGTHS

good at calculating

good problem solver

good at researching, experimenting, or organizing ideas

thinks logically

can figure things out

finds better ways to do things

ART STRENGTHS

good at visualizing or imagining

good sense of choosing colors

good at creating own designs

good at drawing, sculpting, or building things

good at putting things together so they will look right

good at noticing small details

good at making or reading maps

MUSIC STRENGTHS

good at playing an instrument

good at making up songs

moves well to music

sings well

good sense of rhythm and timing

good at remembering tunes and words to songs

PHYSICAL STRENGTHS

good at sports

moves body with speed or grace

good at dancing

good at using hands to fix things, or use tools, equipment, or machines

good eye-hand coordination

SUPPLEMENTARY ACTIVITY #1

Remembering Good Experiences

Objective   Students will be assisted in remembering their good experiences through completing sentence stems.

Materials   Supplementary Activity #1 Handout -   "Remembering Good Experiences"

Procedure   Set the stage for this activity by sharing a few **good experiences** of your own from your childhood. Begin the activity by reading aloud the following sentence stems, calling on student volunteers to complete the stems with good experiences of their own. (You may wish to model the activity by volunteering to finish the first sentence yourself.)

- I tried something I ordinarily wouldn't have the time I . . . .
- I stuck with a job that was hard to do and finally finished it the time I . . . .
- I was glad I practiced the time I . . . .

Next, distribute copies of the Handout, "Remembering Good Experiences." Tell students to choose seven of the sentence stems to complete with examples of their own good experiences. Remind them to read each completed sentence to themselves to be sure it makes sense and is a complete sentence. Suggest that students who wish to earn "extra credit" can complete **ten** of the sentence stems instead of seven.

SUPPLEMENTARY ACTIVITY #1 HANDOUT

Remembering Good Experiences

1. Nobody else noticed, but I felt good the time

    _____

    _____

2. I didn't put someone down even though I felt like it the time

    _____

3. I really listened to another person's point of view when it was
    different from mine the time _____

    _____

4. I learned from a mistake the time_____

    _____

5. I avoided making excuses or blaming someone else for what I
    did the time _____

    _____

6. I told the truth even though I was afraid I'd get in trouble the
    time _____

    _____

7. I tried to get along better with my family the time _____

    _____

8. I controlled my temper in a difficult situation the time _____

    _____

9. When I was little people were proud of me when _____

    _____

10. It felt good to think about others the time _____

    _____

11. I realized I was good at _____ the time _____

    _____

12. I was afraid (but did it anyway and felt great) the time _____

    _____

SUPPLEMENTARY ACTIVITY #2

Who Do You Think of When You Hear the Strength Word . . .

Objective   Students will name classmates who they think demonstrate specific strengths.

Materials   Supplementary Activity #2 Transparency - "Strength Words"

Procedure   Place the transparency on the overhead with all the words covered. Uncover each word, one at a time, and read it aloud. Then ask questions such as the following:

- "Who can think of a person in our class who is **energetic**?"
- "Who in our class is nearly always **organized**?"
- "Who do you think of when you hear the word **imaginative**?"
- "Who in here is very **responsible**—you could trust them to take good care of something that's important to you?"
- "Who do you think is a very **patient** person in this room—someone who is willing to wait without complaining?"
- "Who in here is **outdoorsy**? Think of someone who likes to do things outside like hike or climb trees."

When you call on students who raise their hands, ask them to look at the person they think has the quality you've just named and say that person's name out loud for all to hear.

As you go through the list, ask students to listen carefully so they can try to name classmates who haven't been mentioned yet.

SUPPLEMENTARY ACTIVITY #2 TRANSPARENCY

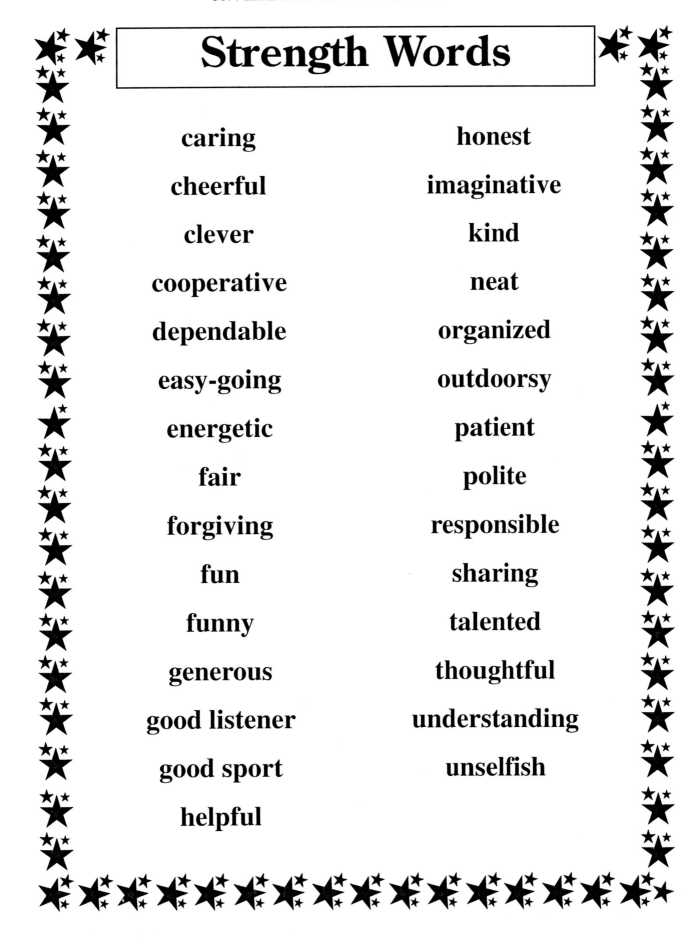

Strength Words

caring	honest
cheerful	imaginative
clever	kind
cooperative	neat
dependable	organized
easy-going	outdoorsy
energetic	patient
fair	polite
forgiving	responsible
fun	sharing
funny	talented
generous	thoughtful
good listener	understanding
good sport	unselfish
helpful	

SUPPLEMENTARY ACTIVITY #3

Looking for a Partner's Strengths

Objective

Students will practice good listening skills while listening to a partner's good experience.

Students will identify the strengths hidden in their partner's good experience.

Materials

Blank transparency and pen (optional)

Handout #1 from Lesson 1 - "My Trail of Good Experiences"

Handout #3 from Lesson 1 - "Memory Triggers for Good Experiences"

Handouts #1, #2, and #5 from the lesson

Blank "Strength Detective Report" (Handout #4 from the lesson) for each student

Procedure

Tell students they are going to be "Strength Detectives" for each other. They will do this by working with the Learning Partners, with whom they'll share good experiences and fill out "Strength Detective Reports."

Before students begin, go over the following good listening strategies with the class. You may wish to write these on a blank transparency or ask a student volunteer to help you demonstrate good listening by modeling these skills:

- Look at the person who is speaking.
- Ask questions to find out how the speaker made the good experience happen.
- Say or do something to let the other person know that you understand.
- Think about the strengths that might be hidden in the speaker's good experience.

Have students take their two handouts "Memory Triggers for Good Experiences" and "My Trail of Good Experiences" out of their "Strengths Folders." They may also want to have their copies of "Self Strengths (Short Version)," "People Strengths (Short Version)," and "Some Phrases That Describe Strengths" for reference during the activity.

Students should now take these papers and go sit with their Learning Partners. The shorter of each of the two partners will share first. They should choose a good experience from one of their two pages and tell their Learning Partners about it. They will have six minutes to share. Remind the listening partner to follow the good listening guidelines. Suggest that the listener might also want to ask the speaker questions such as the following (you may wish to write these on the chalkboard or the transparency):

- How old were you when this happened?
- Was this hard to do?
- How did you feel about this experience?
- Did anyone else know about it? Did they say anything?

After five and a half minutes have elapsed, tell the speakers that they have 30 seconds to finish. When the time is up, instruct the partners to switch roles so the other partner can share a good experience.

After both Learning Partners have shared, distribute the "Strength Detective Reports" to each student to fill out about their Learning Partner's experience. Have the students give their Learning Partners the reports they made for them. Students should put their "Strength Detective Reports" in their "Strength Folders." You may also wish to allow the students to share these reports verbally.

SUPPLEMENTARY ACTIVITY #4

Detecting Your Own Strengths

Directions:

Try being your own "Strength Detective." The reason you enjoy an activity and do it well is because you have certain talents, skills, or strengths. Think of some things you have done well and liked doing. Write them on the lines at the left. Then write your talents, skills, or strengths that helped you do these things well on the lines at the right.

**Some things I have done well
and enjoyed doing:**

**Talents, skills, or strengths
that helped me do it well
and enjoy it:**

1. _____

1. _____

_____

_____

_____

_____

2. _____

2. _____

_____

_____

_____

_____

3. _____

3. _____

_____

_____

_____

_____

4. _____

4. _____

_____

_____

_____

_____

Building a Strength Word Vocabulary

Objective

Students will learn to recognize and use a number of new vocabulary words that describe personal strengths.

Students will continue to identify these strengths in themselves and others.

Materials

Blank transparency and pen

Transparency #1 from Lesson 2 - "Self Strengths (Short Version)"

Transparency #2 from Lesson 2 - "People Strengths (Short Version)"

Handouts #1A-#1E - "Strength Word Dictionary" (stapled in booklet form)

Transparency #1 - "Looks Like—Sounds Like"

Transparency #2/Handout #2 - "Finding My Strengths in the Dictionary"

Handout #3 - "Using Your Strength Word Dictionary"

Completed "Strength Detective Reports" in the "Strength Detective Box"

Notebook paper (optional)

To the Teacher

In this lesson students will build a sight/comprehension vocabulary of words that describe strengths. This expanded vocabulary will provide them with a larger bank of descriptors as they continue to look at good experiences and identify their own strengths and the strengths of their classmates. Because it contains so many elements of a language arts lesson, this and the following lesson can be integrated into your language, spelling, and creative writing programs.

This lesson provides students with a "Strength Word Dictionary." It also employs a game format for vocabulary drill which allows for participation by students of varying verbal skill levels. The lesson begins with a review of strength words and phrases taught in the previous lesson. The guessing-game format used in the review is used throughout the lesson.

The "Strength Word Dictionary" contains forty-one descriptors arranged alphabetically with definitions and/or synonyms. A sentence which contains the strength word is included in each entry.

Students are encouraged to have fun with their dictionaries, surprising others with the "big words" they know. The purpose of the dictionary is not for all students to master all the words, but for students to broaden their vocabularies of strength words according to their varying abilities.

The guessing-game format involves to use of the "Strength Word Dictionary" as students look up words and become familiar with the layout. The difficulty of the task is gradually increased as students become more familiar with their dictionaries. It is important that students be able to handle and use their dictionaries comfortably before playing the second game, "Strength Word Pop-Up," otherwise they may find the fast pace of the game frustrating.

The "Strength Word Pop-Up Game" will be most successful if students do not have to rely too heavily on their dictionaries. While playing the game, students who are less gifted verbally can be provided opportunities to participate in several ways:

- Give the definition of one of the simpler words, then call on a less verbal student; the rules of the game allow you to call on **any** student who "pops-up," not on the **first** student.
- Call on less verbal students to make up sentences for the second point in the game.
- Call on less verbal students to identify classmates who display the strength in question for the third point.
- Occasionally preface a clue with, "Now this **next** clue is only for students who haven't 'popped-up' yet (or who haven't answered yet)," and tailor the clue to the less verbal students.

At the end of the lesson, students are asked to recall good experiences and find in their dictionaries strengths they used in making those experiences happen. It will be important for you to model carefully the "thinking through" of this process, as well as to reserve distributing the handout until the end of the thinking time, so that students won't omit the thinking step and go immediately to the writing.

The lesson ends with sentence stems used as a stimulus for verbal review and a short homework assignment in which students demonstrate their comprehension of strength words by completing sentences and drawing pictures.

Supplementary Activity #5 also provides a list of more difficult words, "Challenging Strength Words," for extra credit work to stimulate your most verbally gifted students.

Lesson Presentation

Strength Detective Reports

STRENGTH DETECTIVE REPORTS

We've been looking at our good experiences and the good experiences of our classmates in order to find our strengths. You've been good "Strength Detectives" the past few days. I've seen you spying on each others' strengths and filling out "Strength Detective Reports." I'd like to read you some. *Choose several "Strength Detective Reports" to read to the class. Compliment the student on his or her strength and acknowledge the classmate who filled out the report for a good job of "strength detecting." Give the reports to the students who used the strengths to put in their "Strengths Folders."*

THE NEED FOR A GOOD VOCABULARY OF STRENGTH WORDS

Transp. #1 and Transp. #2 from Lesson 2

There are lots of different words we can use when we describe our strengths; here are some of the words we've been using. *Use Transparencies #1, "Self Strengths (Short Version)," and #2, "People Strengths (Short Version)," from Lesson 2 for the following exercise. Put Transparency #1 on the overhead and say:* **One of the strength words on this page could be used to describe a girl named Mary. Mary always finishes her assignments, even if she has to take them home to complete them. When she tells her mother she'll wash the dishes, she doesn't stop until she's done. Which one of these strength words describes Mary?** *Call on a student to identify the strength "finishes things." Continue to review the definitions of the strength words on these two transparencies in the same way. You may wish to use the following scenarios:*

For "Self Strengths"

Chan can always make even the most ordinary story interesting. He's also able to convince his friends of his point of view when they have a difference of opinion. *(good with words)*

(continued)

Marcus has the neatest notebook in the class. When the teacher says, "Please get out your homework," or "Take out the maps you were working on last week," Marcus always knows exactly where his paper is. At home he has all his things placed neatly on shelves and in special boxes. *(organized)*

Danielle is known in her family as a live wire. She has lots of pep and is always doing something. She's always ready to go somewhere or do something new. When her cooperative learning group has an assignment, she's anxious to get started and always willing to do her part. *(energetic)*

For "People Strengths"

When someone needs help learning to do something new, the teacher often asks Willie to help. He's always willing to explain the instructions again when someone doesn't get it the first time. He doesn't seem to mind when they're slow at getting something done. *(patient)*

Britt never seems to mind sharing her things. When she has cookies in her lunch, she often gives one to her neighbor. When someone doesn't have a pencil, she often says, "Here—use one of mine," even before she's asked. *(generous, sharing, unselfish)*

You may wish to call on a few student volunteers to make up examples of their own for the rest of the class to guess before proceeding with the lesson.

INTRODUCING THE STRENGTH WORD DICTIONARY

When we know a lot of different strength words, we can do a better job of describing our own and others' strengths. Remember the example about Britt who liked to share her cookies at lunch? Because we know so many strength words, we can say more than "she shares"; we also can use the words "unselfish" and "generous."

As we grow older our vocabulary grows, too. We learn to use longer and more interesting words. Today I'm going to give you a special dictionary to help you increase your vocabulary of strength words. You can have a lot of fun with this dictionary, impressing your friends with the hard words you know. You can even use some of them on your family. Imagine your mom's surprise if you were to say, "Mom, you're a <u>dedicated</u> and <u>persevering</u> worker," instead of, "Mom, you're a hard worker!"

Handout #1A
Handout #1B
Handout #1C
Handout #1D
Handout #1E

Distribute stapled copies of Handouts #1A-1E, "Strength Word Dictionary." As you can see, your "Strength Word Dictionary" is packed with different ways of describing strengths. Look through it a little bit. Some of these are very hard words! A few are even high school words. I don't want you to worry about learning all these words at once. We'll start by playing some games with them and you'll find that some will stick in your mind. Let's start with a guessing game to practice using your new dictionaries.

THE "STRENGTH DEFINITION GAME"

In this game you will give students definitions of strength words from their dictionaries, and they will match them by giving you the correct strength words. In order to simplify their "skimming" task, you will tell them which page to skim in their dictionaries.

I'm going to give you a definition of one of the strength words in your dictionary. I'll say the meaning; you tell me the word. Look in your dictionary to make sure you have the right word so you can spell it correctly. I'll tell you which page the word is on. The page numbers are in the upper righthand corner.

Students can participate in this game in one of two ways. Choose the one that is most appropriate for your class:

Blank Transp.

- *Ask students to put their finger on the correct word and hold up their dictionaries when you give a signal. Call on a student to give the correct word. Write this word on a blank transparency and have students jiggle their dictionaries if they chose correctly.*

- *Instruct students to tear several sheets of notebook paper in half. If necessary, model the folding and tearing. Have students use both sides of each half sheet to save paper. Give the definition, then ask students to write the word they think you are defining in large letters on a half sheet, which they will hold up when you give a signal. Call on a student to give the correct word. Write the word on the transparency and have students hold up their papers if they guessed correctly. (Use this second option if most students can write fast enough for the game to proceed at a lively pace. Or students who have difficulty writing rapidly can write just the first three or four letters of the word.)*

Ready? Here's the first strength word definition. It's on page _(#)_ and it means _(definition)_ . Find the strength word that means _(definition)_ and (put your finger on it / write it on your scratch paper). *Give students a reasonable amount of time to find the word, then give the signal for them to show their answers. Call on a student to say the word. Write it on the transparency, reminding the rest of the class either to "jiggle" or hold up their papers if they got it right. You may wish to provide reinforcement by suggesting that students put a tiny star by the word if they got it right.*

Continue playing this guessing-game as above. After giving five to seven definitions, call on several student volunteers to come to the front of the room to give clues.

MAKING THE GAME MORE CHALLENGING

After the volunteers are finished, say: **Just for fun, let's change the game a little. Let's make it a little harder. This time, instead of reading you the definition, I'm going to give you a sentence with the strength word missing. You see if you can figure out what the missing strength word is and (put your**

finger on it/write it on your scratch paper) the same way you did before.

Read the following sentences or make up sentences of your own, giving the dictionary page number if necessary. If students give a synonym, ask them to explain their answer. Accept all reasonable answers. You may also wish to <u>prompt</u> for synonyms or other words that might also be correct.

- **Darren can help his friends work out their disagreements with each other; he's a good _____.** *(negotiator)*

- **Gretta doesn't get upset very easily. She's usually in a good mood. She's _____.** *(easy-going)*

- **You can tell Angelina a secret and know that she'll never tell anyone else. She's _____.** *(trustworthy)*

- **When it comes to running the obstacle course on the playing field, George White Eagle is the class champ. He never seems to trip running through the tires and he can shinny up a rope better than anyone else in the class. He's really _____.** *(coordinated)*

- **Brad is the one everyone tells their troubles to. He listens quietly and says things that make you feel he understands. Brad is a very _____ person.** *(sympathetic)*

- **Sally Ann likes to spend as much time as she can playing soccer, so she doesn't waste a minute during the time she has to spend doing her chores and homework. She keeps her mind on what she's doing so that she can get the most done in the least amount of time. Sally Ann is an _____ worker.** *(efficient)*

CLARIFYING DIFFICULT VOCABULARY WORDS

You're doing very well with these new strength words. Have any of you learned any new strength words you didn't know before today? *Call on students volunteers to tell their newly learned words. Ask if they'd like to use them in a sentence or paraphrase their meanings to practice what they've just learned.*

In a minute we're going to divide into teams and play another game. But first I want you to look carefully through your dictionary and put a small pencil mark by any word that you aren't sure about. *Allow students time to do this.*

Transp. #1

I think the game will be a lot more fun for you if we practice the words you're curious about before we play. *Show Transparency #1, "Looks Like—Sounds Like."* **Who will volunteer to be the first one to give us a word you're curious about?** *Call on a volunteer and write the strength word in the box at the top of the transparency.*

Read the definition of the word from the "Strength Word Dictionary." **This is a good strength word. We want to be sure we understand it so we can use it to describe our strengths or someone else's.** *Point to the column labeled "Looks like."* **If you saw someone using this strength, what kinds of things might you see her or him <u>doing</u>?** *Call on a student to suggest a scenario. Write it in the "Looks like" column.* **That's a good example of this strength.** *Point to the "Sounds like" column.* **Now, tell me what kinds of things might you hear a person who had this strength <u>saying</u>?** *Write student responses in the "Sounds like" column. Continue in this way until the strength word has been described to your satisfaction.*

Erase the transparency (or save it and use another) and continue this procedure with the remainder of the words students have marked in their dictionaries.

STRENGTH WORD POP-UP—A VOCABULARY GAME

Good job! I think you know most of these strength words well enough now for us to play the "Strength Word Pop-Up Game."

This is how the game goes. I'll divide the class into two teams. *You may have the students sit at their desks and simply have a dividing line down the middle of your classroom. However, since this is a skill game, you may want to carefully balance the two teams by moving students around. If you have the space, students can bring their chairs to opposite sides of the room. If you do have students move, tell them to take their dictionaries with them.*

Blank Transp.

Team 1 will have the first turn. I'll put the definition of a strength word on the overhead and read it. If you are on Team 1 and you know what the strength word is, you will "pop-up"—stand up—so I'll know you have the answer. I'll choose one of the pop-ups to tell me the strength word.

If Team 1's pop-up gives me the right word, Team 1 will get a point—but, be careful! If you pop-up when you aren't sure, you may give the wrong word. When that happens, the turn will go to Team 2 and they will pop-up if they know the answer. If the team member I call on can give the correct strength word, Team 2 gets the point.

Whichever team correctly names the strength word, it will then be the other team's turn to pop-up if they can give us a good sentence using the strength word. The sentence has to be a good one. It can't be something like, "He is <u>thoughtful</u>." The sentence has to show that you know the meaning of the word. So for the word "thoughtful," you could say, "Someone who takes out the trash without being asked is a <u>thoughtful</u> person." The team can earn a point for giving a good sentence. If they don't give a good sentence, the other team gets to pop-up and try.

There's one more way to win a point. After one of the teams has used the word in a good sentence, then the other team has a chance for a point. They can get this last point by naming someone in the class who they think has that strength and giving an example of when they used it. Members of the team will pop-up when they're ready to tell who it is <u>and why they think so</u>. For example, they could say "_(name)_ is thoughtful <u>because</u> she helped a second grader find the library last week."

At the end of the game, we'll add up the score and the winning team will . . . . *Choose a reward such as: getting to line up for lunch first, receiving five minutes of free time, or whatever reinforcement is appropriate for your class.*

Choose a Scorekeeper and divide the class into two teams. You may want to start with the words students are more likely to know and progress to more difficult ones. When a word is missed, wait a turn or two and then use it again.

USING THE "STRENGTH WORD DICTIONARY" TO FIND PERSONAL STRENGTHS

When you've finished the game and students have returned to their regular seats, say: I want you to use your "Strength Word Dictionaries" one more time today—this time for yourselves. I want you to take your time and look carefully through all these great new strength words to find two of them that you think describe you best.

Here's the way I want you to do this. Try to think if there was a time when you used each strength to create a good experience for yourself. Put a little mark by the strength words you remember using. Then choose the two strength words that you remember using the most or that seem the most like you. *Model looking through the "Strength Word Dictionary," thinking out loud about times you used some of the strengths to do something you felt good about. Allow students time to make marks in their dictionaries and to select their two strength words. Choose two strength words of your own.*

Transp. #2

When you've found your two special strength words, I want you to write them carefully and neatly in BIG letters in the two strength boxes when you get this next handout. Like this . . . . *Put Transparency #2, "Finding My Strengths in the Dictionary," on the overhead and print two of your strengths in the small boxes.* **On the lines below each of your strength words I'd like you to describe a time when you used that strength.** *Model on the transparency by writing a time you used each strength on the lines under that strength's box. Read the entry aloud:* **"I was (strength) the time I (action/event) ,"** *emphasizing the fact that it makes a complete sentence about your strength.*

Handout #2

Distribute Handout #2, "Finding My Strengths in the Dictionary," and circulate around the room, assisting those who need help with their dictionaries. Have students put their completed handouts in their "Strengths Folders."

A DICTIONARY HOMEWORK ASSIGNMENT

Handout #3

You should all be feeling very proud of yourselves today; you've learned some pretty hard words! This is going to be a great help as we look for our own strengths and help each other find theirs. I have a short dictionary homework assignment for you—it has a little bit of drawing and a little bit of writing. You'll want to take your "Strength Word Dictionaries" home with you so you can look up the words on this handout. *Distribute Handout #3, "Using Your Strength Word Dictionary."*

Let's pretend the first sentence said, "We can say Felix is ar-tistic because he . . . ." You might finish this sentence by writing, "can draw things so that they look real." After you'd written this, you'd need to read it to be sure it made a good sentence. Let's see if it is. "We can say Felix is artistic

because he can draw things so that they look real." Is that a good sentence? Does it explain why we can say Felix is artistic? *Allow for student response.*

On your papers it says, "We can say Felix is thorough because he . . . ." You'll need to look up the word "thorough" to be sure you know what it means. Then you'll finish the sentence so that it explains why we can say Felix is thorough. Be sure to read the sentence when you're finished to make sure it sounds right. When you've finished the sentence, make a small drawing that represents Felix being thorough.

Tomorrow I'll ask some of you to share your sentences with the class.

LESSON REVIEW

Process the lesson by asking students to complete one of the following sentence stems:

- *A new strength word I learned today is . . . .*

- *A strength word I'll use to compliment someone else today is . . . .*

- *I learned . . . .*

- *I liked . . . .*

- *I wish . . . .*

SUPPLEMENTARY ACTIVITIES

Use the Supplementary Activities to reinforce the skills taught in this lesson:

- *"Strength BINGO"*
   (Supplementary Activity #1)

- *"Make a Path of Strength Words—Short Version"*
   (Supplementary Activity #2)

- *"Strength Baseball"*
   (Supplementary Activity #3)

- *"Creating Strength Vocabulary Game Shows"*
   (Supplementary Activity #4)

- *"Challenging Words Concentration Game"*
   (Supplementary Activity #5)

Strength Word Dictionary

adventurous
willing to take chances; daring; bold
Mary hopped from stone to stone across the rushing creek; she's an **adventurous** girl!

confident
sure of oneself; believing in one's own abilities
Jason was **confident** that he'd do well on the science test.

conscientious
doing what one knows is right; honest
Romero's teacher didn't mind leaving the room while he took the science test because she knew he was a **conscientious** kid.

considerate
thoughtful of the rights and feelings of others
"Hey, I'm sorry I bumped into you," Rhonda said to her classmate. Rhonda was **considerate** of other people's feelings.

cooperative
willing to work together with others
When it was time for everyone to pitch in and help with the housework, Alex was always **cooperative** and willing to help.

coordinated
having muscles that work together smoothly
Allison learned to juggle three bean bags when she was only seven. She's really **coordinated**.

courageous
willing to meet danger or difficulty; brave; fearless
The way Mai Lu rescued her cat from the neighbor's big dog was really **courageous**!

creative
able to invent new and original things
Jerry's cooperative learning group had to plan their ideal vacation for social studies, and they asked him to make the travel brochure because he was so **creative**.

HANDOUT #1B

Page 2

Strength Word Dictionary (continued)

dependable
able to be counted on; reliable; trustworthy
At Christmas the teacher asked a **dependable** student to take the class hamster home for the holidays.

determined
having one's mind firmly made up; sticking with something
Josh was **determined** to fix the brakes on his bike if it took him 100 years!

easy-going
dealing with things in a calm manner; unhurried
The kids like to be around Fredrika because she's so **easy-going** and doesn't get stressed-out about things.

efficient
capable of accomplishing a task without waste
The baseball team only had ten minutes to get on the bus, so Coach Johnson wanted someone **efficient** to load the sports equipment.

encouraging
giving help or support; helping others feel hopeful
When my brother or I feel down, we like to talk to our Aunt Reba because she's so **encouraging**.

energetic
liking to move; active; powerful
Ray is so **energetic** that he ran around the gym three times just to warm up for P.E.

enthusiastic
strongly interested; eager
Joe is really **enthusiastic** about computer games; no one in class likes to play more than he.

flexible
able to move and bend easily
Sonia can do cartwheels, backbends, and flips; she's really **flexible**.

HANDOUT #1c

Page 3

Strength Word Dictionary (continued)

graceful

able to move in a smooth, pleasing manner; not clumsy or awkward
One of the most important qualities a dancer needs is to be **graceful**.

imaginative

able to picture something in one's mind; creative
When our cooperative learning group has an assignment, Roberto can always come up with some **imaginative** idea to make the assignment more fun.

independent

able to do things by oneself; not needing to be controlled or guided by someone else
When Tyrone's grandmother asks him to do something, she knows it will get done without her watching over him because he's an **independent** worker.

inventive

able to make up or create something new
One of the parts to his bicycle was missing, so Carl had to be **inventive** when repairing it.

loyal

faithful to a friend or group
Carla never turns against her friends; she's **loyal**.

negotiator

able to help others reach an agreement
Sometimes kids in David's class ask him to help them settle their disagreements because he's such a good **negotiator**.

observant

paying careful attention; alert; watchful
When someone is teaching you how to do something new, it's a good idea to be **observant**.

organized

able to arrange things in a sensible manner; not confused
Andrea is very **organized**, and she can't stand to have her notebook in a mess.

Strength Word Dictionary (continued)

original

able to think up new things; inventive
When it's time for the class to make book reports, Marty always comes up with something **original**.

outgoing

friendly; sociable
Ramona is so **outgoing** that the teacher often asks her to help a new student get acquainted at our school.

patient

able to wait calmly without complaining
Even though Ted couldn't pass the soccer ball very well, his big brother was **patient** with him while he was learning.

persevering

able to continue doing something in spite of difficulty
Jeff couldn't figure out the last story problem, so he took it home to finish it; Jeff is **persevering.**

positive attitude

thinking in a confident way; optimistic
When your team has to play the district champions, it helps to have a **positive attitude**.

punctual

on time; prompt
When Martha says she will come to your house at 4:00, you can always count on her to be **punctual**.

reliable

able to be depended upon; trustworthy
You can count on Luis to do what he says he will do because he's so **reliable**.

responsible

able to be trusted with important matters; able to behave sensibly
Susan's neighbors ask her to babysit because she's **responsible**.

self-disciplined

able to control and guide oneself
Willie practiced his trumpet even when his mother was out of town because he's **self-disciplined.**

Page 5

Strength Word Dictionary (continued)

self-motivated
able to start something alone; able to continue something alone
Mark's mom doesn't have to remind him to do his homework before he watches TV in the evening because he's **self-motivated.**

sensitive
aware of the feelings of others
Ms. Hernandez didn't make the new kid read his report out loud because she was **sensitive** to his feelings.

sincere
truthful; honest
When Eddie gives you a compliment about your pitching, you know he means it because Eddie is **sincere.**

sympathetic
sharing the feelings of another; caring about another's problems
When you're feeling down, it helps to have someone **sympathetic** to talk to.

thorough
taking care of details; finishing completely
Mr. Wong asked Sean to clean out the equipment cabinet because he knew Sean would do a **thorough** job.

thoughtful
considerate of others
Johnny is a **thoughtful** guy who always asks the kid who's left out to be on his team.

thrifty
able to carefully manage money; able to save
Teddy is so **thrifty** that he'll soon have enough money saved from his allowance and birthdays to buy a new snowboard.

trustworthy
dependable; reliable
Monica let LuAnn borrow her brand new music tape because she knew LuAnn was **trustworthy**.

TRANSPARENCY #1

Looks Like—Sounds Like

Looks like: Sounds like:

TRANSPARENCY #2/HANDOUT #2

Finding My Strengths in the Dictionary

Directions:

Look through your "Strength Word Dictionary" to choose two strength words that you feel describe you especially well. For each word, tell about a time when you used that strength.

1. I was [ ]

the time I . . .

_____
_____
_____
_____
_____
_____
_____

2. I was [ ]

the time I . . .

_____
_____
_____
_____
_____
_____
_____

HANDOUT #3

Using Your Strength Word Dictionary

Directions:

In each box below, use your "Strength Word Dictionary" to finish the sentence, then draw a small picture showing yourself or someone else using that strength.

We can say that Felix is **thorough** because he _____	We can say that Angie is **punctual** because she _____
We can say that Garth is **persevering** because he _____	We can say that Goldie is **loyal** because she _____
We can say that Walt is **observant** because he _____	We can say that Rosarita is **inventive** because she _____

Strength BINGO

Objective   Students will use a game format to match strength vocabulary words with their definitions.

Materials   Supplementary Activity #1 Handout   -   "Strength BINGO"

"Strength Word Dictionaries" (Hnadouts #1A-#1E) from the lesson

10-15 cover markers for each student (squares cut from construction paper)

Procedure   Distribute a copy of the "Strength BINGO" form to each student. Tell students to look through their "Strength Word Dictionaries" and choose 24 of their favorite strength words to write in the squares on their BINGO form. While they are filling in their squares, distribute 10-15 markers to each student.

Explain to students that you will be giving them definitions of the strength words in their dictionaries. They are to listen to your clues and decide what the missing strength word is. If they have previously written that word on their card, they are to cover that square with a marker. Tell them that they may use their dictionaries for help if they are not certain of the definitions.

Give your clues in a manner similar to the following:

- If you are willing to take chances, are daring and bold, we can say you are _____. *(adventurous)*
- If you can be trusted with important matters, we can say you are _____. *(trustworthy)*

Students are to shout "BINGO!" when they have a row of five words covered (horizontally, vertically, or diagonally). You may wish to give a small reward to the winner.

As you call out definitions, keep a record of the strength words used so you can check a student's card for accuracy when he or she calls out "Bingo!" Since some of the words have similar meanings, give credit for sensible answers even if they are not the exact word you defined.

SUPPLEMENTARY ACTIVITY #1 HANDOUT

Strength
B I N G O

		FREE		

SUPPLEMENTARY ACTIVITY #2

Make a Path of Strength Words—Short Version

To Learn the Meaning of Some Words That Describe Strengths

Directions:

Begin at either starting shape. Look up the meaning of the first word in your "Strength Word Dictionary." On another sheet of paper, write the word and what it means, and then write a short sentence using the word in a way that would help someone else understand its meaning. When that's done, color the shape the word is in. Choose another word next to the last one, define it, and use it in a sentence. Keep doing this until you have colored a path to the finish line.

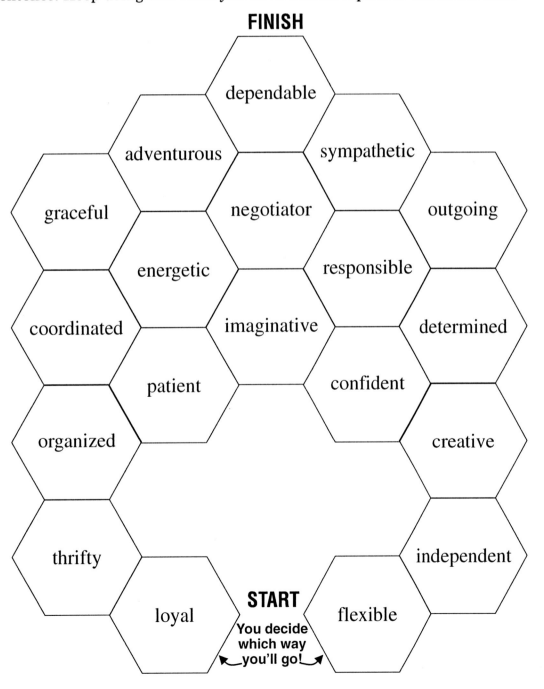

FINISH

dependable

adventurous · sympathetic

graceful · negotiator · outgoing

energetic · responsible

coordinated · imaginative · determined

patient · confident

organized · creative

thrifty · independent

loloyal · flexible

START
You decide
which way
you'll go!

SUPPLEMENTARY ACTIVITY #3

Strength Baseball

Objective   Students will learn the spelling and meaning of a variety of
strength words.

Materials   Handout #1 from Lesson 2   -   "Self Strengths (Short Version)"

Handout #2 from Lesson 2   -   "People Strengths (Short
Version)"

Handouts #1A-1E from the lesson

Markers for four bases

Procedure   Explain to students that they will play "indoor baseball" as they
practice the spelling and/or meaning of strength words. Determine
where home plate and the three bases will be in the room. Students
will need to be able to walk to each base. Divide students into two
equal teams and decide who will be "at bat" first. Sit or stand near
home plate.

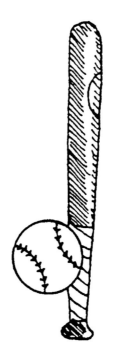

VARIATION 1

Strength Spelling Baseball—As you call, "batter up," a student
comes up to home plate. Ask that student to spell one of the
strength words on the handouts. If he or she does so correctly, the
student may proceed to first base. Ask the next student to spell
another strength word and if he or she does so correctly, that student goes to first base and the student on first moves to second
base. Continue in this fashion. When a student is moved to home
plate by a successful teammate, a home run is scored. Any student
who cannot spell a word "strikes out." After three outs the next
team is up.

VARIATION 2

Strength Definition Baseball—This game is the same as Variation 1, except that students must give the **definition** of a strength
word and use it correctly in a sentence in order to move to first
base.

VARIATION 3

Strength Definition and Spelling Baseball—In this variation, students who can give the definition of the strength word can go to first base. If they can then spell the strength word and use it in a sentence, they can proceed on to second base.

Important: When students are not up to bat, they should **all** be diligently studying how to spell the words on their strength word list or studying the definitions of strength words.

SUPPLEMENTARY ACTIVITY #4

Creating Strength Vocabulary Game Shows

Objective   Students will learn the definitions of strength words.

Materials   Handout #1 from Lesson 2 - "Self Strengths (Short Version)"

Handout #2 from Lesson 2 - "People Strengths (Short Version)"

Handouts #A-#1E from the lesson

Various props

Procedure   Have students meet together in cooperative learning groups or with their Learning Partners. Tell students that they will be creating a new version of a TV game show. This new version will be one where all the questions or activities in the show are about the meaning of strength words. For instance, one contestant or a panel is given the strength word "conscientious" and asked to give its meaning.

Students should devise ways to make the show competitive, decide how answers will be judged, and determine what the prizes will be. Tell students that after they brainstorm some ideas, they must get your O.K. on their final plan. This will allow you to screen out ideas which may be impractical or too involved. Students can use their various strength word handouts for assistance.

Allow students class time to rehearse or to make any props they will need. If they will need contestants from outside their group to be "on their show," they should arrange this with you and their classmates ahead of time.

On the day of the presentations, try to videotape these "shows." Students find it exciting to see their shows "on TV."

SUPPLEMENTARY ACTIVITY #5

Challenging Words Concentration Game

Objective

Students with strong verbal skills will increase their recognition of new strength words through playing a game.

Materials

Supplementary Activity #5 Handout - "Challenging Strength Words"

Construction paper cut into playing cards (all of the same size and color)

Procedure

Have those students who are working with the "Challenging Strength Words" list for extra credit work write those words on blank construction paper playing cards. They should write two cards for each word, being careful that the writing doesn't show through the back of the cards.

Most students will be familiar with the game "Concentration." For those who are not, explain that in this game all the cards are placed face down on a table and mixed around. The student whose turn it is turns two cards face up, leaving them in their position on the playing table. If the cards are a match, the student removes them, puts them in his or her stack and gets another play. If the cards are not a match, the cards are turned face down again and it's the next player's turn. Players are thus challenged to remember where specific cards are so they can create matches. Play continues until all the specific cards have been matched and identified. The player with the most cards in his or her stack at this time wins the game.

SUPPLEMENTARY ACTIVITY #5 HANDOUT

Challenging Strength Words

ambitious
appreciative
articulate

common sense
committed

diplomatic

empathetic
even tempered
expressive

genuine
good communicator
good judgment
good visualizer

intuitive

open-minded
optimistic

peacemaker
perceptive
persistent
persuasive

resilient
resourceful

sociable
self-reliant
supportive

tactful
tolerant

verbal
vivacious

witty

Becoming a Whiz at Using Strength Words

Objective

Students will learn the meanings and usage of more difficult vocabulary words which describe strengths.

Students will use vocabulary words to identify strengths in family members and acquaintances outside the classroom.

Materials

"Strength Detective Box" with "Strength Detective Reports" from Lesson 3

Transparencies #1A, #1B, and #1B - "Strength Squares Trick"

Game Equipment - "Number Cube" (constructed from tagboard or cardboard so that it will roll easily on the floor, or a single die)

Transparency #2 - "The Strength Word Game"

Teacher Pages #1A-#1C - "'Easy' Quiz Questions"

Teacher Pages #2A and #2B - "'Hard' Quiz Questions"

Handout #1 - "I Can See Strengths in Others"

Colored transparent tokens, such as colored squares cut from a transparency or transparent plastic chips, one per team

"Strengths Folders" (each student's)

To the Teacher

This lesson is a companion lesson to Lesson 3, "Building a Strength Word Vocabulary." It is designed to provide practice in using the vocabulary words introduced in that lesson, as well as to continue the emphasis on identifying strengths in oneself and others. The lesson begins with a "magic trick" activity which will appeal to students' natural curiosity and will refocus their attention on the strength vocabulary words. Following the trick, more "Strength Detective Reports" will be read aloud. This reinforces both the students who exhibited the strengths and the ones who identified them, and also encourages continued interest in this unit.

The "Strength Word Game" is the core of the lesson and provides students with a fun drill on the meaning and usage of the words introduced in the "Strength Word Dictionary." The game consists of a "playing board" transparency, the "Number Cube" (or a single die), and the "Easy Quiz Questions" and "Hard Quiz Questions" pages. The class is divided into two or three teams whose players can choose to answer either "easy" or "hard" vocabulary questions in order to roll the cube and advance their team's token.

The questions on both the "easy" and "hard" question pages are ranked in order of difficulty, which allows you to choose a question that will challenge your most gifted student or find one that will give those with learning difficulties an opportunity to succeed. You can make the scoring between teams closer during play by choosing harder or easier questions in either category, according to each player's ability level. You can also get extra mileage out of this game by occasionally asking a student if he or she has ever used the particular strength mentioned to create a good experience for himself or herself.

A homework assignment encourages students to notice strengths in others outside the classroom and requires them to describe the actions they observe in others that show they have these strengths.

You can model this behavior by pointing out strengths in your students occasionally during the school day. You might say things like: "Mary, I notice you are _____. That shows me you must be using the strength of _____. Is that true?" You can use these "teachable moments" to articulate some of the strength vocabulary words you are teaching in this lesson. Finally, you can include these words in your language arts program.

Lesson Presentation

THE STRENGTH SQUARES TRICK

You will want to choose and train in advance a student partner who has good conceptual skills; the class should not know about this advance training. The trick is explained following.

Transp. #1A

Today I'm going to do two things at once—I'm going to amaze you with a marvelous magic trick, and I'm going to give you a chance to use some of your new strength vocabulary words to tell about strengths you see in your classmates. I have a partner in the class who's going to help me with the trick. *Call the student partner to the front of the room. Put Transparency #1A, "Strength Squares Trick," on the overhead. Say:* **My partner has a wonderful talent. He or she can guess which strength word we've chosen from this transparency without even being in the room. If you watch closely, maybe you can figure out how the trick is done.** *Send your partner to stand outside the door. Call on a student to choose one of* *the strength words on the transparency; point to it and repeat it aloud for the class.*

Call your partner in. **Partner, we've chosen a mystery strength word, and we want to see your magic in action. I'm going to point to different strength words on the transparency, and I want you to tell me when I point to the mystery strength word.**

Point to various words on the transparency, asking, "Is it this one?" Your partner will know, and should indicate with any affirmative, when you point to the one that was chosen while he or she was out of the room. Then send your partner out and have the class choose another strength word.

After three or four mystery words have been identified by your partner, ask the class, "Can anyone think of someone in this class who uses this strength a lot?" *Continue asking the students to identify classmates who use each of the mystery strength words as they are identified by your partner.*

HOW THE TRICK WORKS

Your partner will have been trained in advance to see that the nine small squares are arranged in one large square. <u>The place you point to in each of the small squares will indicate the location of the mystery word in the large square.</u> For instance, if you point to the middle of each small square, saying, "Is it this one?" your partner will know that the mystery word is in the middle of the big square; if you point to the top righthand corner of each small square, you will indicate that the mystery word is in the top righthand corner of the large square.

Transp. #1B

After repeating the trick several times, ask the class: **Does anyone think they know the key to this trick? Who has a theory?** *Call on students who wish to guess at how the trick is done. Tell them to test their theories while you and your partner proceed with* *the trick using Transparency #1B, which has different strength words. Vary the nonessential parts of the trick's presentation to disprove erroneous theories. For example, you can vary the number of words you point to before pointing to the mystery word; sometimes ask something other than "Is it this one?"; or point silently. If a student says that he or she has a theory that has worked for three or four times, let him or her try being your partner in order to prove his or her theory.*

Tell the class you'll show them how the trick is done if they pay close attention to the rest of the lesson. It can be helpful to remind students of this promise during the lesson if they begin to be inattentive.

PRIVATE EYE REPORTS

Strength Detective Box

Thinking about all those different strengths reminds me of the "Strength Detective Reports" you've been putting in the "Strength Detective Box." Let's read some of them. *Choose some of the "Strength Detective Reports" from the "Strength Detective Box" to read aloud. Be sure to acknowledge both the student who showed the strength and the student who completed the report for being a good "detective." Give the "Strength Detective Reports" to the students who were observed for them to put in their "Strengths Folders."*

USING THE "HARD NEW WORDS" IN THE "STRENGTH WORD DICTIONARIES"

You've been doing a good job of watching for each others' strengths and of using your new vocabulary words to describe them. Can anyone tell me a new strength word you've learned since we started working with our "Strength Word Dictionaries"? I'd like you to use it in a sentence that lets us know you understand the meaning of the word. *Allow for student response.*

INTRODUCING THE "STRENGTH WORD GAME"

It's fun to use hard new words. Today we're going to play a game which will help you practice using those hard new words you've found in your "Strength Word Dictionaries." We'll divide the class into teams to play this game.

Number Cube

The teams will take turns answering quiz questions about words in the "Strength Word Dictionary" and then will roll a "Number Cube" *(or die)* on the floor. The "Number Cube" *(die)* will tell you how many spaces your team's token can advance on the playing board after you make a correct answer. *Show the "Number Cube" and read aloud the six sides. If using a die, explain that rolling a "6" will mean the team DOESN'T ADVANCE on this roll; this is equivalent to the "Tough Luck!" side of the "Number Cube."*

Transp. #2

There are different things written on some of the squares on the playing board. *Put Transparency #2, "The Strength Word Game," and the transparent team tokens on the overhead. Read aloud some of the directions on the squares.* The team that makes it all the way around the board first landing on the "FINISH" square with an exact role *(or is first to go around twice if you choose to have a longer game)* will be the winner.

TEAM FORMATION

Divide the class into two or three teams and have team members sit together. Have team members number off within the teams to determine their order of play. Assign each team a token and place it on the "START" square of the transparency. Roll the "Number Cube" (or die) to determine which team will go first.

RULES OF PLAY

Teacher Page #1A
Teacher Page #1B
Teacher Page #1C
Teacher Page #2A
Teacher Page #2B

Explain to students that when their turn comes they'll be asked to choose whether they want to answer an "easy" quiz question or a "hard" quiz question. If the player chooses and correctly answers an <u>easy</u> *question, he or she will roll the number cube on the floor* <u>once</u> *and the team's token will advance the number of spaces rolled; if he or she correctly answers a* <u>hard</u> *question, the number cube is rolled* <u>twice</u> *and the team advances twice. If a player rolls "Tough Luck!" ("6" on a regular die), the team does not advance on that roll.*

In order to encourage the students to become more aware of their strengths, you may wish to ask, "Have you ever used that strength to create a good experience for yourself?" when a student correctly answers a quiz question.

AN ASSIGNMENT USING STRENGTH WORDS

After you finish playing the game, say: **Not only are you getting better at recognizing your own strengths and those of your classmates, you're getting really good at using new and difficult vocabulary words to name them.**

Handout #1

I have a little assignment for you. *Distribute copies of Handout #1, "I Can See Strengths in Others."* **I want you to think of three people you know pretty well. They can be people in your neighborhood, in other classes at school, at home—anywhere. Write their names on this handout in the spaces under the word "Who."** *Pause while students each write three names.*

Don't write any more just yet. I want you to think about those three people for awhile. For each person you listed, find the strength word in your "Strength Word Dictionary" which you thinks describes him or her <u>the best</u>. **Write that strength word under the word "Strength." After you've decided which strength word describes them best, write why**

you think they have that strength under the word "Proof." What is it you know they <u>do</u> that lets you know they have that strength?

At the bottom of the page I want you to write four strength words you've learned to use that you didn't know very well before we began these lessons.

For the next few days I want you to continue to look for strengths in yourself and others. We're going to be doing some very special activities in our next lessons.

REWARDING GOOD ATTENTION

If students have been attentive during the lesson, say the following: Because you've done a good job of paying attention during the lesson, now it's time for me to show you how the magic trick was done. *Explain the trick to students, noting that the trick can even be done with empty boxes instead of strength words.*

SUPPLEMENTARY ACTIVITIES

Use the Supplementary Activities at the end of this lesson, as well as more "Private Eye Reports," to provide additional practice of these strength identification skills:

- *"Strengths Football"*
  (Supplementary Activity #1)

- *"Make a Path of Strength Words—Long Version"*
  (Supplementary Activity #2)

- *"Word Jumble"*
  (Supplementary Activity #3)

- *"A Group Story Using Strength Word Synonyms"*
  (Supplementary Activity #4)

TRANSPARENCY #1A

Strength Squares Trick

athletic	helpful	positive attitude
energetic	artistic	fair
hard worker	cooperative	coordinated

Strength Squares Trick (continued)

good listener	generous	cheerful
determined	brave	creative
imaginative	helpful	organized

GAME EQUIPMENT

Number Cube

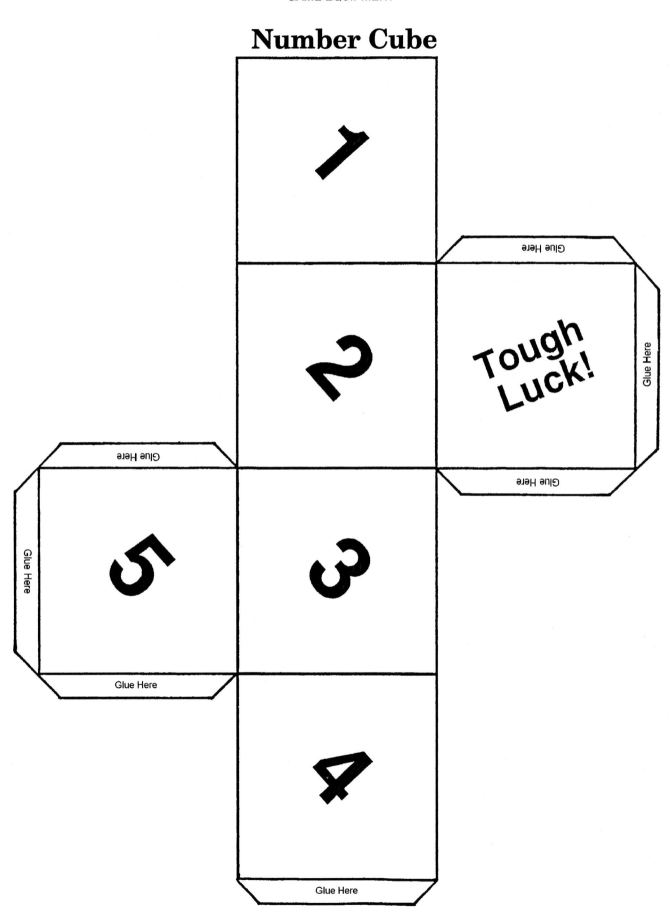

TRANSPARENCY #2

"Easy" Quiz Questions

Students can find the answers to these questions on their "Self Strengths (Short Version)" or "People Strengths (Short Version)" word lists, or in their "Strength Word Dictionaries."

Multiple Choice (correct word is underlined)

What strength word would you use to describe someone who always takes turns and doesn't cheat in games—unselfish or <u>fair</u>?

What strength word would you use to describe someone who loves to move around and is always on the go—cheerful or <u>energetic</u>?

What strength word would you use to describe someone who gets along well with others and makes new friends easily—<u>friendly</u> or kind?

What strength word would you use to describe someone who doesn't let other kids pick on the little kids in the neighborhood—<u>brave</u> or honest?

What strength word would you use to describe someone who is always on time—<u>punctual</u> or fast?

What strength word would you use to describe someone who is able to save his money—generous or <u>thrifty</u>?

What strength word would you use to describe someone who picked up books for someone when she dropped them—athletic or <u>helpful</u>?

What strength word would you use to describe someone who always tells the truth—<u>trustworthy</u> or kind?

What strength word would you use to describe someone who doesn't give up just because something is hard to do—organized or <u>determined</u>?

What strength word would you use to describe someone who gave part of her lunch to someone who lost his—imaginative or <u>generous</u>?

If someone could remember all her math facts and learned her address and phone number in kindergarten, what strength would you say she had—<u>a good memory</u> or was imaginative?

TEACHER PAGE #1B

"Easy" Quiz Questions (continued)

Short Answer

What strength word would you use to describe someone who can play the piano and is learning the guitar? (*musical*)

What strength word would you use to describe someone who loves to use paints and can draw things so they look real? (*artistic*)

What strength word would you use to describe someone who does well in most sports? (*athletic*)

What strength word would you use to describe someone who does something even when he's a little bit scared? (*brave*)

What strength word would you use to describe someone who doesn't mind waiting when others take a long time? (*patient*)

What strength word would you use to describe someone who keeps her things in an orderly way and arranges her notebook so that she can find papers easily? (*organized*)

What strength word would you use to describe someone who is able to work out difficult situations? (*a good problem-solver*)

What strength would you say someone had if he always looked on the bright side and expected things to turn out well? (*a positive attitude*)

What strength word would you use to describe someone who usually finishes first in a race? (*fast*)

What strength word would you use to describe someone who can turn cartwheels and walk on a balance beam without falling off? (*coordinated*)

What strength word would you use to describe someone who can work well in a group? (*cooperative*)

"Easy" Quiz Questions (continued)

Synonyms

What's another strength word that means "unselfish"? *(sharing, generous)*

What's another strength word that means "creative"? *(imaginative)*

What's another strength word that means "trustworthy"? *(honest)*

What's another strength word that means "caring"? *(kind)*

Spelling

nice

fair

kind

brave

strong

"Hard" Quiz Questions

Students can find the answers to these questions in their "Strength Word Dictionaries."

Synonyms

Give me two strength words that can describe someone who dreams up interesting ideas for plays and skits. *(imaginative, creative, inventive, original)*

Give me two strength words that can describe someone who sticks with something and doesn't give up. *(determined, persevering)*

Give me two strength words that can describe someone who tells the truth. *(sincere, reliable, trustworthy)*

Short Answer

What strength word would you use to describe someone who can move her body in a smooth and flowing way? *(graceful)*

What strength word would you use to describe someone who is laid-back and doesn't get upset easily? *(easy-going)*

What strength word would you use to describe someone who sticks with his friends and doesn't turn against them? *(loyal)*

What strength word would you use to describe someone who is able to help two other kids in her neighborhood work out a disagreement? *(a negotiator)*

What strength word would you use to describe someone who can bend and stretch her body easily and is good at gymnastics? *(flexible)*

What strength word would you use to describe someone who likes to tell jokes to people and make new friends? *(outgoing)*

What strength word would you use to describe someone who feels certain he will do well on the science test? *(confident)*

What strength word would you use to describe someone who yells support to a teammate whose turn it is at bat? *(encouraging)*

TEACHER PAGE #2B

"Hard" Quiz Questions (continued)

Short Answer (continued)

What strength word would you use to describe someone who doesn't waste a lot of paper when he cuts out an art project? *(efficient)*

What strength word would you use to describe someone who looks carefully at everything when she goes on a hike? *(observant)*

What strength word would you use to describe someone who doesn't leave a job partly done but always finishes it completely? *(thorough)*

What strength word would you use to describe someone who shares the feelings of someone else? *(sympathetic)*

What strength word would you use to describe someone who is able to start a job or stick with a job by himself without someone else reminding him? *(self-motivated)*

What strength word would you use to describe someone who takes care of her own behavior without someone else watching over her? *(self-disciplined)*

Long Answer

What does *(any word in the "Strength Word Dictionary")* mean?

Give me a sentence that shows you know the meaning of *(any word in the "Strength Word Dictionary")*.

Spelling

Any word in the "Strength Word Dictionary"

HANDOUT #1

I Can See Strengths in Others

Who	Strength	Proof

1 _____ _____ _____

2 _____ _____ _____

3 _____ _____ _____

Four new strength words I didn't know before:

SUPPLEMENTARY ACTIVITY #1

Strengths Football

Objective   Students will learn to recognize and use strength vocabulary words.

Materials   Handout #1 from Lesson 2   -   "Self Strengths (Short Version)"

Handout #2 from Lesson 2   -   "People Strengths (Short Version)"

Handouts #1A-#1E from Lesson 3   -   "Strength Word Dictionary"

Supplementary Activity #1 Transparency   -   "Strengths Football"

Supplementary Activity #1 Teacher Page #1   -   "Kickoffs and Punts"

Supplementary Activity #1 Teacher Pages #2A and #2B   -   "Five-Yard Questions"

Supplementary Activity #1 Teacher Pages #3A, #3B, and #3C   -   "Ten-Yard Questions"

Football Templates   -   cut out of paper for placing on the transparency (found on Teacher Page #3C)

Whistle (optional)

Procedure   This game is designed to resemble a standard U.S. football game, with the exception that there are no "downs."

The game is timed and is played in two "halves" of equal length. Decide the appropriate length of the game for your grade level. Appoint a Timekeeper to note the time of the kickoff and to watch the clock. At "half-time," the team with the ball will give up the ball and kick it off to the other team. The Timekeeper will give a "two-minute warning" before this happens and another warning two minutes before the game ends. (You may also place the Timekeeper in charge of reading kickoff and punt situations from the "Kickoffs and Punts" page, or you may choose to do this yourself.)

Divide the class into two teams of similar ability. Seat the teams on opposite sides of the room. For each team, choose a Team Captain and have the students "number off" to determine the order of play for team members. Have the two Team Captains come to the front of the room. "Introduce" them to each other and have them shake hands. Instruct one Team Captain to call "heads" or "tails" as you toss a coin. The winning Team Captain chooses to "kick" or to "receive" first.

THE KICKOFF—The "kicking" Team Captain now selects a number between one and ten; this number corresponds to a number on the "Kickoffs and Punts" page and determines the kickoff situation. The Timekeeper reads the numbered situation from the page and the ball is moved on the "field" (transparency) to the appropriate yardline. The Timekeeper then marks off the number that was chosen so it cannot be used again. The "receiving" team is now "in possession" and it is their turn to answer questions to try to advance the ball.

CHOOSING YARDAGE QUESTIONS— The player whose turn it is chooses whether to be asked a "Five-Yard Question" or a more difficult "Ten-Yard Question." Select a question from the appropriate sheet and read it aloud. If the player answers correctly, the ball is moved that amount of yardage and the next player on his or her team chooses a question. The ball continues to be advanced five or ten yards at a time until a player misses a question (see "FUMBLES") or the team crosses their goal line to score a touchdown (i.e., six points).

FUMBLES—Missing a question constitutes a "fumble," at which time you will blow your whistle and/or call "Fumble!" The first student **on either team** to raise his or her hand has the opportunity to "recover" the ball by answering the missed question correctly. If the opposite team recovers, they begin answering questions and advancing the ball toward the opposite goal. If a player on the original team raises his or her hand first and answers correctly, that team recovers the fumble and can continue gaining yardage. Each team gets one try at recovering the fumble; if neither succeeds, the original team is forced to punt (see "PUNTS").

PUNTS—If a team is forced to punt, the player who last selected a question now chooses a number between one and ten. The Timekeeper reads the corresponding punt situation from the "Kickoffs and Punts" page. The ball is moved according to the directions on the sheet. The opposing team takes possession of the ball and begins choosing questions to move the ball toward their own goal.

EXTRA POINT—The "extra point kick" following a touchdown is earned by correctly answering a "Five-Yard Question." A correct answer scores the team one more point. If you so choose, each team can designate one player to always be the "Kicker."

PENALTIES—As an option, five-yard penalties can be established for student conduct, such as "Illegal Use of the Mouth" (excessive talking or giving teammates answers).

When giving students questions, note that the categories within both the five-yard and ten-yard question pages increase in difficulty (e.g., naming a synonym is easier than spelling for most students). This is done to allow you to choose questions appropriate for your students' abilities, whether above or below average. For talented students, you may also wish to add your own set of difficult "long-bomb questions" which will score an immediate touchdown or, if missed, be "intercepted" by the other team.

SUPPLEMENTARY ACTIVITY #1 TRANSPARENCY

Strengths Football

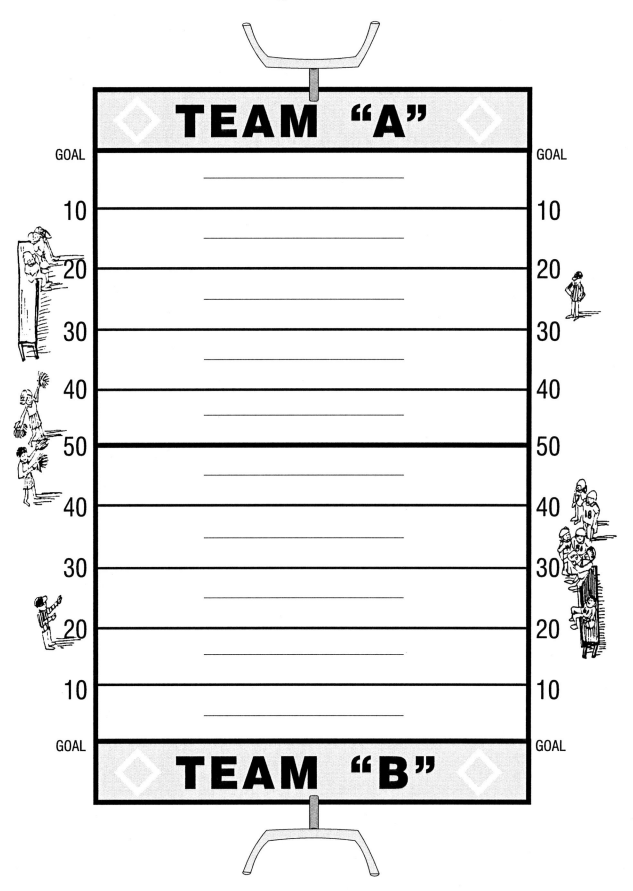

SUPPLEMENTARY ACTIVITY #1 TEACHER PAGE #1

Kickoffs and Punts

 KICKOFFS

1. The ball goes into the end zone. Start play at **their 20** yardline.

2. The ball goes out of bounds. It is kicked again and returned to **the 50**.

3. The ball is caught at their 20 and returned to **their 30** yardline.

4. The ball sails high. It is caught at their 40. The player gets by several tacklers and returns it all the way to **your 25** yardline.

5. The ball goes into the end zone. It is returned to **their 35** yardline.

6. The returner drops the ball! They recover it at **their 15** yardline.

7. The ball spirals into the end zone. The returner goes to the left when everyone else is going to right and returns it to **your 40** yardline.

8. The ball is caught at the 30 and returned to **their 45** yardline.

9. The ball goes through the end zone, so play begins at **their 20** yardline.

10. The ball spirals to their 5 and is returned to **their 25** yardline.

 PUNTS

1. The ball goes into the end zone and they return it to **their 40** yardline.

2. The ball goes **30 yards** and then they return it **10 yards**.

3. The punt is blocked! The other team gets the ball **right where it is**.

4. The ball goes **15 yards**. An opposing player falls on it **right there**.

5. The ball goes **60 yards** and is either returned **10 yards or** to **the 20** yardline.

6. The ball goes **35 yards**. There is **no return**.

7. The ball goes **out of bounds after 20 yards** and play begins there.

8. The ball goes **20 yards**. There is **no return**.

9. The ball goes **45 yards**. It is returned **10 yards**.

10. Your kicker is knocked down! **Keep the ball** and gain **10 yards**.

SUPPLEMENTARY ACTIVITY #1 TEACHER PAGE #2A

Five-Yard Questions

To avoid repeats, you may want to check off these questions as you use them.
Students can find the answers to these questions in their "Strength Word Dictionaries."
Correct answers are underlined.

MULTIPLE CHOICE
(In many cases both words are correct, but one is better.)

❑ What strength word would you use to describe someone who doesn't waste time when he has a job to do? **<u>Efficient</u> or organized?**

❑ What strength word would you use to describe someone who doesn't get upset when her friend takes a long time to get ready to go somewhere? **Sincere or <u>patient</u>?**

❑ What strength word would you use to describe a boy who notices when his friends are feeling down or discouraged? **Cooperative or <u>sensitive</u>?**

❑ What strength word would you use to describe a girl who finishes doing her chores before she goes to the soccer game? **<u>Dependable</u> or confident?**

❑ What strength word would you use to describe someone who dreams up a new design for a car and draws it? **<u>Imaginative</u> or independent?**

❑ What strength word would you use to describe someone who is able to do a backbend and can almost put both heels behind his head? **Graceful or <u>flexible</u>?**

❑ What strength word would you use to describe someone who completely finishes a job and doesn't leave some little part of it undone? **<u>Thorough</u> or thoughtful?**

❑ What strength word would you use to describe someone who works well in a group and doesn't always have to have her way? **Easy-going or <u>cooperative</u>?**

❑ What strength word would you use to describe someone who likes to try things he's never done before? **<u>Adventurous</u> or creative?**

❑ What strength word would you use to describe someone who likes to make a list of the jobs she has to do and scratch each one off as she finishes it? **Observant or <u>organized</u>?**

❑ What strength word would you use to describe someone who doesn't do what his friends are doing if he thinks it's not right or dumb? **Self-motivated or <u>self-disciplined</u>?**

❑ What strength word would you use to describe someone who tells the cashier at the corner store if he gives her too much change? **Considerate or <u>conscientious</u>?**

Five-Yard Questions (continued)

❑ What strength word would you use to describe someone who keeps working on a math problem even when he's gotten it wrong four times? **Persevering** or **reliable?**

❑ What strength word would you use to describe someone who practices her piano lessons even without being reminded? **Determined or self-motivated?**

❑ What strength word would you use to describe someone who got invited to go to a movie but went over to help his friend with his book report instead because his friend's report was due the next day? **Considerate or sincere?**

SHORT ANSWER

❑ What strength word would you use to describe someone who is almost always on time? **(punctual)**

❑ What strength word would you use to describe someone who saved her money for over eight months until she had enough to buy a new stereo tape player? **(thrifty)**

❑ What strength word would you use to describe someone who walked across a log over a stream even though he was scared he'd lose his balance? **(courageous)**

❑ What strength word would you use to describe someone who didn't turn against her friend even when he got in trouble? **(loyal)**

❑ What strength word would you use to describe someone who loves to dance, play sports, help out in his dad's store—anything so long as it's active? **(energetic)**

❑ What strength word would you use to describe someone who helps kids in her neighborhood work out their disagreements when they get mad at each other? **(a negotiator)**

❑ What strength word would you use to describe someone who stays calm when most of his friends are getting upset about this or that? **(easy-going)**

❑ What strength word would you use to describe someone who feels sure of herself and doesn't worry about giving a book report in front of the class or demonstrating a pass for her soccer team? **(confident)**

❑ What strength word would you use to describe someone who tells his friend not to give up, that she's making progress when the friend thinks she'll never learn all her times tables? **(encouraging)**

❑ What strength word would you use to describe someone who is completely fired-up about her team playing for the baseball championship next weekend? **(enthusiastic)**

Ten-Yard Questions

To avoid repeats, you may want to check off these questions as you use them.
You may or may not wish to allow students to use their "Strength Word Dictionaries" to
answer these Ten-Yard Questions. Questions from the "Challenging Strength Words"
handout (Supplementary Activity #5 from Lesson 3) should be reserved for students
who completed that exercise.
Correct answers are in parentheses.

SYNONYMS

❑ Give two strength words that could be used to describe someone you can trust
to do what he says he'll do. **(conscientious, dependable, reliable,
responsible, trustworthy)**

❑ Give two strength words that could be used to describe someone who thought
up a skit for her cooperative learning group to perform for their social studies
project. **(creative, imaginative, inventive, original)**

❑ Give two strength words that could be used to describe someone who notices
when a classmate in P.E. feels left out and asks him to join his team.
(considerate, sensitive, sympathetic, thoughtful)

❑ Give two strength words that could be used to describe someone who sticks
with a job and doesn't give up just because it's hard to do. **(persevering,
determined, thorough)**

❑ Name two strength words that could be used to describe someone who usually
looks on the bright side and expects things to work out for the best.
(confident, positive attitude)

SENTENCE COMPLETION

Show that you know the meaning of this strength word by completing this
sentence: ***"I could tell John/Sally was (strength word) because ____."***

(Use any strength word and write it below to avoid repeats.)

SUPPLEMENTARY ACTIVITY #1 TEACHER PAGE #3B

Ten-Yard Questions (continued)

 DEFINITIONS

For students using the "Challenging Strength Words" handout, select one of the words on that handout and ask the student to define it. For other students, choose a word from any of the other strength word handouts from this unit.

(To avoid repeats, you may wish to write below those words you've used.)

 SPELLING

Have students spell one of the words from one of the strength word handouts from this unit.

(To avoid repeats, you may wish to write below those words you've used.)

SUPPLEMENTARY ACTIVITY #1 HANDOUT #4

Ten-Yard Questions (continued)

 "CHALLENGING STRENGTH WORDS" HANDOUT MULTIPLE CHOICE QUESTIONS

❑ What strength word would you use to describe someone who was careful not to say things that would embarrass others? **Articulate or <u>tactful</u>?**

❑ What strength word would you use to describe someone who was always making people laugh? **<u>Witty</u> or a good communicator?**

❑ What strength word would you use to describe someone who was willing to listen to other people's ideas even if he didn't always agree with them? **Perceptive or <u>open-minded</u>?**

❑ What strength word would you use to describe someone who never took it for granted when someone did something nice for her? **<u>Appreciative</u> or supportive?**

❑ What strength word would you use to describe someone who was able to express his ideas in a very clear way? **Intuitive or <u>articulate</u>?**

❑ What strength word would you use to describe someone who was often able to get her cooperative learning group to agree with her ideas? **Persuasive or <u>persistent</u>?**

❑ What strength word would you use to describe someone who was able to sense what his friend was thinking or feeling even if the friend didn't say anything? **Resourceful or <u>intuitive</u>?**

❑ What strength word would you use to describe someone who was able to figure out a different way to put a model together when some of the parts were missing from the box? **Even tempered or <u>resourceful</u>?**

❑ What strength word would you use to describe someone who calmly explained to her little brother that he couldn't go outside in the snow without his shoes while the little brother was having a temper tantrum? **Empathetic or <u>tolerant</u>?**

❑ What strength word would you use to describe someone who is able to look at the plans for a birdhouse and imagine in his head how it will look when it's put together? **<u>A good visualizer</u> or self-reliant?**

FOOTBALL TEMPLATES

SUPPLEMENTARY ACTIVITY #2

Make a Path of Strength Words—Long Version
To Learn the Meaning of Some Words That Describe Strengths

Directions:

Begin at either starting shape. Look up the meaning of the first word in a dictionary. On another sheet of paper, write the word and what it means, and then write a short sentence using the word in a way that would help someone else understand its meaning.

When that's done, color the shape the word is in. Choose another word next to the last one, define it, and use it in a sentence. Keep doing this until you have colored a path to the finish line.

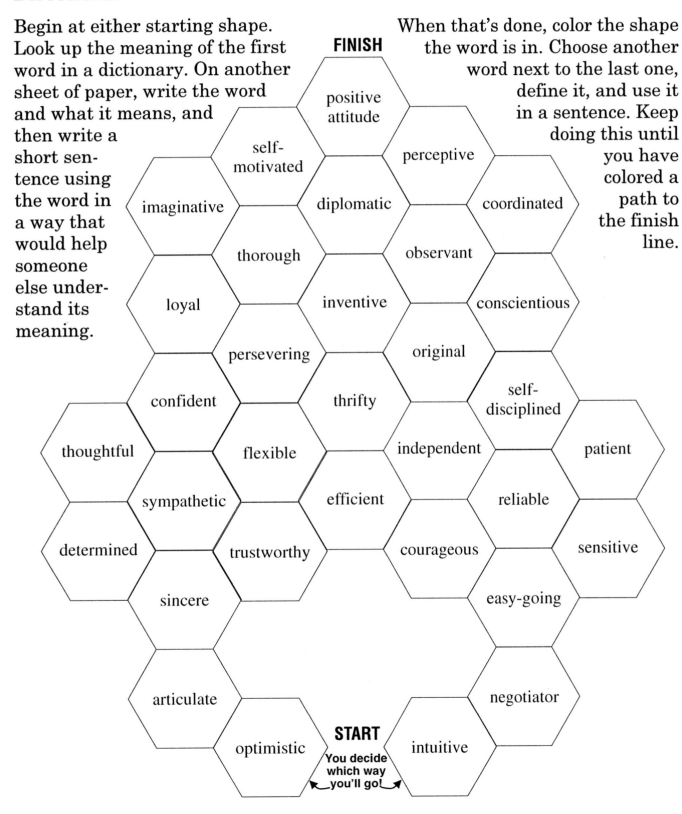

Word Jumble

Objective   Verbally talented students will practice matching "challenging strength words" to their definitions.

Materials   Supplementary Activity #5 Handout from Lesson 3 - "Challenging Strength Words"

Supplementary Activity #3 Handout #1 - "Word Jumble Puzzle"

Supplementary Activity #3 Handout #2 - "Word Jumble Clues"

Crayons or markers

For variation:

- Supplementary Activity #3 Handout #3 - "Blank Word Jumble"

Procedure   Distribute Supplementary Activity #3 Handouts #1 and #2. Have students read the directions on the clue page. As they answer the clues, they color in the appropriate strength word blocks on the puzzle page to reveal the hidden word. Tell them that the hidden word answers the question, "What is something we can use to identify our strengths?" (This hidden word is "WORD.")

VARIATION

Distribute Supplementary Activity #3 Handout #3. Talented students can make up word jumble games for each other by writing words from their "Challenging Strength Words" handout in various shapes on blank word jumble pages. They then should write clues below that are to be matched to the words above and colored according to their instructions. As an example, if a student made up the clue **"thinking in a positive way" (blue)**, then the shape containing the word **"optimistic"** would be colored blue by the student chosen to work the puzzle.

Students making puzzles should not try to create a hidden word or other hidden figure (it is quite difficult to adequately conceal such an item); it is better for the completed puzzle to simply produce a randomly colored pattern.

SUPPLEMENTARY ACTIVITY #3 HANDOUT #1

Word Jumble Puzzle

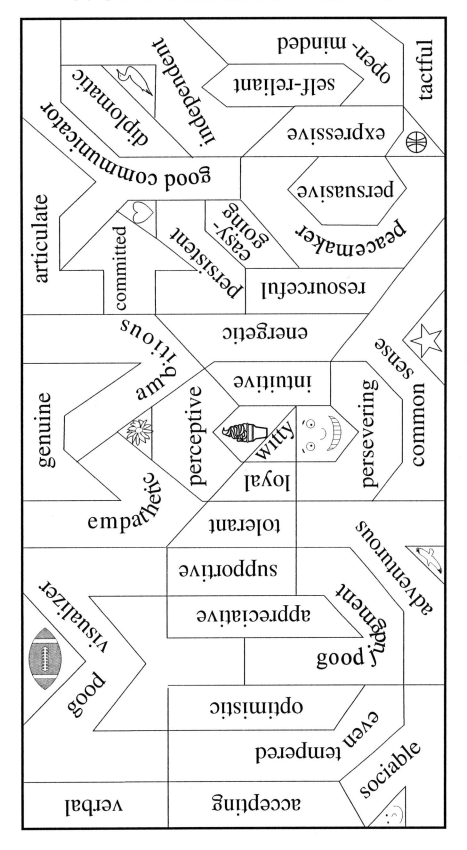

SUPPLEMENTARY ACTIVITY #3 HANDOUT #2

Word Jumble Clues

Directions:

Color the shapes in the Word Jumble Puzzle. Use the clues below to help you find the strength words. When all the shapes are colored, you will see the answer to the question: "What is something we can use to identify our strengths?"

- able to respect other people's ideas, beliefs, and behaviors (yellow)
- able to speak clearly and distinctly (blue)
- having practical judgment or intelligence (green)
- sticking with something even when it's difficult (black)
- willing to take chances; daring (red)
- working toward improvement or advancement (green)
- willing to give courage, help, or confidence to someone else (black)
- good with words (yellow)
- willing for others to be different; tolerant (red)

- skillful in dealing with other people; tactful (blue)
- humorous and amusing (yellow)
- getting along well with others; friendly (blue)
- able to know and understand without being told (black)
- able to give accurate messages by talking, writing, or using gestures (green)
- knowing how to say the right thing without offending someone (green)
- slow to get angry; calm (black)
- able to settle conflicts and disagreements between others (blue)
- able to work without direction; self-reliant (black)

- able to convince others to act or believe as you do (purple)
- grateful; thankful (yellow)
- faithful; trustworthy (black)
- dedicated; determined (red)
- able to continue with something in spite of difficulty; persistent (black)
- sincere, frank, and honest; authentic (red)
- able to form a mental picture of something not seen (blue)
- able to find ways to solve problems quickly (black)
- able to recover strength or good humor quickly; buoyant (red)

- willing to hear other ideas and opinions; free from prejudice (black)
- able to have a hopeful outlook (green)
- dependable, trustworthy (red)
- ability to figure out what is going on by observing (black)
- able to deal with matters in an unworried, unhurried manner (yellow)
- able to show feelings or to put feelings into words easily (black)
- able to feel what someone else is feeling (purple)
- having a lot of energy (red)
- able to make sensible decisions; wise (black)

SUPPLEMENTARY ACTIVITY #3 HANDOUT #3

Blank Word Jumble

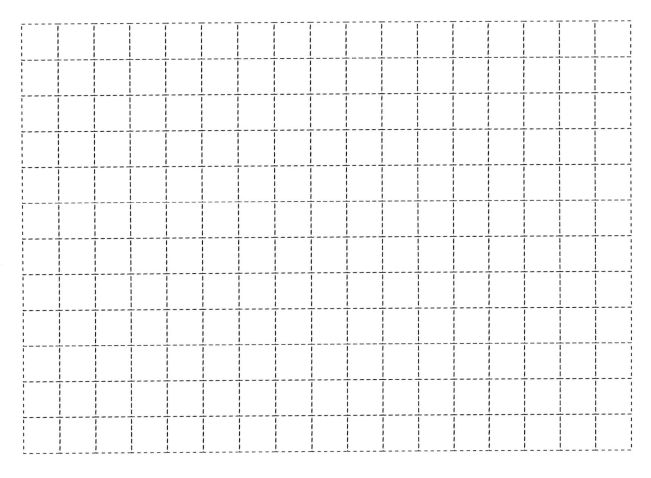

CLUES

_____

_____

_____

_____

_____

_____

_____

A Group Story Using Strength Word Synonyms

Objective   Students will work together to develop a story demonstrating their understanding of strength word synonyms.

Materials   Supplementary Activity #4 Handout - "A Group Story Using Strength Word Synonyms"

Procedure   For this exercise, have students work in cooperative learning groups of four or five students per group. Give each student a copy of the handout.

Explain that each of the words in the two boxes is a synonym for the phrase above the box. Each group will choose either "Kid A" or "Kid B." Their challenge is to work together to write a story about this kid which includes as many of the strength synonyms in the box as they can. For each synonym they include, they'll get one point—but **only** if the synonym is used correctly with an example in a complete sentence.

Set an appropriate time limit for the groups to work. When the time is up, ask each group to select a Reporter to read each group's story.

You can help students to select a Reporter by using the "1, 2, 3, point" method. Call out "1, 2, 3, point," and when you say the word "point," all the students point to the member of their groups they think should present their story. Whoever has the most fingers pointing at him or her is the Reporter in each group.

As the Reporters read the stories, check off the synonyms and award points to the groups as appropriate. The group earning the most points is the winner and may be awarded some special privilege, such as lining up first for lunch.

A Group Story Using Strength Word Synonyms

Kid A sticks with the job until he or she finishes it. He or she is:

determined	persevering
committed	dedicated
a hard worker	persistent
self-disciplined	

Kid B likes doing a really good job on things. He or she is:

organized	careful
a good researcher	conscientious
a good planner	prepared
thorough	
a kid who finishes things	

Using Small Groups for Practice in Detecting Strengths

Objective

Students will participate in small groups, sharing good experiences, practicing good listening skills, and using their new strength vocabulary words to identify others' strengths.

Students will become aware of their own strengths as perceived by others.

Students will continue to expand their repertoire of strength vocabulary words.

Materials

Transparency #6 from Lesson 1   -   "The Definition of a Good Experience"

Handouts #1A-#1C   -   "Strength Corners Game," cut apart into word strips

Transparency #1   -   "More Good Experiences I Remember—An Example"

Handout #2   -   "More Good Experiences I Remember"

Transparency #2   -   "Good Listening Skills"

Transparency #3/Handout #3   -   "Detect-the-Strengths Reports"

Transparency #4/Handout #4   -   "A Word Bank of Self Strengths—Long Version"

Transparency #5/Handout #5   -   "A Word Bank of People Strengths—Long Version"

Handout #6   -   "The Strengths That Keep You Moving!"

Handout #7   -   "Letter to Family Member"

Handout #8   -   "You're On the Ball!"

To the Teacher

In this lesson students have another opportunity to share their good experiences and to develop their ability to identify their own strengths and those of others using their new vocabulary words. This time the students will participate in a small group activity.

After a review of the definition of a good experience, students will participate in the "Strength Corners Game" to practice remembering good experiences and identifying strengths. The process used in previous lessons is reversed in this exercise, as strength words are presented as a stimulus for recalling good experiences. The game also serves as a review of new strength vocabulary words.

The "Detect-the-Truth Game" provides practice in listening well, identifying strengths in others' good experiences, and using new vocabulary words. Before beginning this small group activity, you'll prepare students in two ways: (1) you'll lead them through a short review and a practice exercise in the use of good listening skills, and (2) you'll structure a demonstration model of the small group process. It will be helpful to choose four articulate, analytical, and extroverted students to act out group roles in this demonstration group. These should be students you judge able to do a good job sharing and detecting strengths in others in a "fish bowl" format. If possible, have your class sitting in a circle around this small group.

You can help maintain class attention during this modeling by placing an empty chair in the group of four. Explain that after the listeners in the group have told the speaker the strengths they detected in his or her good experience, any student may go to the empty chair and suggest a strength that hasn't been mentioned.

If this "Detect-the-Truth Game" is well received in your class, you may wish to repeat it as a Supplementary Activity after the lesson.

To encourage family involvement and to facilitate input from an arena other than the classroom, students are asked to take a "homework assignment" to a family member.

The handouts and homework from this lesson will provide more input and "data" for students to use when they summarize their strengths in Lesson 6.

Lesson Presentation

Transp. #6 from Lesson 1

REVIEW OF PREVIOUS LESSON

We've been talking lately about our good experiences and looking for the strengths that helped us create those good experiences. Can someone remind us what we mean by a "good experience"? *Call on a student to reiterate that a good experience is: (1) something they feel they did well; and (2) something they felt proud of doing. (Show Transparency #6 from Lesson 1, "The Definition of a Good Experience," as part of this review.)*

We've been practicing finding other people's strengths by listening to their good experiences. Some of you were "Strength Detectives" at home, and you've been "Strength Detectives" in the classroom looking for strengths in one

another and filling out "Strength Detective Reports." You've also learned a lot of hard new strength vocabulary words that you can now use to describe each others' strengths.

THE "STRENGTH CORNERS GAME"

Today we're going to start our lesson by playing a game in which we practice remembering our good experiences. You're going to have a chance to look at several strength words and to try to remember a time you made a good experience for yourself by using that strength. The game is called the "Strength Corners Game," and this is how it's played.

Handout #1A
Handout #1B
Handout #1C

Choose six students to be "Corner Captains" and have them each draw one of the 18 strength word strips cut from Handouts #1A-#1C, "Strength Corners Game." The Corner Captains each take one strength word strip, along with notepaper and pencil, and go to a "corner" (or place along the side of the room) where they hold up their strength word strips so the rest of the class can see them. The rest of the class studies the six strength words until they think of a time they used one of these strengths to create a good experience for themselves. Then those students who remember using that particular strength go to that "corner" of the room and stand with the Corner Captain. (You may wish to specify a maximum number of students for each spot so one or two Corner Captains aren't inundated with students.)

The students each tell their Corner Captain about their good experience, and the Corner Captain takes notes. When the Captains feel they can summarize the good experiences of the students who came to their corner, they report aloud to the rest of the class, omitting students' names. Students raise their hands when they hear their good experiences summarized. After all the students' experiences have been summarized, the Corner Captains choose six new Corner Captains for the next round of the game. New Corner Captains each choose another strength word strip from the remaining twelve strips. (There are enough strength word strips for three rounds of play.)

After completing the game, say or paraphrase: **That was a lot of fun. You may have remembered a good experience you had forgotten about. Hold up your thumb if that happened to you.** *Allow students to hold up their thumbs.*

CHOOSING THREE FAVORITE GOOD EXPERIENCES

Transp. #1

I have a handout for you to complete right now. You're going to need it for a detective game we're going to play a little later on, so do your best on it. *Show Transparency #1, "More Good Experiences I Remember—An Example."*

I want you to think about some of the experiences you shared during the "Strength Corners Game," or any other good experiences you've remembered, and choose your three favorite ones to put in the bubbles on this handout I'm going to give you. This is the way one student completed the handout. *Read and discuss the three good experiences in the bubbles on the transparency.*

Handout #2

Put your <u>very most</u> **favorite good experience in the "Number 1 bubble," your next favorite in the "Number 2 bubble," and your third favorite in the "Number 3 bubble." You may either draw or write in the bubbles, and you can use any good experience you've ever had—but try to choose your top three favorites. Don't show your paper to anyone else.** *Distribute copies of Handout #2 (the same as the transparency). Give the students time to complete the handout.*

Now that you've drawn or written your top three good experiences, I want you to fold your papers so your Number 1 experience is covered. We're going to save that one for our detective game later. *Model the folding for the class.* **Now turn**

your paper over on your desk and let me tell you what we're going to do with your Number 2 and Number 3 experiences.

PRACTICING GOOD LISTENING SKILLS

Transp. #2

One of the things detectives have learned to be very good at is <u>listening</u>. They have to be able to listen very carefully for clues so that they can solve a crime or a mystery. We'll be doing some good listening when we play our detective game later, so we're going to practice a little bit right now. *Show Transparency #2, "Good Listening Skills," and uncover each guideline as you read and explain it. You may want to give an example of each one.*

Let's do some sharing now and practice these three good listening guidelines. I'll tell you about a good experience I've had and you can practice "good listening" on me. Remember to: look at me while I talk; ask me a question if you don't understand; and be ready to sum up what I tell you when I'm finished. *Tell the class one of your good experiences. Answer any questions, and then call on two or three students to paraphrase your good experience.*

That was very good listening. Now you can practice it with your Learning Partners. Decide which one of you is the shorter partner and let that person be the first speaker. The speaker will have about two to three minutes to tell the listener about the Number 3 good experience on his or her paper. The listener will look at the speaker, ask questions if he or she doesn't understand, and then sum up the speaker's good experience. The Learning Partners will then switch roles and practice again. We'll also do this with our Number 2 experience. Remember to <u>save</u> your Number 1 good experience for our detective game!

Give speakers two to three minutes to tell about their Number 3 good experience. Call "time" to remind those students who have not yet switched roles to do so. Have students repeat this sharing/listening process with their Number 2 good experience on their handouts.

THE "DETECT-THE-TRUTH GAME"

I think you're ready to play our detective game. This game is called the "Detect-the-Truth Game," and it's played in groups of four people. There are three roles in each group: the Speaker, who shares a good experience from the handout, two Detectives, and a Leader. The Leader will have to do two jobs at once, and I'll explain those in a minute. Everyone will have one chance to be the Speaker, and three chances to be a Detective. The Leader will be the same for the whole game.

WHAT THE SPEAKER DOES

When you are the <u>Speaker</u>, this is what you'll do: you'll tell two good experiences—one will be the good experience that was your Number 1 favorite experience on your handout, the one that we saved for this game, but the other good experience will be a <u>fake</u>! You'll <u>make up</u> a "good experience" to tell your group. You'll be trying to trick the Detectives by making your made-up experience sound just as real as your Number 1 favorite experience. The Detectives won't know if you're telling the real experience first or the fake one first. They'll have to use their detective skills to pick out the REAL Number 1 good experience.

WHAT THE DETECTIVES DO

After the Speaker has told his or her two good experiences, then the <u>Detectives</u> will have to do their detective work. When you're a Detective, this is what you'll do. First you'll listen carefully, using the good listening skills we practiced. Then the Leader will have each one of you ask the

Speaker <u>two</u> questions—one about each of the two good experiences. The Speaker can make up an answer about the fake experience, but he or she <u>has to tell the truth</u> about the Number 1 good experience.

WHAT THE LEADER DOES

The person who is the <u>Leader</u> will help the Detectives take turns asking their two questions. After all of the Detectives have asked their questions, then the Leader will ask each Detective, "Which experience do <u>you</u> guess was the real one?" The Detectives will answer, "I think the REAL good experience was _____," telling which one he or she thinks was the true experience.

After each of the Detectives has guessed, then the Speaker will say, "I REALLY DID _____," and tell his or her group which was his or her true good experience.

ADDITIONAL DUTIES OF THE DETECTIVES

Transp. #3

Whether you were right or wrong, Detectives, you'll still have some more detective work to do. You'll need to try to guess the <u>strengths</u> the speaker used to create the Number 1 good experience. When you've guessed these strengths, you'll fill out a "Detect-the-Strengths Report." It looks like this. *Put Transparency #3, "Detect-the-Strengths Reports," on the overhead, modeling how to fill one out.*

**Transp. #4
Transp. #5**

Detectives, you'll write the name of the person you're reporting on here. *Indicate the blank box.* Then you'll think about the Speaker's REAL good experience and try to detect the strengths that you think were hidden in it. I'll give all the Detectives special longer versions of the "Self Strengths" and "People Strengths" lists so you can choose really good strength words to write on your "Detect-the-Strengths Reports." *Show Transparency #4, "A Word Bank of Self*

Strengths—Long Version," and Transparency #5, "A Word Bank of People Strengths—Long Version." **These two lists contain** all **the strength words in your "Strength Word Dictionaries."**

When you start thinking about which strengths the Speaker used to create his or her Number 1 good experience, the first thing you'll do is decide if the Speaker used self strengths or people strengths. then you'll look at either your "self strengths" or "people strengths" word bank list and choose the strengths you think the Speaker used from that strength word list. When you've picked some really good words, write them here where it says, "The strengths I detected." *Indicate the appropriate blank box on the transparency.* **At the top of your report, write your name.** *Indicate the appropriate writing line.*

ADDITIONAL DUTIES OF THE LEADER

The Leader **will do everything the other Detectives do and will also take a turn as Speaker. If you're the Leader, you'll also have extra jobs to do: You'll help everyone remember to take turns speaking and asking questions; and you'll also call on people when it's their turn to talk or ask questions, see that all the reports are filled out, and model good group behavior for the rest of the group. You'll have a big job!**

PRACTICING THE GAME WITH A SMALL GROUP

Handout #3
Handout #4
Handout #5

Are there three people who'd like to help me demonstrate the game for the rest of the class? I'll be the Speaker. I'm going to try to make up a really good fake experience and I'll also tell my true Number 1 experience. The Detectives' job will be really hard, because they won't know which one I'm telling first! I need three Detectives who think they can figure out which of my experiences is the REAL good experience. *Choose three volunteers and give them each a copy of*

Handout #3, "Detect-the-Strengths Reports," as well as Handouts #4 and #5, the two "word bank" lists. They will also need pencils.

If possible, conduct this demonstration in the center of the class. Model telling two good experiences for the class, one real and one made up. Also model the role of the Leader. Help the volunteer Detectives ask good questions. Model repeating the REAL good experience at the end of the guessing period by saying, "I REALLY DID _____." Emphasize the importance of discerning the Speaker's strengths and of choosing strength words from the "word bank" lists, so that the main objective of identifying strengths is not lost in the fun of the game.

PLAYING THE "DETECT-THE-TRUTH GAME" IN SMALL GROUPS

Thanks to our volunteers for giving us this demonstration. Now it's time to break into our groups so everyone can play.

Divide students into groups of four, making sure the demonstration group is split up. Designate a capable Leader in each group. See that each student has a copy of the "Detect-the-Strengths Reports" handout, the two "word bank" handouts, and a pencil.

Circulate around the room, guiding students through the game process when necessary. The "Detect-the-Strengths Reports" should be returned to the Speakers at the end of the game.

GROUP EXPERIENCE DEBRIEFING

To debrief the small group experience, ask students some of the following questions:

- **When you were the Speaker, were you able to make up a fake good experience that was real enough to trick the Detectives?**

- Speakers, did you agree with the strengths the Detectives thought you had?

- Did you discover you had some strengths you hadn't thought about?

- Detectives, what strengths did you discover about the Speaker that you didn't know he or she had?

- Detectives, did you use any really good strength words from your "word bank" lists?

- Leaders, how did your group do at taking turns and filling out their reports?

Have students add any strengths to their own "Detect-the-Strengths Reports" which they feel helped them have their true good experience; ask all students to put their reports in their "Strengths Folders."

PREVIEW OF NEXT LESSON AND HOMEWORK ASSIGNMENT

Our "Strengths Folders" are getting full of all kinds of materials! That's good, because in the next lesson you'll be using all of the materials in your folders to create a summary of your strengths.

Handout #6

I have a homework page for you, and I also have a homework page for your parents! First let me tell you about yours. *Give students Handout #6, "The Strengths That Keep You Moving."* You can use the good experiences from the handout you did today, "More Good Experiences I Remember," or you can think of others that are important to you. Write a few words to describe both experiences on the lines above the car. Use your "word bank" lists to help you pick just the right words to describe your main strengths. Write those strength words on the four lines behind the car—those are the strengths that give you POWER, that keep you moving!

And now for your family members' homework! Won't they be surprised to find out that <u>they</u> have homework? *Distribute Handout #7, "Letter to Family Member," and Handout #8, "You're On the Ball!"* The people in your family know a lot about you and they can help you discover your strengths. Write your name at the top of the handout where it says "Your name," and take it home for someone in your family to fill out. It can be a parent, a big brother or sister, an aunt or uncle, a grandparent—anyone you choose. They'll write down two strengths they see in you and a time when they saw you use each strength. We'll put this soccer ball in your "Strengths Folder" and use it when we make a summary of all your strengths in our next lesson.

SUPPLEMENTARY ACTIVITIES

Use the Supplementary Activities at the end of this lesson to provide additional practice of lesson concepts:

- *"Buddy Strength Mobiles"*
  (Supplementary Activity #1)

- *"The Person, Place, and Strength Game"*
  (Supplementary Activity #2)

HANDOUT #1A

Strength Corners Game

artistic

athletic

brave

coordinated

determined

fair

HANDOUT #1B

Strength Corners Game (continued)

fast

friendly

generous

good with words

hard worker

helpful

HANDOUT #1C

Strength Corners Game (continued)

imaginative

kind

musical

organized

problem solver

responsible

TRANSPARENCY #1

More Good Experiences I Remember—An Example

Directions:

Draw three of your good experiences in the thought balloons.

HANDOUT #2

More Good Experiences I Remember

Directions:

Draw three of your good experiences in the thought balloons.

TRANSPARENCY #2

Good Listening Skills

1. Face the person who is talking and look at him or her.

2. Ask questions if you don't understand.

3. Sum up what the person said to show that you understand.

My good experience was . . . .

TRANSPARENCY #3/HANDOUT #3

Detect-the-Strengths Reports

D E T E C T - T H E - S T R E N G T H S R E P O R T

BY: _____

Name of person reporting about:

The strengths I detected:

D E T E C T - T H E - S T R E N G T H S R E P O R T

BY: _____

Name of person reporting about:

The strengths I detected:

D E T E C T - T H E - S T R E N G T H S R E P O R T

BY: _____

Name of person reporting about:

The strengths I detected:

TRANSPARENCY #4/HANDOUT #4

A Word Bank of Self Strengths—Long Version

adventurous	fast	observant
artistic	finishes things	organized
athletic	flexible	original
		outdoorsy
brave	good memory	
	good thinker	persevering
clever	graceful	positive attitude
confident		problem solver
conscientious	hard worker	
coordinated		responsible
courageous	imaginative	
creative	independent	self-disciplined
	inventive	self-motivated
determined		strong
	musical	
efficient		talented
energetic	neat	thrifty
enthusiastic		thorough

TRANSPARENCY #5/HANDOUT #5

A Word Bank of People Strengths—Long Version

caring	loyal
cheerful	
considerate	negotiator
cooperative	nice
dependable	outgoing
easy-going	patient
encouraging	polite
	punctual
fair	
friendly	reliable
funny	
	sensitive
generous	sharing
good listener	sincere
good sport	sympathetic
good with words	
	thoughtful
helpful	trustworthy
honest	
	understanding
kind	unselfish

HANDOUT #6

The Strengths That Keep You Moving!

Directions:
Write **two** of your top good experiences below.

1. _____

2. _____

Now write the strengths that helped you create those good experiences—the ones that kept you moving!

1. _____

2. _____

3. _____

4. _____

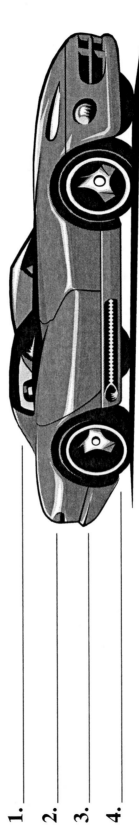

JUST FOR FUN:
Design a license plate that would let people know what your top strengths are.

HANDOUT #7

Letter to Family Member

Dear Family Member,

I am currently teaching some lessons in which the students are learning ways to identify their strengths. While not overlooking the students' needs to overcome their weaknesses, there is much to be gained from helping children understand and appreciate their talents and abilities.

The students are learning to identify their unique combination of strengths by examining their good experiences. They are encouraged to think about and share events of which they are proud. Then they are helped to find the strengths they used to create these good experiences.

By communicating the strengths you see in your child, you can help build self- confidence and increase his or her motivation to improve. A good way to help your child believe in his or her strengths is to point out specific times when you saw these strengths being used. The attached sheet provides space for you to do this. If you will fill this out, we will use the strengths you identify, along with those identified by classmates and adults at school, to help your child create a list of his or her top strengths.

Use any of the following categories to spark ideas about your child's strengths: school subjects or activities; sports; creative, artistic, or musical activities; friendships; family life; work or chores; or hobbies. Here are some examples of comments other parents have made:

> *Strength*: Good Sport
> *A time it was used:* I heard you say "Good game!" to the other team even though you felt bad about losing.

> *Strength*: Sense of Humor
> *A time it was used:* You have a great way of getting us all laughing—like you did last night about the burnt broccoli.

> *Strength*: Good With Your Hands
> *A time it was used:* I'm amazed at the way you can fix things.
> You put that broken model together and it looks like new.

You might want to set aside regular times for focusing on the strengths or positive qualities of all your family members. These times can be during family dinners or on birthdays or holidays. After experiencing having their strengths pointed out to them, children are usually able to name strengths of others.

Thank you for helping remind your child that you honor his or her diverse talents and skills.

Sincerely,

HANDOUT #8

You're On the Ball!

Directions:

Your family members probably know a lot about your strengths. Ask a member of your family to write in the spaces on the ball two of your strengths and a time they saw you use them.

Your name _____

STRENGTH:
_____
_____

A time it was used:_____
_____
_____
_____
_____
_____

The person
who identified
these strengths is:

_____
_____
_____

STRENGTH:
_____

A time it was used: _____
_____
_____
_____
_____

SUPPLEMENTARY ACTIVITY #1

Buddy Strength Mobiles

Objective

Students will acknowledge each other's strengths by creating a mobile that identifies the strengths of a fellow classmate.

Materials

Handouts #1A-#1E from Lesson 3 - "Strength Word Dictionary"

Index cards or squares of heavy paper, each with a different student's name (one for each student) written on both sides. These cards should also have a hole punched in the center at the top and bottom of the card so the mobile will hang straight (see illustration).

String or yarn

Squares of construction paper, two or three for each student

Dark colored markers or crayons

Procedure

Prepare students for this activity by telling them that you are pleased to see everyone in class working hard to make the class a comfortable and safe place for all students to discover their strengths. In this activity, students will each help a classmate to discover some of his or her strengths.

Each student will be assigned another classmate as their "buddy." Do this by passing out the index cards or squares of heavy paper you've prepared with student names on both sides. Be sure that those students whose strengths may be less obvious are assigned to your more compassionate or perceptive students.

Give each student several pieces of string or yarn and two (or three) squares of colored construction paper. Have the students look carefully through their "Strength Word Dictionaries" to choose two (or three) strength words that sound the **most** like their "buddy." When the students choose these strengths they must be sure they can think of a time when their "buddy" used that strength; later they'll be asked to tell these examples to the class to help explain their choices. Tell the students you'll help anyone who is having difficulty deciding on words or thinking of examples.

When students have decided on the two (or three) words, they should write each word on a different paper square, writing the same word on both sides. Have students string the squares of paper together with the buddy's name at the top. After the students have finished the mobiles, have them each stand before the class with their buddy and tell which strengths they chose for his or her mobile and why, presenting the mobile to their buddy before they both sit down.

SUPPLEMENTARY ACTIVITY #2

The Person, Place, and Strength Game

Objective
Students will practice thinking of ways that strengths can be used to create good experiences.

Materials
Blank transparency and pen (optional)

Supplementary Activity #2 Card Page #1 - "Person Cards"

Supplementary Activity #2 Card Page #2 - "Place Cards"

Supplementary Activity #2 Card Page #3 - "Strength Cards—Easy Words"

Supplementary Activity #2 Card Page #4 - "Strength Cards—Hard Words"

Supplementary Activity #2 Card Page #5 - "Strength Cards—Harder Words"

Supplementary Activity #2 Card Page #6 - "Strength Cards—Hardest Words"

Procedure
The basic game is played as follows:

The students draw one card from each of the three piles. The first card will identify a person. The second card will name a place. The third card names a particular strength. The students' task is to make up a scenario describing how they could use the **strength word** they drew to create a good experience in the **place** named on the card and with the **person** named on the card. For example, if the strength drawn was "generous," the place "the playground," and the person "someone you don't usually play with," the scenario might be that the student used the strength of being generous to invite another student he or she doesn't know well to join a game on the playground. As a result, the student made a new friend.

The game can be played in a number of ways. For example:

VARIATION 1

Ask a student to draw one place, one person, and one strength card. Write the contents of each card on the chalkboard or overhead. Ask for student volunteers to suggest scenarios using the place, the person, and the strength written on the chalkboard or overhead.

VARIATION 2

The students can be divided into small cooperative learning groups. Each group can draw a card from each pile and then use the person, place, and strength card drawn to present a scenario or role-play describing a good experience to the class.

VARIATION 3

Divide the class into two teams and play the game as a relay. A member from each team takes turns drawing the three cards and coming up with a scenario that uses the strength to create a good experience involving the person and place on the card. If the team member can do it, a point is gained for his or her team. Or students from each team could work in pairs to try to gain a point for their team in this manner.

SUPPLEMENTARY ACTIVITY #2 CARD PAGE #1

Person Cards

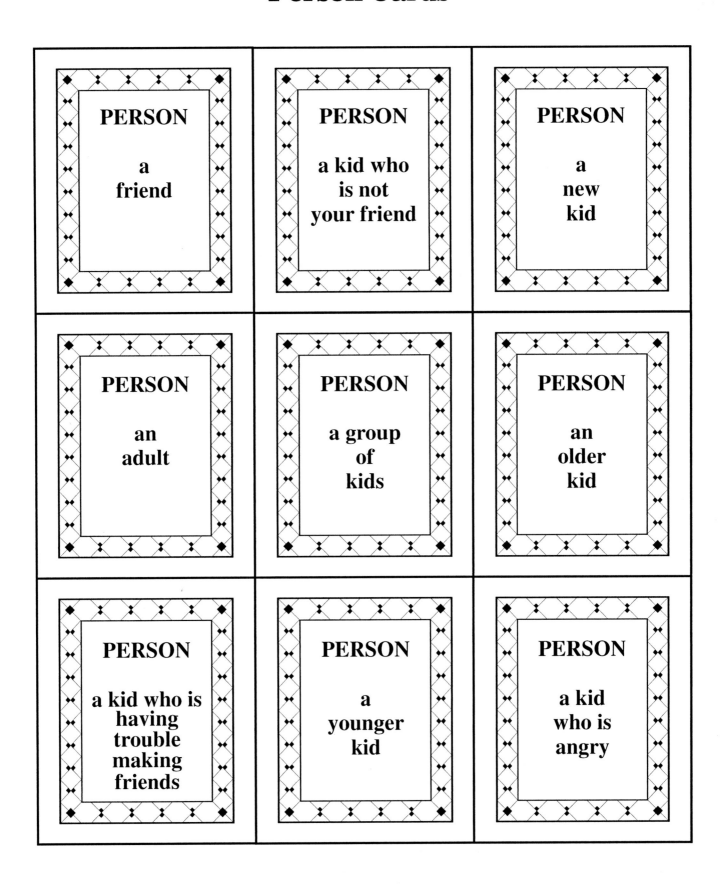

PERSON a friend	**PERSON** a kid who is not your friend	**PERSON** a new kid
PERSON an adult	**PERSON** a group of kids	**PERSON** an older kid
PERSON a kid who is having trouble making friends	**PERSON** a younger kid	**PERSON** a kid who is angry

SUPPLEMENTARY ACTIVITY #2 CARD PAGE #2

Place Cards

PLACE

in
your
classroom

PLACE

on the
playground

PLACE

in the
lunchroom

PLACE

at a
friend's
house

PLACE

at an
after school
activity

PLACE

at a
park

PLACE

at your
house

PLACE

at a
party

PLACE

on
vacation

SUPPLEMENTARY ACTIVITY #2 CARD PAGE #3

Strength Cards—Easy Words

STRENGTH helpful EASY	**STRENGTH** forgiving EASY	**STRENGTH** good sport EASY
STRENGTH fair EASY	**STRENGTH** caring EASY	**STRENGTH** generous EASY
STRENGTH understanding EASY	**STRENGTH** brave EASY	**STRENGTH** kind EASY

SUPPLEMENTARY ACTIVITY #2 CARD PAGE #4

Strength Cards—Hard Words

STRENGTH cheerful HARD	**STRENGTH** considerate HARD	**STRENGTH** honest HARD
STRENGTH problem solver HARD	**STRENGTH** patient HARD	**STRENGTH** unselfish HARD
STRENGTH good sport HARD	**STRENGTH** cooperative HARD	**STRENGTH** imaginative HARD

SUPPLEMENTARY ACTIVITY #2 CARD PAGE #5

Strength Cards—Harder Words

STRENGTH encouraging HARDER	**STRENGTH** self- disciplined HARDER	**STRENGTH** positive attitude HARDER
STRENGTH outgoing HARDER	**STRENGTH** truthful HARDER	**STRENGTH** supportive HARDER
STRENGTH peacemaker HARDER	**STRENGTH** wise HARDER	**STRENGTH** gentle HARDER

SUPPLEMENTARY ACTIVITY #2 CARD PAGE #6

Strength Cards—Hardest Words

STRENGTH diplomatic HARDEST	**STRENGTH** genuine HARDEST	**STRENGTH** tactful HARDEST
STRENGTH optimistic HARDEST	**STRENGTH** empathetic HARDEST	**STRENGTH** loyal HARDEST
STRENGTH negotiator HARDEST	**STRENGTH** open-minded HARDEST	**STRENGTH** sense of humor HARDEST

Creating a Summary of Strengths

Objective

Students will learn to avoid common ways of discounting their strengths.

Students will discern their most dependable strengths with the help of their teacher and peers.

Materials

Transparencies #1A and #1B - "Things We Say to Ourselves That Stop Us From Believing In Our Strengths"

Transparency #2 - "A Summary of My Strengths—An Example"

Handout #1 - "A Summary of My Strengths"

Transparency #3A/Handout #2A and Transparency #3B/Handout #2B - "Strengths That Just Keep Showing Up!"

Handout #3 - "My Strengths Forms" (cut apart)

Poster #1 - "Remind Yourself of Your Strengths"

"Strengths Folders" (each student's)

Post-It Notes or paper squares

Index cards (optional)

To the Teacher

The main objective of this lesson is for students to determine their most dependable strengths. Because it is a common practice for humans to discount their own and others' strengths, this lesson begins with an overview of four common strength discounting errors and ways to avoid them. Students then complete work-sheets that enable them to assess which strengths seem to occur most frequently in association with their good experiences.

As part of this assessment, students are asked to look for patterns of strengths by filling out a "strength grid" that reflects the data in their good experiences handouts. For most people it takes many years to discover truly "dependable" strengths; these cannot usually be discerned until a person reaches the last years of high school. Although your students will not have acquired the abstract thinking skills needed to analyze their strengths for consistent patterns, they may be able to see the beginnings of strengths that will become "dependable strengths" at a later time.

After students have completed their "assessment" handouts, you will meet with each of them in a small group setting to review the work in their "Strengths Folders" and their final assessment sheets. At that time an effort will be made to reach a group consensus as to the three or four recurring strengths that seem to be present in each student's good experiences. These groups have the potential of making a significant impact on students' self-esteem, as students experience the attention of you and their peers working with them to discern their main strengths. This group activity can also create a bond between students and build a sense of good will and community within the classroom.

After a summary of strengths has been completed for each student, you may wish to capitalize on it by allowing the students to print their strengths on index cards and then tape these to their desks. The students can write the cards in the form of "I'm a kid who is . . ." or some similar "I statement." You can remind the students to read these statements to themselves a few times each day. Putting up the poster, "Remind Yourself of Your Strengths," will also serve as a reminder. The "strengths summary" handout will also be used in Lesson 7 as the students prepare a formal presentation of their strengths.

Lesson Presentation

REVIEW OF HOMEWORK

For homework, you looked at two of your good experiences and decided which strengths you thought helped you have those good experiences. *Have the students that out their homework page entitled, "The Strengths That Keep You Moving!" (Handout #6 from Lesson 5).* **Would anyone like to share one of their good experiences and the strengths that keep them moving?** *Allow for student response.* **Would anyone like to describe or show us the license plate they designed to "sum up" their strengths?**

LESSON OVERVIEW

Today we're going to do something important with our "Strengths Folders"—we're going to use all the things we've been saving in them to help us discover our top three or four strengths. These are the strengths we use over and over, the strengths that we can usually count on to help create good experiences for ourselves.

We're also going to meet in small groups. We'll share our soccer ball handouts with our groups and talk about the strengths our families have been finding in our good experiences. The group members will all help each other pick out their very best strengths.

SOMETIMES WE SAY THINGS THAT STOP US FROM BELIEVING IN OUR STRENGTHS

Finding your strengths can be a lot of fun—but did you know that finding their strengths is <u>hard</u> for some kids? Even though they're very good at some things and have some very important strengths, some kids say things to themselves that keep them from believing in their strengths. Let me tell you about some of the things kids tell themselves so that they don't believe in their strengths.

ERROR #1: IF I DON'T DO IT WELL EVERY TIME, IT'S NOT A REAL STRENGTH

**Transp. #1A
Transp. #1B**

Use Post-It Notes or paper squares to cover the thought bubbles on Transparencies #1A and #1B, "Things We Say to Ourselves That Stop Us From Believing In Our Strengths," and put #1A on the overhead projector. Point to the boy at the top of the transparency. This is Arturo. One day after P.E. he put the sports equipment away without being asked. The coach noticed what he had done and said, "You're so <u>thoughtful</u>, Arturo! You always try to help out." Arturo started to smile, but then he remembered that he'd left for school that morning without taking out the trash for his mother. Instead of feeling good about what the coach said, <u>this is what Arturo said to himself to keep himself from believing in his strength.</u> *Uncover the top left-hand bubble and read:* "<u>I'm not that way ALL the time.</u>"

How many of you have ever done what Arturo did—told yourself you really weren't good at something just because you weren't good at it every single time? Would anyone like to tell us about a time you said, "I'm not that way all the time," to yourself when you or someone else noticed a strength? *Allow for student response. (You may need to tell an experience of your own to remind the students that it's safe to share.)*

The truth is that you can have a strength even though you don't use it every time. What if one of your strengths is that you're brave? Let's say that you're usually willing to try new things, but one time you were afraid to try something. Does that one time mean you can't say that one of your strengths is being brave? *Pause.* Of course not! No one is perfect all the time!

So, if Arturo finds himself thinking, "I'm not that way all the time," what can he think instead that will help him to believe in his strength? *Allow for student response. Uncover the right-hand though bubble above Arturo's smiling face and read his thought aloud:* "<u>NOBODY's perfect all the time!</u>" *Ask for the students to suggest other similar things to say and write these above Arturo's head.* When someone feels that he or she must not <u>really</u> have a strength because once in awhile they don't use it, these are the kinds of thoughts they can think to help them realize that the strength really is there.

ERROR #2: IF I'M NOT THE BEST AT IT, IT'S NOT A REAL STRENGTH

Now, let me tell you about Georgina. Georgina also stops herself from believing in her strengths. She loves to do math and she's quite good at it. But when the other kids in the class praise her for how many problems she gets right, do you know what Georgina says to herself? *Uncover the lower left-hand thought bubble and read:* "<u>He's BETTER at it than I am.</u>" That's right! Because there's someone in Georgina's class who can do math even better than she can, she doesn't let herself believe in her math strength.

Raise your hand if you've ever stopped yourself from be-lieving you were good at something just because someone else was even better at it than you were. *Allow for a show of hands.* **There will <u>always</u> be people who are better than you at some things! It's not necessary to compare yourself with others to decide if you have a strength or not. You can be proud of something because you've done it better than <u>you</u> ever have before!**

Can you give Georgina some ideas of things she could say to herself to help her believe in her strength? *Allow for student response. Then uncover the second thought bubble above Georgina smiling and read aloud:* **"<u>Just because HE's good at it, that doesn't mean it's not MY strength, too!</u>"** *You may also want to add some of the students' responses above Georgina's head.* **If Georgina will think these kinds of thoughts, she'll be able to believe in her strengths.**

ERROR #3: MY STRENGTH ISN'T REAL IF OTHERS DON'T SEE IT

Transp. #1B

Put Transparency #1B on the overhead. **There's something else we often say to ourselves to keep ourselves from believing in our strengths. Yasir does this one.** *Point to Yasir.* **Yasir is a pretty good ball-player. He's really good at stealing bases, is a fair hitter, and he's a <u>great</u> fielder. One day Yasir caught a fly ball and a teammate yelled, "You're a great ball-player, Yasir!"**

Yasir <u>could</u> have felt good about his strength, but he imme-diately remembered a time last week when a couple of other kids made fun of the way he swung when he was at bat. <u>Those</u> kids had said he was terrible. So this is what Yasir thought to himself. *Uncover the upper left-hand thought bubble and read:* **"<u>SOME PEOPLE think I'm not very good at this</u>." Yasir didn't feel good about his playing that day; all he could think of was what those other kids had said. How**

many of you have ever kept yourself from believing in your strengths the way Yasir did? *Ask the students to raise a thumb if they've ever been criticized by a person about something they were usually pretty good at doing.* It's not a good idea to let a few people cause you to decide you're not good at something. You need to pay at least as much attention to the people who <u>do</u> think you have a strength as you do to the people who say you <u>don't</u>. What are some things Yasir could have thought to himself instead? *Allow for student response. Uncover the thought bubble above Yasir smiling and read aloud:* "<u>There are OTHER people who think I AM good at it!</u>" *Write the students' responses above Yasir as well.* If Yasir will tell himself these kinds of things, he'll be able to believe in his strengths.

ERROR #4: THINGS THAT COME EASILY AREN'T REAL STRENGTHS

There's one more thing that people often say to themselves that stops them from believing in their strengths. Look at Yoriko. She's so flexible she can do a handstand and then go on over into a backbend! She's also better at jump rope than anyone else in her grade. But do you know what Yoriko says to herself when her classmates compliment her? *Uncover the lower left-hand thought bubble and read aloud:* "<u>This can't be a REAL strength because I don't even have to TRY hard.</u>" How many of you have ever told yourself that something that was easy for you wasn't a real strength? *Allow for a show of hands.*

Something doesn't have to be hard for you to do in order for it to be a strength. If you use that strength to create good experiences for yourself, it's <u>very valuable</u>. Be happy that you have a natural talent! Who can think of some things Yoriko could tell herself instead? *Allow for student response. Uncover the thought bubble above Yoriko smiling and read aloud:* "<u>Something doesn't have to be hard for me to do</u>

<u>for me to feel good about it!</u>" *Write the students' responses above Yoriko's head as well.* **If Yoriko will tell herself these kinds of things, she can feel good about her natural talent!**

SUMMARY

We've seen that there are many things you can think or say to yourself that put down your strengths and keep you from feeling good about them. As you look through your "Strengths Folders" today, try to take a fair look at the strengths others thought they saw in you. Don't eliminate a strength just because: *(point to the left-hand thought bubbles on the two transparencies as you say)* (1) you're not that way all the time, (2) someone else is better at it, (3) someone else doesn't think you have the strength, or (4) it's easy for you. You gave Arturo, Georgina, Yasir, and Yoriko good advice today. Remember it for yourselves when you're looking for your own strengths.

PREPARING A SUMMARY OF STRENGTHS

Today we're going to spend some time looking at all the things in our "Strengths Folders" and making a careful decision about our best strengths—those strengths that we use over and over to create good experiences for ourselves. This will be very valuable information, so we're going to take our time and do a good job of it.

In our last lesson you picked your top three favorite good experiences and put them on a handout, "More Good Experiences I Remember" *(Handout #2 from Lesson 5)*. We're going to start our search for our top strengths by looking at that page. Will you take it out of your "Strengths Folders" please? *Give the students time to retrieve their handouts.*

I'd like you to think one more time about all the good experiences you remember having. You'll want to look at the three top experiences on this handout, and you'll want to think about the other good experiences you listed on some of your other handouts—"My Trail of Good Experiences" *(Handout #1 from Lesson 1),* "Memory Triggers for Good Experiences" *(Handout #3 from Lesson 1),* and "Good Experiences I'd Forgotten About Until Now" *(Handout #3 from Lesson 2).*

Transp. #2

Show Transparency #2, "A Summary of My Strengths—An Example." I'm going to give you another handout that looks just like this, where you'll list your five <u>all-time best</u> good experiences. After you've written down each of your five very best good experiences, think very carefully about the strengths you used to create those good experiences and list them next to the experience. Try to list two or three strengths for each experience, the way this person did. *Read each good experience on the transparency and its corresponding strengths.*

After you've written your five best good experiences *(point to these on the transparency)* and listed the strengths you used to make them happen *(point to them),* I want you to do something else: Read over all the strengths you've listed *(point to the column on the right)* and choose <u>the three or four you are most proud of</u>. Remember—this ISN'T bragging. This is noticing something TRUE about yourself and feeling good about it! Write those three or four favorite strengths here at the bottom of the page. *Indicate the lines on the transparency.*

Handout #1

Discovering your top strengths is very important, so you'll want to take your time and think about it carefully. You may want to use your "word bank" lists from your "Strengths Folders" to refresh your memory of strength words. *Distribute Handout #1, "A Summary of My Strengths."*

Allow the students time to complete the handout. Circulate around the room to help less organized students sort through their various handouts.

NOTING STRENGTHS WHICH REOCCUR

When the students have completed their handouts, say, **I've been glad to see how hard you've been working at looking through all your good experiences to find your top strengths.**

Now I'm going to ask you to look at your strengths in a different way. This next handout will help you to see if you have some strengths that show up again and again. These often can turn out to be strengths of yours that you'll be able to depend on to help you do new things.

Transp. #3A
Transp. #3B

This is what the handout will look like. *Show Transparency #3A, "Strengths That Just Keep Showing Up!"* **Across the top of the handout are the titles of most of the pages in your "Strengths Folders."** *Read these titles aloud.* **In a minute you'll take out each of these and look for the strengths listed on them.**

If, for example, you show yourself being coordinated in sports on your "My Trail of Good Experiences" handout, you'll put a little line next to the word "coordinated" under column 1. If one of the "Strength Detective Reports" in your "Strengths Folder" says you used the strength of being "artistic," you'll put a little line next to "artistic" under "Strength Detective Reports," or column 6. *Model putting a tally mark on the transparency. Then show Transparency #3B.* **If your soccer ball handout says you have the strength of being "helpful," you'll put a tally mark in the "helpful" box under "You're On the Ball!", or column 8.** *Model this and continue modeling until your class understands how to survey the handouts in their "Strengths Folders" and tally the strengths listed* *in each on this handout.* **When you're finished, you may see that some of your strengths keep showing up again and again.**

Handout #2A
Handout #2B

Give students Handouts #2A and #2B, "Strengths That Just Keep Showing Up!" and allow them time for completion of this survey. Circulate around the room to answer questions and assist those students who are experiencing difficulty with this task of organizing information.

If there is not sufficient time for the following small group activity, you may wish to stop the lesson at this point and continue with the activity next time.

MEETING IN SMALL GROUPS

If you have the option of training three or four parents to facilitate small groups, all students can be involved in the following small group activity at once. If not, meet with one group at a time while the rest of the class works on an academic assignment or a Supplementary Activity from one of the lessons at their desks. Small groups can consist of five to six students. Instruct the students to bring their complete "Strengths Folders" to their group, as well as the two handouts they just completed: "A Summary of My Strengths" and "Strengths That Just Keep Showing Up!"

Handout #3

Look through each group member's "Strengths Folder," giving special attention to its contents and taking notes on scratch paper or writing directly on a copy of Handout #3, "My Strengths Forms," for each student. Read the student's handout "You're On the Ball!" aloud to the group and make positive comments about what the family member has written about the student. Also read aloud particularly complimentary "Strength Detective Reports." Survey the two handouts, "A Summary of My Strengths" and "Strengths That Just Keep Showing Up!", and compare them to feedback the student has received from others.

Involve both the student and the other group members in reaching a consensus about the student's top three or four strengths, saying, for example:

- *"Joshua, I see 'hard worker' mentioned in three of your 'Strength Detective Reports.' Do you think we should write it down as one of your main strengths?"*

- *"What do you think, group? Do you think 'energetic' is a strength Joshua shows a lot? Does it sound like Joshua to you?"*

- *"Joshua, which strength sounds the <u>most</u> like you—'reliable' or 'artistic'?"*

- *"Group, this 'Strength Detective Report' says Joshua shows the strength of being 'determined.' <u>I've</u> seen Joshua be 'determined'; have you seen him be 'determined'?"*

Your tasks will be to tie together any loose ends as the group discusses each student's strengths and to help the group arrive at a consensus of strengths that the student agrees describe him or her. Write these strengths on the "My Strengths Form" and give it to each student for his or her "Strengths Folder."

(If a student has a shortage of data in his or her "Strengths Folder," you may want to enlist the help of the small group in brainstorming a few strengths for his or her list based on their knowledge of this student. The group members may want to refer to their "word bank" lists for this task.) Repeat this procedure for each remaining small group of students.

Repeat this procedure for each remaining small group of students.

PREVIEW OF THE NEXT LESSON

It's been fun to work with each of you in discovering your strengths. This is a very talented class—I'm proud to be your teacher! I also want to compliment you on doing such a good job helping each other in the small groups.

This sheet titled "My Strengths Form" is a very important document; it represents several weeks of hard work you did in finding your strengths. It also lists the strengths you can count on in yourself to help you create good experiences for yourself again and again.

In our next lesson we're going to use this list of strengths to write our letters of application for the DizzyWorld job that we talked about in the first lesson. And just for fun, we'll set up a pretend interview so that those of you who want to can actually interview for the job!

SUPPLEMENTARY ACTIVITIES

Use the Supplementary Activities at the end of this lesson to provide additional practice of unit concepts:

- *"Strengths Letter Search"*
  (Supplementary Activity #1)

- *"Writing a Cinquain"*
  (Supplementary Activity #2)

TRANSPARENCY #1A

Things We Say to Ourselves That Stop Us From Believing In Our Strengths

1. Arturo

2. Georgina

TRANSPARENCY #1B

Things We Say to Ourselves That Stop Us From Believing In Our Strengths (continued)

3. Yasir

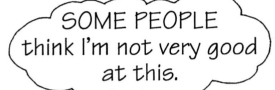

4. Yoriko

TRANSPARENCY #2

A Summary of My Strengths—
An Example

Good Experiences	Strengths I Used to Make Them Happen
1. I won an art contest and won a trip for four to Tillicum Village (worth $49.99).	good with colors imaginative artistic
2. I ran a mile race and only two 8th graders beat me with twice the size legs.	energetic coordinated strong fast
3. I learned to read.	good with words hard worker patient
4. I helped a friend when he got hit on the head with a rock.	friendly helpful caring
5. I learned to swim.	patient determined coordinated

Strengths I am most proud of:

coordinated

friendly

patient

HANDOUT #1

A Summary of My Strengths

Good Experiences	Strengths I Used to Make Them Happen
1.	
2.	
3.	
4.	
5.	

Strengths I am most proud of:

_____

_____

_____

TRANSPARENCY #3A/HANDOUT #2A

Strengths That Just Keep Showing Up!	1 My Trail of Good Experiences	2 Memory Triggers for Good Experiences	3 Good Experiences I'd Forgotten About Until Now	4 Detect-the-Strengths Reports	5 More Good Experiences I Remember	6 Strength Detective Reports	7 The Strengths That Keep You Moving!	8 You're On the Ball!	TOTAL
Artistic									
Athletic									
Brave									
Caring									
Confident									
Coordinated									
Creative									
Determined									
Dependable									
Energetic									
Enthusiastic									
Fast									
Generous									
Good Memory									
Good Sport									
Good Thinker									
Good With Hands									
Good With Numbers									
Good With Words									

TRANSPARENCY #3ʙ/HANDOUT #2ʙ

Strengths That Just Keep Showing Up! (continued)	1 My Trail of Good Experiences	2 Memory Triggers for Good Experiences	3 Good Experiences I'd Forgotten About Until Now	4 Detect-the-Strengths Reports	5 More Good Experiences I Remember	6 Strength Detective Reports	7 The Strengths That Keep You Moving!	8 You're On the Ball!	TOTAL
Hard Worker									
Helpful									
Imaginative									
Kind									
Loyal									
Organized									
Patient									
Positive Attitude									
Problem Solver									
Reliable									
Responsible									
Self-Disciplined									
Self-Motivated									
Thorough									
Thoughtful									

HANDOUT #3

My Strengths Forms

My Strengths

_____
My Name

_____

_____

_____

_____

and I have lots more, too!

My Strengths

_____
My Name

_____

_____

_____

_____

and I have lots more, too!

POSTER #1

REMIND YOURSELF OF YOUR STRENGTHS

SUPPLEMENTARY ACTIVITY #1

Strengths Letter Search

Objective   Student will guess the letters in a word that describes a
             classmate's strength.

Materials   None

Procedure

This activity works like the "Wheel of Fortune" game show. It reinforces students' awareness of different strength words and how they are spelled.

Explain to students that the class will be playing a game in which they guess the letters in a word that describes one of their classmate's strengths. Ask for a volunteer who is willing to have others try to guess his or her strength. This student will whisper the word to you and how it is spelled. He or she can refer to his or her "word bank" lists, if necessary. The student volunteer will then draw on the chalkboard a long rectangle divided into the same number of boxes as there are letters in his or her strength word. (Check this for accuracy.)

That student then calls on his or her classmates to try to guess the letters in the word and, as soon as they are able, to guess the word itself. As students guess correct letters, these are written in the appropriate boxes. If a letter is repeated in the word, all the repetitions are filled in when the letter is first guessed. Incorrect letters are written outside the rectangle to help the students remember which letters have already been guessed. When the word is guessed, the student who claimed it as a strength then gives an example of a time he or she used this strength to create a good experience.

VARIATIONS

To familiarize students with more difficult or less frequently used strength words, you may choose to be the one writing the strength words on the chalkboard. In this variation, to win the game a student who guesses the word must also be able to give an example of how this strength could be used to create a good experience in general. An even better response would be if the student could relate a time he or she actually used this strength.

If you are confident of students' accuracy in being the person spelling the word at the chalkboard, this activity can also be done in smaller groups. In this format, each student takes a turn at asking other group members to guess his or her strength.

SUPPLEMENTARY ACTIVITY #2

Writing a Cinquain

To write your cinquain, follow the directions below.

First line: Write your name. ___Sarah_____

Second line: Add two words that describe your strengths. For example:

_____Loyal_____ , _____fun_____

Third line: Write three action words (verbs) that describe your strengths. For example:

___Running___ , ___smiling___ , ___helping___

Fourth line: Compare yourself to something else. For example:

___Cheerful like the sun_____

Fifth line: Write the strength word that describes you best. For example:

___Athletic___

TO FINISH: Decorate the page with a border or drawing.

Here are four other students' examples of cinquains.

Richard
Friendly, fun
Running, flying, darting
Speedy like a bird
Tough

Mary
Fair, nice
Playing, skipping, running
Fast like a cheetah
Happy

Cheryl
Kind, generous
Skating, dancing, running
Draws like an artist
Friendly

Kevin
Smart, caring
Playing soccer, cleaning, helping
Busy as a bee
Energetic

Owning Strengths and Being Able to Prove Them

Objective   Students will prove that they have particular strengths by citing instances in which they have used them.

Materials   Transparencies #1A and #1B -   "These Kids Have Strengths and They Can Prove It!"

Transparency #2 - "Letter of Application—An Example"

Handout #1   - "Letter of Application"

Handout #2   -   "DizzyWorld Personnel Team Interview Questions"

Handout #3   - "DizzyWorld Letter"

Handout #4   - "DizzyWorld Design Team Award"

Students' "think pads"

"Strengths Folders" (each student's)

To the Teacher   Students come "full circle" in this lesson, proving their strengths by describing the good experiences they've created for themselves. Using their copies of the "My Strengths Form" and their collection of good experiences in their "Strengths Folders," the students will write a letter of application for the fictional job at DizzyWorld they were told about in Lesson 1. The students will state their qualifications (strengths) for the job, proving they have these strengths by citing past good experiences where they have used them. These application forms will serve as a rough evaluation of the students' understanding of this unit and their involvement in it.

An optional mock interview activity adds to the authenticity of the simulated job application theme. It also gives the students an opportunity to make accurate, positive statements about themselves and to present a case for their strengths without bragging or sounding conceited. Follow-up activities such as receiving a "letter from DizzyWorld," being presented with a certificate as an official member of the "Design Team," and the creation of an optional amusement park mural all extend the theme.

Lesson Presentation

In our last lesson we searched through all the materials in our "Strengths Folders" and carefully tallied each strength word in order to find the ones that kept showing up repeatedly. We met in small groups and helped each other decide which strengths sounded the most like us. Then we made a list of those strengths. I hope you've been reminding yourself of your strengths often since our last lesson.

PROVING YOUR STRENGTHS

In our first lesson we talked about an imaginary company named DizzyWorld that wanted to hire some kids to help them come up with new rides for a new theme park. Let's pretend this job really exists. It will be fun and pay a lot of money—but to get it, the kids who apply will have to be able to prove they have the qualities it takes to do the job!

You've worked hard at determining what your strengths are. With all you've done, you should be able to sit down and write your letter of application to the DizzyWorld managers. You're ready to tell them what your strengths are and why they should hire you.

But here's the tricky part—what if they ask you to <u>prove</u> your strengths? For instance, what if you tell them that one of your strengths is that you're "responsible," and they say, "Great! We need responsible kids in our design department!" but then they say, "By the way—what <u>proof</u> do you have that you're responsible?" What could you say to prove to them that you really <u>are</u> a responsible person? *Allow for student response.*

USING GOOD EXPERIENCES TO PROVE YOUR STRENGTHS

If you were a grown-up, you'd probably tell about times you used your strengths in another job. The DizzyWorld managers know that kids your age won't have had a lot of job experiences. So they're interested in hearing about times you did something well and things you've done you're proud of—and these, of course, are your <u>GOOD EXPERIENCES</u>!

Transp. #1A

Put Transparency #1A, "These Kids Have Strengths and They Can Prove It!" on the overhead, covering all but the first example. **Here are some examples of how other kids have given some proof of their strengths.** *Read the first example.* **Can anyone else tell some other experiences that could be used to prove being responsible? You can tell a good experience of your own, or you can make one up.** *Call on a student volunteer and write the response on the blank next to "Responsible."*

Transp. #1B

Use as many examples from Transparencies #1A and #1B as necessary to teach your class how to use their good experiences to prove their strengths. Use the "every pupil" response technique: ask all students to write their responses on their "think pads," and then either call on several students to read their responses aloud or have all the students share their responses with their Learning Partners.

WRITING LETTERS TO DIZZYWORLD

**Transp. #2
Handout #1**

It's now time to write your letter of application to DizzyWorld! You've pinpointed your best strengths, and you've learned how to use your good experiences to prove them. I'll give you something to make the letter writing really easy for you. *Show Transparency #2, "Letter of Application—An Example" and read it to the students, then distribute Handout #1, "Letter of Application."*

To write your letter, all you have to do is write down your top strengths and give examples of times you used them.

For each of your top strengths, choose those examples—your good experiences—that you're proudest of and that prove you have that strength. When you choose which strengths you'll write down on your application, be sure to pick strengths and examples that will show you are a kid of high quality. These will prove to them that they won't be sorry if they choose you for the job!

OPTIONAL MOCK INTERVIEWS

Handout #2

After students have completed their letters of application, you may want to plan some mock interviews. If so, choose two students to be the "DizzyWorld Personnel Team." Seat them both on one side of a table, interview-style, and give them each copies of Handout #2, "DizzyWorld Personnel Team Interview Questions." Choose a volunteer to be the "secretary" who escorts each "applicant" into the interview and introduces him or her to the two interviewers.

All the applicants will bring their "Letters of Application" handouts into the interview. The "DizzyWorld Personnel Team" members will take turns asking the applicant questions from Handout #2; the applicant can refer to his or her letter of application when proving his or her strengths. At the end of the interview, one member of the "DizzyWorld Personnel Team" will tell the applicant, "We'll let you know the results of this interview by letter. Thank you for applying." The applicant will then leave his or her application letter with the team, being sure to thank them for the interview before leaving.

LESSON SUMMARY

As a way of reviewing and summarizing the lesson, ask the students the following questions:

- **How did you feel when you were writing your letter of application and interviewing for the job?**

- Do you think you'd have felt any differently if you were interviewing for a real job?

- How well do you think you'd have done writing a letter like this or interviewing for a job like this before you learned to find your strengths?
    1. Would you have listed the strengths you put down today?
    2. How would you have proven your strengths to someone?

- How do you think being able to know and prove your strengths could help you in your life right now?
    1. Are there any jobs you could apply for where you could earn some extra money?
    2. Are there any privileges you could get (from your mom, a coach, etc.) by being able to prove some of your strengths?

- Do you know a way to use the strengths you've discovered to help yourself do new or difficult things?

FOLLOW-UP ACTIVITIES

Use the application letters as a way to evaluate each student's ability to identify his or her strengths and to apply the lesson concepts. Tell students that in the next few days they will be receiving notification letters from the "DizzyWorld Personnel Team" letting them know if they've been selected for a DizzyWorld position.

Handout #3
Handout #4

After evaluating the applications, give Handout #3, "DizzyWorld Letter," to any student who has made a reasonable effort to complete the job application. Each student "hired" by DizzyWorld should also receive a copy of Handout #4, "DizzyWorld Design Team Award," to signify his or her acceptance as an official member of the "DizzyWorld Design Team." (A nice touch is to run off Handout #4 on parchment paper, if available.)

You may also want to let interested students actually design a wall mural of an addition to an amusement park, showing various imaginative rides, theme restaurants and shops, etc. This mural activity could also lend itself well to an accompanying creative writing assignment.

PREVIEW OF THE NEXT LESSON

In our next lesson we'll be having a "Celebration of Strengths." We'll do this by having each of you decide how to make a presentation to the class to show everyone just what your best strengths are. You'll have lots of choices of different ways to make your presentation.

I think you'll be surprised to see all the talents and strengths in this class. When we're through you'll realize that <u>everyone</u> here has good qualities they can be proud of!

SUPPLEMENTARY ACTIVITIES

You can extend the lesson by using the Supplementary Activities at the end of the lesson:

- *"Design a Sweatshirt"*
  (Supplementary Activity #1)

- *"Times I Used a Strength"*
  (Supplementary Activity #2)

TRANSPARENCY #1A

These Kids Have Strengths and They Can Prove It!

Strengths They Have	Past Experiences They Had That Proved It
Reponsible	I took care of my neighbors' dog, cat, and plants while they were on vacation. I showed my parents I can babysit my sister alone.
Self-Discipline	I saved my allowance for six weeks instread of blowing it on candy each week. I wanted to give a kid a put-down and I didn't.
Patient	I knitted a whole scarf. I taught my brother to swim even though he kept messing up.
Artistic	I can draw these real good bugs. I drew some Disney characters with some oil paints.
Coordinated	I ran a mile race and only two 8th graders beat me with twice as long legs. I learned to carve wood with my Swiss Army knife.
Tough	I survived my parents' divorce. I made it through first grade even though I didn't have any friends.
Brave	I went on a long plane trip alone. I was the narrator of a play in front of the whole school.

TRANSPARENCY #1B

These Kids Have Strengths and They Can Prove It! (continued)

Strengths They Have	Past Experiences They Had That Proved It
Determined	I jogged a whole mile and back. I had to practice every day but I finally learned to play a hard song on the piano.
Kind	I cleaned up the house when my mom was sick. I helped a friend when a kid was picking on him. I taught a little kid how to play football.
Creative	I made different things out of dough and sold them. I built a miniature house out of video boxes. I made up a song.
Good With Numbers	I learned all my times tables. I got a "100" on a very hard math test. I learned how to multiply when I was only in second grade.
Hard Worker	I learned all my spelling words four weeks in a row. I built an entire tree house that was big enough to sleep in. I wrote a six-page report not counting the pictures.

Letter of Application—An Example

Director of New Projects
DizzyWorld
Orlando, FL 32822

November 16
(date)

Dear Sir or Madam:

I am applying for the position of Consultant on New Ideas for DizzyWorld. After you read about my strengths, I'm sure you'll agree I'm just the person for the job. The following is a list of my top strengths and examples of experiences where I have actually used these strengths.

1. Strength: _patient_

   Examples of times I used this strength:
   I had to be patient when I didn't have any friends in first grade but
   I waited it out because I knew I'd get some eventually.
   I let others finish talking before I say my ideas.

2. Strength: _creative_

   Examples of times I used this strength:
   I learned to sew several different kinds of clothes and jumpsuits for my
   dolls.
   I made up an entire skit and did it for my class.

3. Strength: _artistic_

   Examples of times I used this strength:
   I made different things out of dough and sold them with my friend.
   I designed a symbol for a T-shirt logo contest and won.

4. Strength: _brave_

   Examples of times I used this strength:
   I scared away a dog that bites anything that moves.
   I stood up for a kid nobody likes.

I hope you will consider me for this position. You won't regret it.

Sincerely,

Anya

HANDOUT #1

Letter of Application

Director of New Projects
DizzyWorld
Orlando, FL 32822

_____
(date)

Dear Sir or Madam:

I am applying for the position of Consultant on New Ideas for DizzyWorld. After you read about my strengths, I'm sure you'll agree I'm just the person for the job. The following is a list of my top strengths and examples of experiences where I have actually used these strengths.

1. Strength: _____

    Examples of times I used this strength:

    _____
    _____
    _____

2. Strength: _____

    Examples of times I used this strength:

    _____
    _____
    _____

3. Strength: _____

    Examples of times I used this strength:

    _____
    _____
    _____

4. Strength: _____

    Examples of times I used this strength:

    _____
    _____
    _____

I hope you will consider me for this position. You won't regret it.

Sincerely,

HANDOUT #2

DizzyWorld Personnel Team
Interview Questions

- What qualities do you think are important for this job?

- Why should we hire you?

- Give another example of why you think you have the strengths you say you do.

- Tell me about something else you've done in your life you are proud of.

- This job requires that you work well with others as a team member. Do you have any strengths that would help you do this?

- Do you already have ideas for designing the new theme park addition to DizzyWorld?

HANDOUT #3

DizzyWorld Letter

DizzyWorld

Dear Job Applicant:

Congratulations on being selected to be part of our new design team for DizzyWorld! You were selected because you proved to us that you had many valuable strengths.

We would like to employ you to design an entire new "land" and three new rides. As you know, like DisneyWorld, we already have Main Street, Adventureland, Fantasyland, Tomorrowland, New Orleans Square, and others. We were thinking of making School-Land, Mountain-Land, Arctic-Land, Dinosaur-Land, or Wild Horses-Land, but we think you might come up with something else that kids would like better.

Once you've decided on the land, make up three new rides. Two rides should be for the new land you've created. We'd like the third ride to be based on a recent movie which kids like.

You might want to work on this project with the other design team employees we've selected. We look forward to seeing what you create for us!

Sincerely,

Michelle Moose
Director of New Projects
DizzyWorld

HANDOUT #4

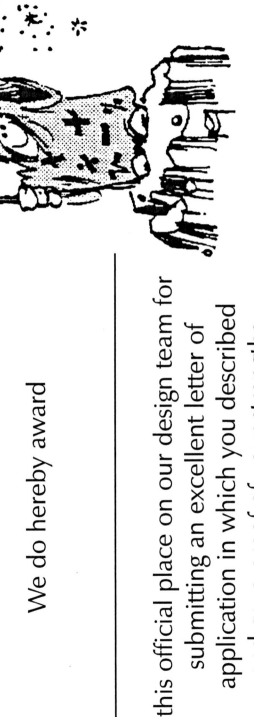

DizzyWorld
Design Team Award

We do hereby award

this official place on our design team for submitting an excellent letter of application in which you described and gave proof of your strengths.

Michelle Moose, Director of New Projects

Date

SUPPLEMENTARY ACTIVITY #1

Design a Sweatshirt

Directions:

Design a sweatshirt showing one of your particular strengths. You can use words and pictures.

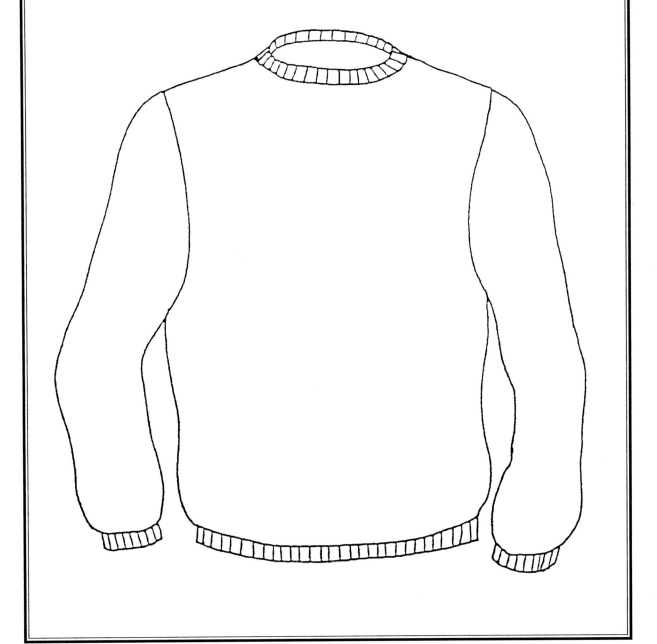

SUPPLEMENTARY ACTIVITY #2

Times I Used a Strength

Directions:

Choose one of these to write about:

I was kind when

_____
_____
_____
_____

I was generous when

_____
_____
_____
_____

I was brave when

_____
_____
_____
_____

Putting It All Together—A Celebration of Strengths

Objectives

Students will select strengths important to them and choose a modality for presenting them to the class.

Students will use a public presentation to celebrate the discovery of their strengths.

Materials

Transparency #1A/Handout #1A and Transparency #1B/Handout #1B - "Many Ways to Show My Strengths—Final Project Ideas"

Transparency #2/Handout #2 - "My Final Project Plan"

Transparency #3/Handout #3 - "Presentation of Strengths Evaluation Forms"

Handout #4 - "Strengths Award"

Transparency #4 - "You Have Hidden Strengths"

"Strengths Folders" (each student's)

Parchment paper (optional)

Ribbon (optional)

Gold stars (optional)

To the Teacher

This lesson is designed to encompass several class periods. It is a lesson that involves "putting it all together" through creating a public presentation of strengths. Students will review their strengths and determine which of these they want to demonstrate to the class. They are asked to select strengths which have special meaning for them and create a well thought-out plan for a presentation.

The students may do their presentations alone, with a partner (such as a Learning Partner), or as part of a small group. After they have decided on an approach, they will show you their "final project plan" and obtain your approval. The students should also be shown the "Presentation of Strengths Evaluation Forms" before they begin their project so that they will know the criteria their classmates will use in evaluating their presentation. This will help ensure careful preparation and creativity.

Explain to the students that, if they decide to team up with others and make their presentation with a partner or as a group, they will have to find a way for each person in the group to demonstrate his or her strengths so that each person can be evaluated individually by his or her classmates. The students may volunteer to help other students by being part of their presentations, but if the student's strengths aren't highlighted in these, they must do another presentation of their own. Give the students as many days as you think are necessary to develop and work on their presentations.

Each student will evaluate the presentations of all his or her classmates. Because of the large number of evaluations, you probably will not want to cut them apart and return them to each presenter. An alternative method is to photocopy the evaluation forms on both sides of a page. Then put all the completed evaluation forms in a large box and allow the students to look through them during their free time.

On the day chosen for the "Celebration of Strengths," you can create a celebratory mood by asking the students to bring treats to share during the presentations. On this day, emphasis is on celebrating the fact that each student in the room has excellence in them.

The Supplementary Activities that follow this lesson can be used for those students who have trouble creating a presentation project on their own or for those who let their project go until the last minute and need help putting something together. You may also want to extend some of the follow-up activities in this lesson into your language arts or art activities.

Lesson Presentation

PRESENTATION IDEAS FOR SHOWING STRENGTHS

Say or paraphrase: **Now it's time to get ready for our "Celebration of Strengths" party. Each of you will be choosing some of your strengths that you've discovered these past weeks to present to the class in the form of a final project.**

One purpose of doing this is to practice telling others your strengths. Who can tell us why this might be a useful thing to practice telling others about your strengths? *Allow for student response. If students don't mention it, point out that this is what they will need to do when the time comes for them to apply for a job. It also makes it easier to create and work together in a team.* **Another reason we are going to do this is so we will know**

each other a little better and appreciate each other more. And perhaps the <u>best</u> reason of all to demonstrate our strengths is that it can help us to feel good about ourselves!

You've worked very hard remembering your good experiences and finding the strengths that helped you make those good experiences happen. Now let's look at some fun ways you could choose to demonstrate those very special strengths.

**Transp. #1A
Transp. #1B**

Place Transparencies #1A and #1B, "Many Ways to Show My Strengths—Final Project Ideas," on the overhead and go over the ideas under each category. When discussing the "Use WORDS . . ." category, you may want to call attention to the "Strength Autobiopoem" and "A Commercial About a Friend's Strengths" Supplementary Activities at the end of this lesson.

If the students want to perform in some way, remind them that, along with their performance (e.g., playing an instrument, demonstrating jump-rope tricks, etc.), they will need to identify and tell about the strengths they used to perfect the skill before they demonstrate it.

When discussing the "WORK WITH OTHERS . . ." category option of demonstrating strengths, explain to the students that they will need to: (1) complete their "final project plan" by themselves to decide on the strengths and ideas for demonstration that are most meaningful to them, and (2) get teacher approval if they want to work with others. (This is to ensure that each student gives a sufficient amount of time and thought to his or her own strength demonstration process.)

**Handout #1A
Handout #1B**

I'm going to give you a copy of these idea lists so you can spend some time deciding which one would be the most fun way for you to demonstrate your strengths. *Distribute copies of Handouts #1A and #1B, "Many Ways to Show My Strengths—Final Project Ideas."*

STUDENTS DECIDE WHAT STRENGTHS THEY ARE GOING TO PRESENT

Say or paraphrase: **Now that I've given you some suggestions about how you might demonstrate your strengths, take a few minutes to review the strengths you listed on your "A Summary of My Strengths" sheet** *(Handout #1 from Lesson 6)* **and DizzyWorld "Letter of Application"** *(Handout #1 from Lesson 7).* **As you look over these strengths, your job is to pick three or four strengths that you'd like to demonstrate to the class. These strengths might be the ones you've used the most or the ones that mean the most to you for some reason. You will be stating why you chose them on your "My Final Project Plan" handouts which I'll give to you in a few minutes.**

STUDENTS FILL OUT A FINAL PROJECT PLAN

**Transp. #2
Handout #2**

After students have had time to decide what strengths they'll present and how they'll present them, show Transparency #2, "My Final Project Plan." Model how to fill out the form by completing one on the overhead. Give the students a copy of the form (Handout #2) and have them work individually to complete Steps #1-3. Make sure they take sufficient time to think seriously about their most meaningful strengths and how they might want to demonstrate them.

Explain that they'll all need to have their plans approved by you before starting their projects, to ensure that everyone is on the right track. Students who wish to work with others will need to have at least Steps #1 and #2 completed and approved before they start asking others to work with them. If students want to work with others, remind them that their demonstration should reflect strengths that are possessed by <u>all</u> of the participants, or a student may assist someone else and then do his or her own demonstration. Tell the students that their final project presentations should be at least five minutes in length.

INTRODUCING THE STRENGTHS EVALUATION FORM

Show Transparency #3, "Presentation of Strengths Evaluation Forms." Say or paraphrase: **After each presentation is given in front of the class, everyone will fill out one of these evaluation forms for the people involved in the presentation. I'm showing you this now so that you can see how you'll be evaluated. You will want to keep this in mind as you plan your presentation.** *Read over the items on the form one at a time. Model filling out an evaluation form for an imaginary presenter. Say or paraphrase:* **As you can see, it's important that you take some time to really think about your presentation and decide if it will clearly demonstrate your strengths. You need to put some time, energy, and creativity into your preparation. If you'd like a copy of this form to think about while you plan your presentation, I'll give you one.** *Give those students who so desire a copy of the "Presentation of Strengths Evaluation Forms" (Handout #3).*

FURTHER PREPARATIONS FOR THE "CELEBRATION OF STRENGTHS"

The rest of this session can be spent with the students completing their "final project plans" and beginning preparation for their demonstrations. You may either allocate additional class time to project preparation or assign it as homework.

At this time, you may want to set up a refreshment and clean-up committee for the "Celebration of Strengths" party, depending on how you decide to conduct the final session.

THE DAY OF THE PRESENTATION OF STRENGTHS

On the day of the "Celebration of Strengths" party say or paraphrase: **Today is the day we've all been looking forward to! You've been studying about your strengths for several weeks and today we'll get to see each of you present some of** your special strengths to the class. Lots of work has gone into planning these fun and interesting presentations, and it's going to be fun to see which strengths you've chosen to demonstrate and how you're going to do it!

Saying your strengths out loud is an important way to get comfortable talking about your good points. Because of that, I'd like each of you to say your strengths to the class at some point in your presentation. People who work in a group will each need to say which strengths they're demonstrating. Of course, if you're only helping out in a group, you won't tell about your strengths until you do your own demonstration.

Now, remember—this isn't bragging! Who can remind us about the difference between bragging and feeling pleased about your good points? *Allow for student response. If the students don't mention it, point out the following:* You won't be saying you're better than others—you're just stating some of the strengths you have that have helped you have your good experiences. It's natural and healthy to let yourself feel good about your positive qualities. It's been said that high self-esteem is one of the things you need to be successful in life. The reason discovering your strengths is so important is because knowing and remembering them helps you to have high self-esteem.

EVALUATING THE PRESENTATION

**Handout #3
Transp. #3**

Pass out copies of Handout #3, "Presentation of Strengths Evaluation Forms," and put Transparency #3 of the same form back on the overhead. Let's go over the "Presentation of Strengths Evaluation Forms" one more time to be sure you understand what you'll be doing. After each presentation I'll give you a minute or two to rate the presentation. You'll rate it by reading each of the criteria and deciding whether to circle a 1, which is low, a 2, which is medium, or a 3, which is high.

Let me give you an example. *Read each criterion and create examples showing how to determine a rating.*

Be sure you write down your name as evaluator and the name of each person doing the presentation. You will need to rate each person individually, even if the person does his or her presentation as part of a group. If you're just helping in a group but not using it for your presentation, tell the class so they'll know not to evaluate you with the rest of the group, that you'll be doing your presentation later. Remember, the purpose for evaluating each other is not to be critical, but to give a person credit for how much time and work they put into their presentation and to note whether you can tell what the person's strengths are after the presentation. Let's get started!

GIVING "STRENGTHS AWARDS"

Handout #4

Begin having students do their demonstrations. Usually students will volunteer, but you may want to schedule the presentations, especially if some of them involve bulky props or elaborate set-ups. After each presentation, give each presenter Handout #4, "Strengths Award," and offer a word of congratulations. You may want to run the awards off on parchment or put a gold sticker on them and then roll them up and tie them with ribbon.

THE BENEFITS OF FOCUSING ON STRENGTHS

Transp. #4

Show Transparency #4, "You Have Hidden Strengths." Say: **It's important for each of you to remember that you've only scratched the surface of your particular package of strengths. You still have many hidden strengths and talents just waiting to be discovered.**

The time you've spent noticing the strengths in others can also be a benefit to <u>you</u>. People are usually happier when they pay attention to the positive things in others, instead

of looking at each others' faults. If we spend the rest of the year looking at the strengths in ourselves and in each other instead of criticizing ourselves and putting others down, we can create a year we'll never forget!

SUPPLEMENTARY ACTIVITIES

Use the Supplementary Activities at the end of this lesson to provide additional practice of lesson concepts:

- *"Strength Autobiopoem"*
    (Supplementary Activity #1)

- *"A Teeny-Tiny Book of Strengths"*
    (Supplementary Activity #2)

- *"Talk Shows About Strengths"*
    (Supplementary Activity #3)

- *"A Commercial About a Friend's Strengths"*
    (Supplementary Activity #4)

TRANSPARENCY #1A/HANDOUT #1A

Many Ways to Show My Strengths— Final Project Ideas

Use WORDS to show your strengths:

Make a crossword puzzle of your strengths for the class to complete.

Write a poem. (Try an Autobiopoem or Cinquain. Ask your teacher for handouts.)

Write a commercial that advertises your strengths or those of a friend. (Ask your teacher for a handout.)

Write a make-believe newspaper article describing you and your strengths.

Pretend you are 25-years old and coming back to school to speak to a class. Tell how you have used your strengths since leaving school.

Write about how you will use your strengths to create a good life for yourself and others.

Use PUZZLES, RIDDLES, or COMPUTERS to show your strengths:

Use a computer to make something that shows what your strengths are.

Develop a code to describe your strengths.

Make up some riddles about your strengths.

Use ART to show your strengths:

Make a collage of pictures about your strengths. You can cut them out of magazines or newspapers.

Make a poster that shows us what your strengths are.

Do a painting, mural, or drawing that depicts your strengths.

Make a cloth banner that shows your strengths.

Design a series of cartoons that describe your stsrengths.

Design a coat-of-arms that shows your strengths.

Many Ways to Show My Strengths— Final Project Ideas (continued)

Use MUSIC to show your strengths:

Make up a rap or song about your strengths.

Play an instrument and tell which strengths helped you learn to play it.

Use ACTION to show your strengths:

Do a charade or pantomime of your strengths and have the class guess them.

Perform karate, ballet or other dance, gymnastic moves, or jump-rope moves and tell which strengths helped you learn that skill.

Use sports equipment, tools, or other items to show your strengths.

WORK WITH OTHERS to show your strengths:

Lead the class in some activity that relates to your strengths, like demonstrating how to make a new friend or how to get over a fight with a friend.

Compare and contrast your strengths with a friend. Each write down your strengths and then see how they are alike or different. Both of you tell the class about it.

Pretend you're on the "Good Morning America" show and have someone interview you in front of the class about your good experiences and strengths. You write the interview questions.

TRANSPARENCY #2/HANDOUT #2

My Final Project Plan

1. Strengths that I'm going to demonstrate to the class:

    _____

    _____

    Why I chose these strengths:

    _____

    _____

2. How I'm going to demonstrate my strengths to the class:

    _____

    _____

    _____

3. Materials I will need:

    _____

    _____

    _____

4. If working with others, who I will be working with:

    _____

    _____

    Since teacher approval is required, has my teacher
    agreed to let them work with me on this?

    ❑ Yes

TRANSPARENCY #3/HANDOUT #3

Presentation of Strengths Evaluation Forms

Presentation of Strengths Evaluation Form

Name of person(s) giving presentation: _____

_____

Name of evaluator: _____

	LOW		HIGH
• Strengths were said with pride.	1	2	3
• The presentation showed that time and thought were put into it.	1	2	3
• The presentation was carefully prepared.	1	2	3
• The presentation clearly explained the person's strengths.	1	2	3
• The presentation showed creativity and originality.	1	2	3

TOTAL POINTS: _____

Presentation of Strengths Evaluation Form

Name of person(s) giving presentation: _____

_____

Name of evaluator: _____

	LOW		HIGH
• Strengths were said with pride.	1	2	3
• The presentation showed that time and thought were put into it.	1	2	3
• The presentation was carefully prepared.	1	2	3
• The presentation clearly explained the person's strengths.	1	2	3
• The presentation showed creativity and originality.	1	2	3

TOTAL POINTS: _____

HANDOUT #4

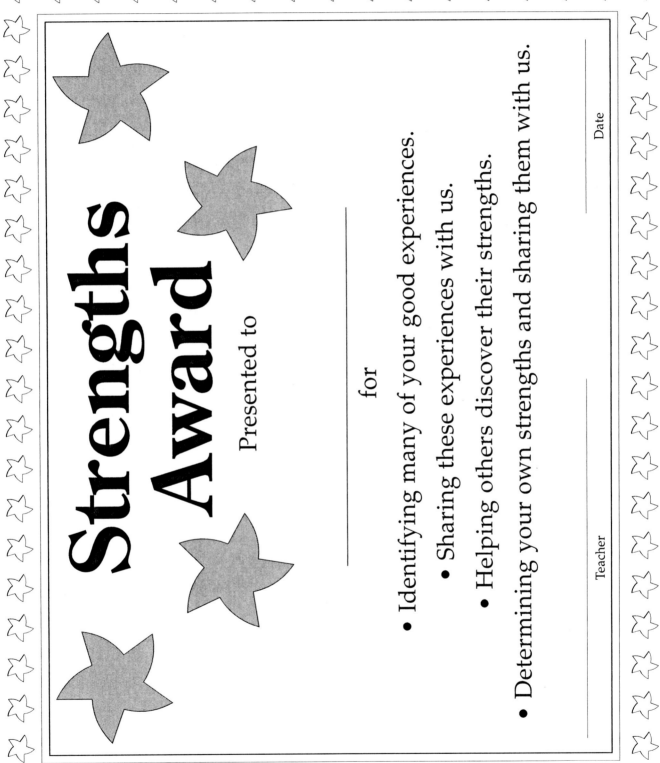

Strengths Award

Presented to

for

- Identifying many of your good experiences.
- Sharing these experiences with us.
- Helping others discover their strengths.
- Determining your own strengths and sharing them with us.

Date

Teacher

TRANSPARENCY #4

You Have Hidden Strengths

You may think you already know all the things you do well

BUT
you have hidden strengths inside of you you haven't even imagined yet!

SUPPLEMENTARY ACTIVITY #1 HANDOUT #1

Strength Autobiopoem

Follow these directions and you will discover you can write a poem about your strengths. Write the things that are in dark print on your paper. Look at the poem on the next page to see an example of how to complete each line.

Line 1:   **Your first name** only

Line 2:   **Two strengths** which describe you

Line 3:   **(Son/Daughter) of . . .**

Line 4:   **Who was proud when (he/she) . . .**

Line 5:   **Who felt great when . . .**

Line 6:   **Who was glad (he/she) kept trying when . . .**

Line 7:   **Who realized (he/she) was good at something when . . .**

Line 8:   **Who felt kind the time (he/she) . . .**

Line 9:   **Who was afraid but did it anyway when . . .**

Line 10:   **Who made someone happy when . . .**

Line 11:   **Who stuck with something that was hard when . . .**

Line 12:   **Who learned by (himself/herself) to . . .**

Line 13:   Two more **strengths**

Line 14:   **Your last name** only.

SUPPLEMENTARY ACTIVITY #1 HANDOUT #2

Strength Autobiopoem Sample

Larry

Kind, coordinated

Son of Andy and Mary

Who was proud when he caught his first pop fly in baseball

Who felt great when he caught his first fish

Who was glad he kept trying when he learned to jump off a ramp with his bike

Who realized he was good at something when he learned to dribble a basketball with his left hand

Who felt kind the time he taught his little brother to swim

Who was afraid but did it anyway when he read a report in front of the class

Who made someone happy when he was nice to a kid nobody liked

Who stuck with a job that was hard when he learned his times tables

Who learned by himself to ride a skateboard

Determined, good sport

Larson.

SUPPLEMENTARY ACTIVITY #2

A Teeny-Tiny Book of Strengths

You can easily carry around this little book of your strengths because it is very, very small!

This book will have 16 tiny pages. Each page will have room for a picture and a few strengths words. To make your teeny-tiny book:

1. Fold a piece of paper in half, then fold it in half again three more times.

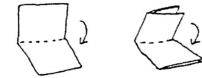

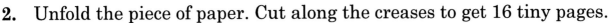

2. Unfold the piece of paper. Cut along the creases to get 16 tiny pages.

3. On one page, draw the front cover for your book. On each of the 15 other pages, draw a picture of one of your strengths.

4. Staple the book together. Then open it and for each strength write on the page next to the picture a few words that tell about how you use that strength. You may have to use teeny-tiny writing!

If you want to, you can pass the book around the class for others to read. It's also a great book to tuck into your pocket or notebook to remind you of your own special strengths.

Talk Shows About Strengths

Objective   Students will interview their classmates regarding their good experiences and the strengths they used to create them.

Materials   A microphone (or a prop that simulates one)

Videotape recorder/camcorder (optional)

TV, VCR, and videotape (optional)

Procedure   Have the students get together in small groups or pairs. Ask them to replicate an interview sequence of a television program like "Good Morning America." In each group, one student will be the interviewer and the remaining students will be the show's guests. Guests will answer the interviewer's questions about one or more of their good experiences and the strengths they used to create those experiences. For example, the interviewer might ask, "Could you tell me what some of your good experiences have been? What strengths helped you create your good experiences?"

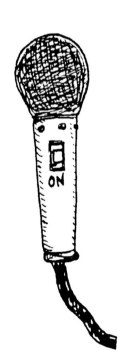

If you would like to add more challenge to this activity, you might suggest the interviewers to ask detailed questions, such as, "How could you use that strength now to create another good experience for yourself?" The interviewers should also be encouraged to probe a little about the strength being used, asking questions such as, "When you say your strength was being **athletic**, did you also use strengths like being coordinated or flexible or fast?" or "How **exactly** did you use your strength in this good experience?"

Using a real or pretend microphone makes it much easier for the students to pretend this is really a TV show.

OPTION

For an optional presentation, videotape these "shows." Then show the video to the students within the next few days. Seeing themselves and their peers "on TV" is exciting for students, and using this method also allows you to stop the action and discuss strengths without having to interrupt the live performances to do so.

A Commercial About a Friend's Strengths

Objective
Students will prepare a commercial that advertises the strengths of a friend.

Materials
Supplementary Activity #4 Handout #1A and #1B - "My Friend's Strengths"

Construction paper (12" x 18" sheets)

Felt tip pens or crayons

"Roller Movie Theater" materials (see the directions on Handout #1A)

Procedure
Have the students work in pairs interviewing one another using copies of the handout. Explain the importance in TV commercials of creating something that will appeal to the audience, and discuss any techniques used in TV commercials you feel might be helpful for the students to consider. Tell the students that their job will be to create commercials that will use interesting ways to tell about their friends' strengths.

The commercials can be shown to the class in a "roller movie" format.

SUPPLEMENTARY ACTIVITY #4 HANDOUT #1A

My Friend's Strengths

Directions:

Here are directions for creating a roller movie theater:

1. Take a cardboard box and cut out a rectangular shape slightly smaller in size than the 12" x 18" sheets of construction paper you will use for your friend's "strength commercial" in the bottom panel.

2. Stand the box on end, and cut two holes on the sides of the box at both the top and bottom, as shown in the illustration.

3. Insert two wooden dowels or round sticks.

4. Using four or five sheets of 12" x 18" construction paper, put pictures and words on each sheet of paper to tell about a special strength of your friend interviewed. Tape the sheets together end to end.

5. To present your commercial, tape one end of your commercial paper to one dowel and the other end to the second dowel, rolling it up so that the first picture is in view in the opening.

6. Roll the movie from one frame to the next. "Sell" your friend to the audience by showing the advertisement and reading the words you wrote under each picture.

Ask your friend to tell you all he or she can about good experiences he or she has had and about the strengths that helped him or her to have these good experiences. Use the questions on the next page as a guide.

SUPPLEMENTARY ACTIVITY #4 HANDOUT #1B

My Friend's Strengths (continued)

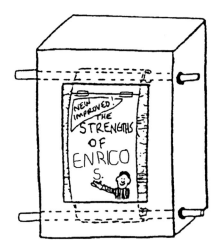

Friend's Name: _____

1. In what school subject do you have the most strengths?

    _____

2. In what sports and hobbies do you have strengths?

    _____

3. What are some things you do at home that show your strengths?

    _____

4. Tell about a time you were proud of something you did.

    _____

5. Tell about something you plan to be successful at some day.

    _____

Using My Strengths to Create New Successes

Objectives

Students will use their strengths as a springboard for setting new goals.

Students will learn and use a number of strategies for reaching their goals.

Materials

Transparencies #1A and #1B - "Determination"

Transparency #2/Handout #1 - "Using Your Strengths to Create New Good Experiences"

Transparencies #3A, #3B, and #3C - "Possible Goals That Could Help Me Have More Good Experiences"

Transparency #4/Handout #2 - "I've Done It Before—I Can Do It Again"

Transparency #5 - "Strategies for Reaching Goals"

Transparency #6 - "Remember a Good Experience—Imagine an Even Better One"

Handout #3 - "I Can Do It! Using Self-Talk to Reach My Goal"

Handout #4 - "How I Will Reach My Goal"

Transparency #7 - "Things That Might Stop Me From Reaching My Goal"

Handout #5 - "Using My Strengths to Overcome Obstacles to Goals"

Handout #6 - "My Ladder to Success"

Handout #7 - "How I'm Doing"

Handout #8 - "I Did It!"

Handout #9 - "Goal Achievement Award"

Transparency #8 - "Your Value As a Person Doesn't Depend On How Well You Do"

To the Teacher

One reason for helping students discover their strengths is to help them find the courage to risk and try new things. In this lesson students are encouraged to use those strengths which they've discovered underlie their past good experiences to help them achieve new goals. It is left up to the students to decide what this new area of challenge will be. They are asked to set their goal in the area of schoolwork, after-school activities, or interpersonal relationships.

Students are asked to set a goal not in one of their areas of weakness, but in an area where they already have some strength. All of us have been trained to look for our weaknesses and try to overcome them; we all know the discouragement of this approach. By setting goals in areas where the students already have some ability and have already had some good experiences, the risk of failure is minimized. The students learn how to create new successes using their existing strengths.

Students are encouraged to set specific short-term goals. They are given a series of strategies to help them reach their goals. Two of these strategies are recalling past successes and good experiences, and imagining themselves reaching goals. These, along with encouraging self-talk, will be effective tools for helping students establish a belief in themselves. These strategies are among those commonly used by champion athletes and successful people in all walks of life.

Students may not immediately see the usefulness of these strategies and are not likely to practice them without your encouragement. By providing time for systematic practice of these techniques, however, students will eventually experience the boost in performance these strategies can bring about and become self-motivated to use them. It will be helpful for the students to focus on their goals for two to three weeks. During this time, try to provide a few minutes at the beginning and end of each day so the students can read their goals, remember past successes, practice imagining themselves reaching their goals, and encourage themselves with positive self-statements.

Lesson Presentation

LESSON PREVIEW

Say or paraphrase: **You've spent a lot of time looking at your good experiences and discovering your strengths. By now most of you have a pretty good idea of what your particular strengths are. Today you're going to see how you can use some of your strengths to accomplish new things and to have more good experiences.**

Later in this lesson, you're going to be asked to choose an area where you want to have more good experiences. This will be an area where you've already been able to make good things happen for you. You'll be asked to decide on something you'll <u>do</u> in this area to make more good experiences happen. Then you'll set a goal and use the strengths you already have to help yourself meet that goal. The goal could be something you will do during school or do after school, or it could be a way you'll act with others. Let me show you what I mean.

USING STRENGTHS TO ACCOMPLISH NEW THINGS

Transp. #1A

You all have certain strengths that have helped you have some of your good experiences in the past. *Put Transparency #1A, "Determination," on the overhead.* Many of you have used your strength of determination to help you do certain things well—you stuck with something and tried and tried again until you got it.

One example of this could have been learning to ride your bike without training wheels, when you got back on again and again after you tipped over. It might have been learning your math facts, when you practiced them over and over until you remembered them. It might have been showing up for every practice in basketball even though there were some times you didn't feel like going. Today we're going to talk about how you can use strengths like determination to create more good experiences for yourself.

Transp. #1B

You can use your strength of determination to make more good experiences for yourself in the future. *Show Transparency #1B, "Determination," and point to the figure playing baseball.* For example, you may want to set a goal for yourself to become a much better baseball player. What are some ways the strength of determination could help you meet that goal? *Allow for student response. Help the students discover that determination might be expressed by practicing regularly; by not missing practices or games; by seeking instruction from others and practicing their pointers; etc.*

Point to the girl sitting at her desk. **What if your goal was to be one of the finalists in a spelling bee? How could you use the strength of determination to accomplish that goal?** *Allow for student response. Lead students to see that determination could help them to practice spelling with a partner; to get someone at home to call out words to them; to write the spelling words over and over while spelling aloud; etc.*

Here's a little different example. What if your goal was to buy your own sewing machine that had all the latest attachments, but it was very expensive. How could the strength of determination help you reach that goal? *Allow for student response. Help the students see that determination could help them to find ways of making money (yard work, paper route, babysitting, etc.); to do jobs even if they didn't want to so they could earn the money; to save their money when they were tempted to spend it on something else; etc.*

What if you and your friends had the goal of building your own club house? *Direct the disussion as for the other examples.*

In all four of these examples, these kids each set a goal to have a good experience in the future; then they used their strength of determination to meet their goals. You can do the same thing using your own strengths.

IDENTIFYING NEW "SELF STRENGTHS"

**Transp. #2
Handout #1**

Show Transparency #2, "Using Your Strengths to Create New Good Experiences," and give students Handout #1 of the same title. Say: **Many of you have used strengths other than determination to accomplish things in the past. As we talk about each strength, circle those that you feel you might have used,** even if you haven't written them down on any of your strength lists before.

Progress through the transparency by saying: **Some of you have discovered you're <u>enthusiastic</u>; you get excited about what you're doing or about learning new things. Others of you have discovered that you're the kind of person who's <u>organized</u> and that this has helped you accomplish things or have good experiences. Some of you may have discovered that you have a <u>positive attitude</u>. You tell yourself that things are going to work out, or that you <u>can</u> do things even if they're hard, and this has helped you create good experiences. Others of you have discovered that you're <u>good with words</u>—schoolwork may be pretty easy for you. Still others of you have discovered you're <u>good at problem solving</u>; you're able to figure things out and find a way to get things done. Some of you have realized that you can be <u>self-</u>disciplined. You've been able to get yourself to do even hard things without others having to tell you to do them. There may be some people in here who've discovered you can count on yourself to be <u>"tough"</u> when you need to; you've been able to keep yourself going and to do what you needed to get done even though it was hard or scary sometimes. Some of you have found you have the strength of being <u>thorough</u>. You don't let things go until the last minute. You start early and take care of every detail so you can do the kind of job that you're proud of.**

All of the strengths we've talked about so far are "self strengths," strengths you can use in many different ways to overcome obstacles to things you want to do. These strengths can be used to improve schoolwork or after-school activities. *Point to the figures to the right of the arrow.*

Take out your "A Summary of My Strengths" sheets from one of our previous lessons *(Handout #1 from Lesson 6)*. **Look over your strengths and see if you have listed any other**

strengths that aren't on this sheet that could help you try new things. Write them on the lines provided. *Ask for student volunteers to share any strengths they added to their handout.*

IDENTIFYING NEW "PEOPLE STRENGTHS"

Now, let's read through this list of "people strengths." Some of you have discovered you have many strengths that help build friendships. You can use these strengths to do better at getting along with people. Maybe you'll decide you want to improve your relationship with a brother or sister, or with a kid at school you don't know well. If you have some of these people strengths already, it will be much easier for you to do that. *Go through each "people strength" as you did with the "self strengths" above, defining the word and pointing out times students may have used these strengths to build relationships. Bridge these strengths to the present by pointing out to the students that they can use them to have more good experiences with other people.*

USING GOAL SETTING TO CREATE GOOD EXPERIENCES

As I explained earlier, I'd like you to choose an area in which you'd like to have more good experiences. Think of something you could do that would really make you feel good. This goal might be in the area of one of your school subjects, after-school activities, or friendships.

You should pick an area where you've already had some good experiences and where you've discovered you have some strengths. If you're already a little bit good at something, you have more courage to try new things in that area. It's easier to improve strengths you already have than to try to improve weaknesses.

PRACTICE IN IDENTIFYING SCHOOL GOALS

Transp. #3A

Let's pretend the area you've chosen is to improve your schoolwork. You'd feel happier if you had more good experiences at school. *Put Transparency #3A, "Possible Goals That Could Help Me Have More Good Experiences," on the overhead.* **Can anyone think of a goal that could help you or someone else have more good experiences with school-work? What would help?** *Call on students to suggest actions that could help them do better on schoolwork, such as: finishing their work in class, doing homework before watching TV, studying longer before every test, etc. Write appropriate suggestions on the transparency. (You may wish to ask the students to set possible goals for improvement in specific subjects, such as math, spelling, reading, etc.)*

If you set one of these goals and used your strengths to help you reach it, what kind of new good experiences could you have? *Write student comments on the bottom half of the transparency.*

PRACTICE IN IDENTIFYING AFTER-SCHOOL GOALS

Transp. #3B

Place Transparency #3B by the same title on the overhead. **Many of you do after-school activities, such as playing sports or music. What if you wanted to set a goal that would help you have more good experiences <u>after</u> school? What are some goals you could set?** *Lead the students to suggest goals such as: not missing practice sessions; not goofing-off during practice; paying close attention to explanations or instruction; practicing on their own; spending less time watching TV so they have more time for practice; etc. Write appropriate suggestions on the transparency.*

If you set one of these goals and used your strengths to reach it, what kind of new good experience could you have after school? *Write student responses on the bottom half of the transparency.*

PRACTICE IN IDENTIFYING SOCIAL GOALS

Transp. #3c

What about the area of friendships and getting along with other kids? I guess you'd all like to have good experiences in this area! *Put Transparency #3C of the same title on the overhead.* **What are some goals you could set for yourselves that would help you have more good experiences with other kids at school, in the neighborhood, or anywhere?** *Lead the students to suggest goals such as: not giving put-downs; controlling their temper; not gossiping or tattling; keeping secrets; giving a specific number of compliments each day; being a better listener by not interrupting; avoiding getting in fights with _____ (someone specific); etc.*

If you set one of these goals and used your strengths to reach it, what are some new good experiences you could create for yourself? *Write student response on the bottom half of the transparency.*

If you haven't already decided on the area in which you want to have more good experiences, take a moment and choose this area now. *Pause.*

SETTING SPECIFIC PERSONAL GOALS

**Handout #2
Transp. #4**

Now let's think of some goals for future good experiences in the area you chose. *Give students Handout #2, "I've Done It Before—I Can Do It Again," and place Transparency #4 (of the same title) on the overhead.* **When you decide on your goals, you'll want to make them as <u>specific</u> as possible. It can be really depressing to decide you want to do something and then not make it, and this usually happens because people set goals that aren't specific enough.**

Write "I'll get all A's," and "I'll be nicer to people," on the transparency. **Goals like "I'll get all As" or "I'll be nicer to people" usually don't work. You need to break your goal down into** "bite-sized chunks." If you want to improve your swimming speed, you need to have a specific goal like, "I will do a lap one second faster each day" instead of "I'll swim faster." If you want to raise your grade in a certain subject, you need to have a specific goal like "I'll do my class assignments and homework each day."

How could we break these two goals on the transparency down into bite-size chunks? *Help the students rephrase the two goals written on the transparency in specific terms.* Now these two goals are specific enough to work on; they tell you exactly what you need to do. Would anyone like to share their own goals with the class? *Call on students and write their goals on the transparency. If some students' goals are too lofty, help them reword them so that the goals are more specific, realistic, and attainable.*

Point to the date blank at the bottom of the transparency. People are more likely to reach a goal if they include a target date for completion. If you don't reach your goal by the date you set for yourself, there's no reason to feel bad. Maybe you chose a tough goal for yourself. Just give it a little more thought and set a new target date.

STUDENTS SET THEIR GOALS

Now it's time for you to pick your specific goals that will help you have more good experiences in the area you chose. Be sure to make your goal something that won't be too easy to do. Before you decide on your goal, you might want to take a moment to remember a good experience you've had in the past that was hard for you to do, something that required some extra hard work or determination to make it happen. Pick a goal that would be like that. *Have the students review their "A Summary of My Strengths" handouts again if they need help remembering such an experience.*

Guide the students through the completion of the handout, paying special attention to making goals specific and setting reasonable target dates.

STRATEGIES FOR REACHING GOALS

Transp. #5

Now we're going to talk about some tricks or techniques you can use to help make sure you make the goal you've set. *Put Transparency #5, "Strategies for Reaching Goals," on the overhead. Cover all but the first strategy.*

The first technique is to <u>remind yourself of your goal</u>. One of the main reasons people don't make their goals is because they simply forget about them. I'm going to ask you to read your goal to yourself at the beginning and the end of each day for the next week or so to help you remember it. *Uncover the next strategy and read it to students. Then say:* **It really helps to try to <u>remember clearly how good it felt in the past</u> to accomplish something you were proud of.** *Uncover the third strategy and say:* **An even more powerful way to use your imagination is to <u>picture or see yourself reaching your new goal</u>.**

Transp. #6

Uncover the fourth strategy and say: **It also helps to <u>think about how good it will feel when you reach your goal</u>.** *Show Transparency #6, "Remember a Good Experience—Imagine an Even Better One," and review strategies 2, 3, and 4 on Transparency #5 once more by relating them to Transparency #6.*

Transp. #5

Show Transparency #5 once again. Say: **There are two other powerful strategies you can use to help yourself reach your goal.** *Uncover strategies 5 and 6. Say:* **It helps a lot to <u>say encouraging things to yourself</u>, like "I can do this!"**

Handout #3

You also can use this kind of "self-talk" to get yourself restarted if you get off track. Let me show you what I mean. *Distribute Handout #3, "I Can Do It! Using Self-Talk to Reach My Goal."*

These are the kinds of things that champion athletes and other successful people say to themselves over and over when they're working on a goal. <u>You</u> can use this technique, too. Let's silently read through the two lists. Circle the "self-talk" statements you like. When you get to the bottom of each list, add any other statements that you think would work for you. *Allow the students time to read through the lists and circle the statements they like.*

Now, for each list I'd like you to put a star by your very favorite statement in that list. When both you and your Learning Partner are done, share your choices with each other. *You may wish to have several students share their favorite statements with the class. (The students may want to copy these statements onto a card and to tape to their desks for future reference.)*

Handout #4

Give the students Handout #4, "How I Will Reach My Goal." This handout will help you tie together everything we've just been talking about. It will be a reminder to you of the tricks you can use to reach your goal. Begin by writing your goal on this handout and the strengths you'll use to reach that goal. *Walk the students through the rest of the handout. Tell them they'll be looking at this sheet at the beginning and end of each day, when they practice imagining their goal.*

USING STRENGTHS TO OVERCOME OBSTACLES TO GOALS

Transp. #7

Show the students Transparency #7, "Things That Might Stop Me From Reaching My Goal." Say: Almost everyone who tries to reach a goal runs into obstacles or difficulties at times which make it hard for them to stick with their goal. What are some things that might stop you from sticking with a goal until you reach it? *Call on students to offer suggestions. Elicit from the students the following obstacles and write them on the boulder: forgetting, old habits, other things that are more fun, a goal that's not specific, needing help but not getting it, becoming bored, being too tired, having a goal that's too hard. (The students may also have other good ideas to add.)*

The minute you're tempted not to do what you told yourself you would do, you need to quickly remind yourself of the strengths you used in the past to get things done. You need to say things to yourself like:

- **"I'm tough."**

- **"I have a lot of determination."**

- **"I've done hard things before; I can do hard things again."**

- **"I've used my self-discipline before; I can use it now."**

- **"I'm the kind of kid who sticks with things."**

- **"I've done things I've been proud of in the past. I can do this now."**

- **"I've been kind to others before, even when I didn't feel like it. I can do it again."**

Handout #5

It helps to think ahead and try to figure out the kind of obstacles that might stop you from reaching your goal. Then they're not as likely to sneak up on you. When you notice one of those obstacles, remind yourself of your strengths—that's the best way to overcome a temptation to stop moving toward your goal. *Give the students Handout #5, "Using My Strengths to Overcome Obstacles to Goals." Review the directions with them, asking them to write their goal, the problems or difficulties they anticipate they may have as they try to reach their goal, and the strengths they have that they will use to overcome these obstacles. Allow the students time to complete the handout.*

HANDOUTS TO HELP STUDENTS REACH THEIR GOALS

**Handout #6
Handout #7**

Help the students make specific plans regarding what they will do each day to reach their goals by having them complete Handout #6, "My Ladder to Success." Also give them Handout #7, "How I'm Doing," to keep a daily record of their progress.

**Handout #8
Handout #9**

Whenever a student has completed his or her goal, give the student Handout #8, "I Did I!" to fill in as a reminder of his or her success, and fill out and present the student with Handout #9, the "Goal Achievement Award."

LESSON SUMMARY

If you talk to any championship athletes or successful people and ask them the secret of their successes, they're very likely to tell you that they set small goals—often each day—and little by little they accomplish big things. They'll probably also tell you that they didn't always reach every one of their goals, but that they failed now and then.

Hardly anyone meets all the goals they set. That's because each one of us is a mix of strengths and things that need improvement. When you don't make a goal, don't waste energy putting yourself down for it. Winners forget the past and start over. They focus on their strengths instead of their weaknesses. They focus on what they can do now, not on what they didn't do then.

Transp. #8

It's great to know your strengths so you can try to have more good experiences, but those aren't the most important things for you to know. *Show the students Transparency #8, "Your Value As a Person Doesn't Depend On How Well You Do," covering the right half. Discuss the pictures on the left half of the transparency.* The most important thing for you to know and to remember is that <u>you're valuable just because you're you!</u> *Uncover the right half of the transparency.*

SUPPLEMENTARY ACTIVITIES

Use the Supplementary Activities at the end of the lesson to provide reinforcement of the skills and strategies taught:

- *"See Yourself Reaching Your Goal"*
  (Supplementary Activity #1)

- *"Reviewing My 'Strengths Folder'"*
  (Supplementary Activity #2)

Determination

Helped You Have Good Experiences in the Past

Determination

Can Help You to Have More Good Experiences in the Future

Using Your Strengths to Create New Good Experiences

Directions:

Circle the strengths that have helped you have good experiences in the past. Add any not listed.

You can use these strengths to help yourself accomplish new things in the future like:

Self Strengths
- Enthusiastic
- Organized
- Positive Attitude
- Good With Numbers
- Good With Words
- Problem Solver
- Self-Disciplined
- Strong
- Thorough
- _____
- _____

Improving your schoolwork or after-school activities

People Strengths
- Caring
- Considerate
- Friendly
- Generous
- Good Listener
- Loyal
- Nice
- Supportive
- _____
- _____
- _____
- _____

Having better friendships

TRANSPARENCY #3A

Possible Goals That Could Help Me Have More Good Experiences

Schoolwork

POSSIBLE GOALS:

1. _____

2. _____

3. _____

4. _____

Good Experiences I Could Have if I Did One or More of These

TRANSPARENCY #3B

Possible Goals That Could Help Me Have More Good Experiences (continued)

After-School Activities

POSSIBLE GOALS:

1. _____

2. _____

3. _____

4. _____

Good Experiences I Could Have if I Did One or More of These

TRANSPARENCY #3c

Possible Goals That Could Help Me Have More Good Experiences (continued)

Friendships

POSSIBLE GOALS:

1. _____

2. _____

3. _____

4. _____

Good Experiences I Could Have if I Did One or More of These

TRANSPARENCY #4/HANDOUT #2

I've Done It <u>Before</u>— I Can Do It <u>Again</u>.

A Goal That Could Help Me Have More Good Experiences

Directions:

Write out what you will do or draw a picture showing yourself using your strengths to accomplish this goal.

I will meet my goal by _____.
(date)

TRANSPARENCY #5

Strategies
for Reaching Goals

1. Read my goal twice a day.

2. Remind myself of past times when I accomplished something I was proud of.

3. Picture or see myself reaching my goal.

4. Think about how good I will feel when I reach my goal.

5. Say encouraging things to myself, like "I can do this!"

6. Use self-talk to restart when I get off-track.

TRANSPARENCY #6

Remember a Good Experience— Imagine an Even Better One

HANDOUT #3

I Can Do It!

Using Self-Talk to Reach My Goal

Things I can say to encourage myself:

- "If I try hard, I can do it."
- "I'll make it."
- "I've done hard things before. I can do hard things again."
- "I have all the strengths I need to do this."
- "This is easier than things I've done before."
- "I'll take it one step at a time."
- "If I put in the time, I can do it."

Things I can say to myself when I get off-track:

- "I'll keep trying until I make it."
- "If I practice it, I'll learn it."
- "I can start again."
- "I can use my strengths to keep going."
- "I haven't put enough time into this yet."
- "I'll do better next time."
- "Everyone makes mistakes."
- "Just because I got off-track doesn't mean I can't start again."

HANDOUT #4

How I Will Reach My Goal

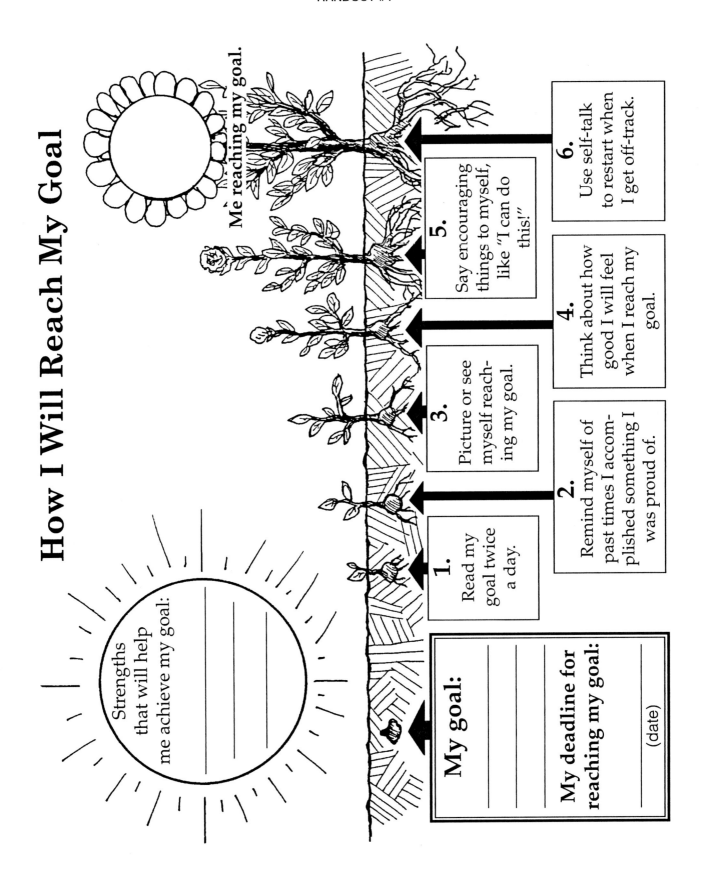

Strengths that will help me achieve my goal:

Me reaching my goal.

1. Read my goal twice a day.

2. Remind myself of past times I accomplished something I was proud of.

3. Picture or see myself reaching my goal.

4. Think about how good I will feel when I reach my goal.

5. Say encouraging things to myself, like "I can do this!"

6. Use self-talk to restart when I get off-track.

My goal:

My deadline for reaching my goal:

(date)

TRANSPARENCY #7

Things That Might Stop Me From Reaching My Goal

HANDOUT #5

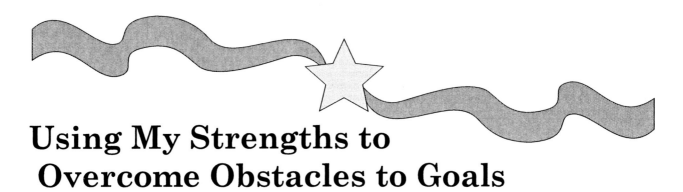

Using My Strengths to Overcome Obstacles to Goals

Most people working towards a goal run into obstacles along the way. Overcoming these obstacles requires strengths like determination, being self-disciplined, trying again, being strong, sticking to a schedule, and having a positive attitude.

Think about the obstacles you might run into in reaching your new goal. For example, you might forget about your goal, or you might be tempted to watch TV or play Nintendo or do something with your friends instead of working on a schoolwork goal. If you're working on a friendship goal, you might be tempted to give up if someone says "no" when you ask them to do something with you, or if you see him or her whispering to someone else.

In the boxes below:
1. Write down your goal.
2. Write down your guesses regarding obstacles you think you'll run into in trying to reach your goal.
3. List the strengths you'll use to overcome these obstacles.

My Goal	Obstacles I Might Face	Strengths I Will Use to Overcome These Obstacles

What do you think are your chances of reaching your goal?

❑ slim   ❑ 25%   ❑ 50%   ❑ 75%   ❑ 100%

Why do you think so? _____

_____

HANDOUT #6

My Ladder to Success

What I will do each day this week to help myself reach my goal:

My Goal

Friday

Thursday

Wednesday

Tuesday

Monday

Start Climbing Here

Examples

Completing daily assignments

Helping someone each day

Checkling out books for an assignment

Reading 15 minutes each night

HANDOUT #7

How I'm Doing

Directions:

For each time that you did something to reach your goal, color one of the suns.

If you ignored or forgot about your goal, color one of the rainclouds.

My goal is to try to:

_____

	I did something towards my goal.	I ignored or forgot my goal.
M	☀ ☀ ☀ ☀	☁ ☁ ☁ ☁
T	☀ ☀ ☀ ☀	☁ ☁ ☁ ☁
W	☀ ☀ ☀ ☀	☁ ☁ ☁ ☁
TH	☀ ☀ ☀ ☀	☁ ☁ ☁ ☁
F	☀ ☀ ☀ ☀	☁ ☁ ☁ ☁
	I can do **even better** next time!	I'll **remember more often** next time.

HANDOUT #8

Wow! ————————— Yeah!

I DID IT!

I made my goal of: _____

_____

_____

_____

To make it I had to: _____

_____

_____

_____

_____

When I made it I felt: _____

_____

_____

_____

Some of the strengths that helped me achieve this
were: _____

_____

_____

_____

HANDOUT #9

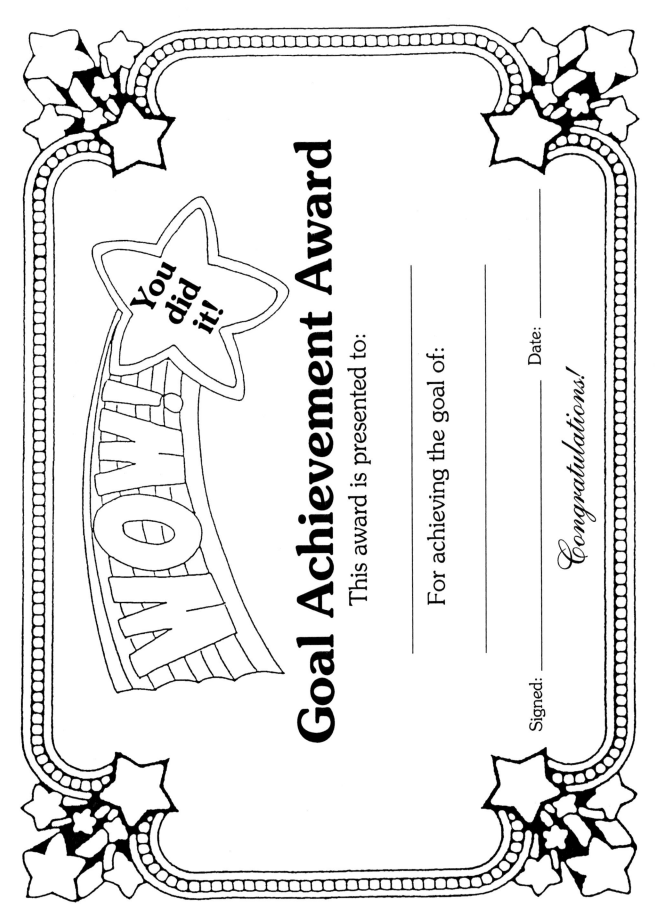

Goal Achievement Award

This award is presented to:

For achieving the goal of:

Date:

Congratulations!

Signed:

TRANSPARENCY #8

Your Value As a Person Doesn't Depend On How Well You Do

How well you do can make you feel **happy** or **sad**,

You're valuable because there's never been anyone on this planet just like you.

but it has nothing to do with your **value** as a person.

You're valuable just because you're you.

SUPPLEMENTARY ACTIVITY #1

See Yourself Reaching Your Goal

Objective   Students will remember a good experience from the past and actively imagine themselves accomplishing their goal in a similar way in the future.

Materials   Writing paper

Pencils

Drawing paper

Markers or crayons

Procedure   Tell students they are going to use their memories and imaginations to help them accomplish the goal they set for themselves in the lesson. Lead them through the following exercise, pausing between thoughts in order to allow them time to fill in details in their imaginations. Say something similar to the following:

> Now I'd like to show you how to practice using your imagination to remember a time you accomplished something in the past and how good you felt about it. You might want to close your eyes. Think back to one of your favorite good experiences. . . . Think of something you worked hard on that you were really proud of. . . . Try to remember a past good experience that is similar to the goal you're working on now. For example, if you're working on a school-work goal, remember a past good experience or success in some area of schoolwork. . . .
>
> See yourself as clearly as you can. Remember what it felt like to do all the things you did to make this good experience happen. . . . See yourself using the strengths that helped you create this good experience. . . . Feel how good you felt. . . . Notice yourself holding your head up and being proud of what you did. . . . Then tell yourself, "Just as I was able to do this, I'll be able to accomplish my new goal, too."

Continue the exercise, this time leading students to imagine accomplishing their goal in the future:

Now let's do what Olympic champions do—imagine ourselves reaching a new goal. "Watch a movie" of yourself in your imagination, looking and acting just the way you want to look and act as you work towards your goal. . . . Notice everything you do to reach your goal. . . . Notice each little step you take. . . . See yourself using your strengths to stick to the job of working to reach your goal. . . . Picture any obstacles or problems that might come up and then see yourself using your strengths to solve them. . . .

Now see yourself reaching your goal. . . . Feel how happy you are inside when you're able to do what you set out to do. . . . See others congratulating you on what you've accomplished. . . . Tell yourself you've been clever to use the strengths you've used in the past to give yourself another good experience. . . . When you are ready, open your eyes.

Give the students drawing paper and ask them to illustrate their inner "movie," including as many details as they can. Then ask them to write a paragraph describing in their "movie" what their goal was, what obstacles they overcame, how it felt to succeed, what others said or did to congratulate them on their accomplishments, and what they said to themselves about the strengths they used to meet their goals. The students may or may not want to share their illustrations and paragraphs with the class.

SUPPLEMENTARY ACTIVITY #2

Reviewing My "Strengths Folder"

My Favorite Strength Handout

Name _____

Title of Handout _____

_____

I chose this one because _____

_____

The best thing about this handout is _____

_____

One thing I learned from completing this handout is_____

_____

Something other people could learn about me from this handout is _____

_____

If I could make this handout even better, I would do that by _____

_____

What's Your Reaction to My "Strengths Folder"?

 My Name _____

Please write your comments in the space below.

PARENT	AN ADULT I LIKE	A FRIEND

A P P E N D I C E S

Appendix A:

Evaluation Form

Appendix B:

The ASSIST Program Scope and Sequence
and
ASSIST School-Wide Monthly Themes

Evaluation Form

Directions:

How did you like these lessons on ways to find your strengths? Complete five of the following sentence stems:

1. I learned . . . .

2. This unit helped me . . . .

3. The main idea seemed to be . . . .

4. What I'll remember most is . . . .

5. I was surprised . . . .

6. The best part was . . . .

7. Some other things I liked were . . . .

8. I didn't like . . . .

9. I changed my mind about . . . .

10. I really felt good when . . . .

11. I hope that . . . .

12. A question I have is . . . .

13. A way I'm going to use what I learned is . . . .

14. The specific time I will use what I learned is . . . .

15. If you teach this again, I suggest . . . .

The ASSIST Program Scope and Sequence

Kindergarten	Grade 1	Grade 2	Grade 3	Grade 4	Grades 5-6
Teaching Friendship Skills: Primary Version · · · · · Recommended list of children's books	*Teaching Friendship Skills: Primary Version* · · · · · Lessons 1-3; Appendix A: Using Literature to Enhance Students' Understanding of Friendship	*Teaching Friendship Skills: Primary Version* · · · · · Lessons 4-8; Appendix B: Friendship Games	*Teaching Cooperation Skills* · · · · · Lessons 1-7	*Teaching Friendship Skills: Intermediate Version* · · · · · Lessons 1-7; Appendix A: Multiple Intelligences Friendship Center; Appendix B: Using Literature to Enhance Students' Understanding of Friendship; Appendix C: Friendship Games	*Helping Kids Handle Anger* · · · · · Lessons 1-9
Building Self-Esteem in the Classroom: Primary Version · · · · · Recommended list of children's books; Lesson 1 and Kindergarten Workbook	*Building Self-Esteem in the Classroom: Primary Version* · · · · · Lessons 1-6; Student Workbook (First Grade)	*Helping Kids Find Their Strengths* · · · · · Lessons 1-7 (Primary Version)	*Building Self-Esteem in the Classroom: Intermediate Version* · · · · · Lessons 1-3; Student Workbook (Intermediate)	*Helping Kids Find Their Strengths* · · · · · Lessons 1-9 (Intermediate)	*Building Self-Esteem in the Classroom: Intermediate Version* · · · · · Lessons 4-9; Self-Esteem Activities for Older or More Capable Students (Unit Five)
Creating A Caring Classroom · · · · · Climate-Building Activities (Primary)	*Creating A Caring Classroom* · · · · · Warm-Up Activities (Primary)	*Creating A Caring Classroom* · · · · · Climate-Building Activities (Primary)	*Creating A Caring Classroom* · · · · · Warm-Up Activities; Holiday Activities	*Creating A Caring Classroom* · · · · · Classroom Management Procedures	*Teaching Cooperation Skills* · · · · · Lessons 8-11
	Helping Kids Handle Anger · · · · · Lessons 1-3		*Helping Kids Handle Anger* · · · · · Lessons 4-9		*Helping Kids Handle Anger* · · · · · Lessons 10-15

ASSIST School-Wide Monthly Themes

S E P T E M B E R

Creating A Caring Classroom
"Warm-Up Activities"
"Climate-Building Activities"

O C T O B E R

Building Self-Esteem in the Classroom
Lessons 1-9 (Primary Version)
Lessons 1-9 (Intermediate Version)

N O V E M B E R

Teaching Cooperation Skills
Lessons 1-9

D E C E M B E R

Helping Kids Handle Anger
Lessons 1-10

Creating A Caring Classroom
"Holiday Activities"

J A N U A R Y

Teaching Friendship Skills
Lessons 1-5 (Primary Version)
Lessons 1-4 (Intermediate Version)

F E B R U A R Y

Teaching Friendship Skills
Lessons 6-8 (Primary Version)
Lessons 5-6 (Intermediate Version)

M A R C H

Helping Kids Handle Anger
Lessons 1-3 (Primary)
Lessons 5-9 (Intermediate)

A P R I L

Helping Kids Find Their Strengths
Lessons 1-7 (Primary)
Lessons 1-9 (Intermediate)

M A Y

Teaching About Sexual Abuse